THE LAST WHALER

Capt. Nicholas Stevensson Karas

authorHOUSE®

AuthorHouse™
1663 Liberty Drive
Bloomington, IN 47403
www.authorhouse.com
Phone: 1-800-839-8640

© 2010 Capt. Nicholas Stevensson Karas. All rights reserved.

No part of this book may be reproduced, stored in a retrieval system, or transmitted by any means without the written permission of the author.

First published by AuthorHouse 9/27/2010

ISBN: 978-1-4520-7439-9 (sc)
ISBN: 978-1-4520-7529-7 (e)
ISBN: 978-1-4520-7528-0 (hc)

Library of Congress Control Number: 2010913078

Printed in the United States of America

This book is printed on acid-free paper.

Because of the dynamic nature of the Internet, any Web addresses or links contained in this book may have changed since publication and may no longer be valid. The views expressed in this work are solely those of the author and do not necessarily reflect the views of the publisher, and the publisher hereby disclaims any responsibility for them.

About the cover.... The painting entitled An American Ship In Distress was done in 1841 by English artist Thomas Birch. He moved to the United States and settled in Philadelphia. His reputation was built on a large number of depictions of ships and marine scenes. All that is known about the ship comes from its Philadelphia hailport. The ship is typical of three-masted barks that dominated the American merchant marine service during the mid-19th century. Tranquility, the whaleship in this novel, is almost an exact duplicate. The difference is that the whaleship would have three whaleboats in davits on their port sides and one on the starboard side. The painting is used here with the grateful permission of The Putnam Foudation, Timken Museum of Art, 1500 El Prado, San Diago, CA 92101.

I must go down to the seas again,
to the lonely sea and the sky,
And all I ask is a tall ship
and a star to steer her by,

           Sea Fever ....John Masefield

PROLOGUE

The discovery of oil in Pennsylvania in 1859 had a devastating effect on the whaling industry in the United States. However, its death knell had already been rung.

From meager beginnings in the 1670s along the shores of eastern Long Island, Shinnecock and Montauk Indians took pity on Quakers driven from New England by intolerant Puritans. The Indians showed them how to salvage whales washed ashore and used as food and oil and eventually to search for them in canoes and boats near shore.

However, to go beyond the horizon and last for more than a day to hunt whales they needed ships. Sag Harbor on the South Fork was their only deep-water port. Eventually, experienced Sag Harbor whalers were enticed to bring their knowledge to New England's prolific number of deep-water ports. As a result, New England, too, flourished.

Whaling in America reached its zenith in 1848 when 735 whaleships with more than 70,000 men sailed from four major Northeast ports. But, on the down side, the explosive search for whales and their oil to light the lamps of this nation and smooth the start of the industrial revolution had reduced a once large population of these behemoths to scattered sightings in both the Atlantic and Pacific oceans. Thereafter, few "greasy ships" ever returned to port.

The first whaleship owners were ever-industrious Quake entrepreneurs. In Sag Harbor they formed "The Company," a loose assortment of ship owners, ship chandlers, whale oil supportive industries, retired whaleship captains, widows and farmers and fisher Quakers with a little money on their hands to invest.

By the end of the Civil War the Sag Harbor Company had lost

several vessels to Rebel Raiders and had but one remaining whaleship, *Tranquility*. Many in the Company wanted to immediately turn it into a coastal merchant ship but the majority agreed to have it make one last sail for whales.

Ever since the first Quakers landed on eastern Long Island Shinnecock and Montauk Indians were a valued part of the crew, especially as harpooners. However, in 1865 no Shinnecocks wanted to sign onto a three- or four-year voyage on vessels whose return was always in jeopardy and whose profit might not exist.

The superstitious 30-man crew of a whaleship, composed of "bums and greenies" in the ship's forecastle, was considering jumping ship before it departed because no Indian was in the crew. On a cold, late-December night in 1865, just before *Tranquility* was to sail, the 1st mate was ordered to kidnap an Indian. Both the Indian and the ship were not heard of again until February 1942 when, at age 91, he was discovered living on an isolated island in the Fiji Group.

This is the story of a 16-year old Indian, well-educated by standards of the period, who within four years at sea rose from being an impressed cook's helper to 4th mate, one of the ship's five officers.

He was under the aegis of an experienced whaleship captain who failed on this trip because of his innate ability to make quick, correct decisions. The protagonist is his brother, a ship's master in his own right; a disburser whose quest for profit often put him at odds with the captain; and his antagonistic nephew who acted as temporary 4th mate and wanted to command the whaleship.

The Last Whaler is their story. *Tranquility*, in 1865, was the next to the last whaleship to sail from Sag Harbor. And, the Indian, in 1942 was the last purebred Shinnecock alive.

The Course of the

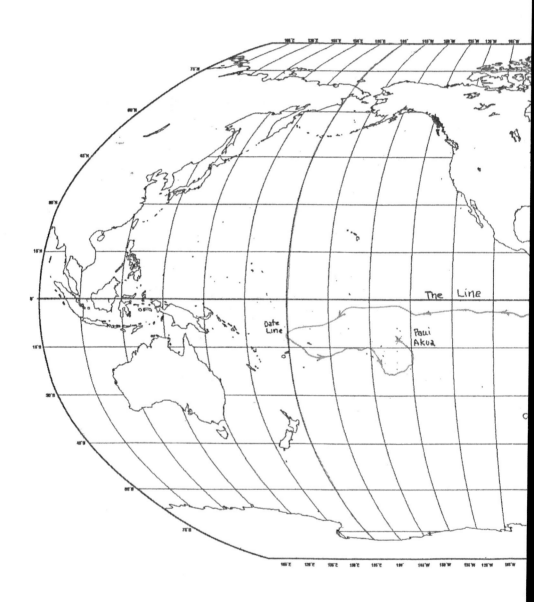

Whaleship *Tranquility*

Chapter 1

The Abduction

Friday December 2, 1865
Sag Harbor. L.I., N.Y.

Ice-cold water begins to affect Ben-quam's ability to concentrate. It rises above his knees as he slowly walks over the soft, muddy bottom of a small tidal pond the Shinnecocks call *Neish-Mimipeek* (Eel Pond). Through a small outlet, its level rises and falls with that of Great Peconic Bay. The sun had set a half-hour ago and the teen-aged Indian now has difficulty seeing his way. He slowly feels the bottom ahead by constantly stabbing the mud with the tri-prong-headed spear.

"Just one more," he says with trembling lips. "Just one more and I can go home."

Eleven eels are strung together through their gills by a long cord that is tied to his belt. They float and sink behind him as he walks. Occasionally, he breaks through thin, skim ice that is just forming. It is a cold December evening. On the verge of quitting, he suddenly feels the telltale wiggle of an eel on the end of his spear.

Quickly he adds it to the stringer. As he walks out of the water he begins searching the horizon south of the pond for a break in the line of scrub pines that dominate the land. He finds it and climbs a well-worn path up a slight hill. The Shinnecocks call the path *Niamuck*, "the-place-between-the-bays." Centuries of Indians created it by dragging their wooden dugout canoes back-and-forth from North Sea (Peconic Bay) to South Bay (Shinnecock Bay). Whites call it Canoe Place. The path rises but a few feet onto a level plain and joins the Montauk Trail. The Trail is a sandy, dirt road, rutted by wagon wheels and horse tracks. Far to the east, it begins at Montauk Point and ends on the banks of the East River across from Manhattan.

Benquam shivers in the cold night air. For warmth he begins running slowly to the east, toward his reservation. As he does, he thinks how his mother and aunt will smoke the eels for days. Both families will have a traditional Christmas treat. He wishes he had speared more when his thoughts are suddenly interrupted by the sound of horses and a wagon on the road behind him. He turns, and in the last vestiges of a fading twilight sees two men on the rig. He thinks they must be lost. They near him and stop.

"Do you need help?" he asks the driver, a bearded man. He does not answer nor does he see a third man jump off the back of the wagon. The man silently, quickly comes forward. In his hands is an open burlap bag. He pulls it over Benquam's head. A second man jumps off the seat and wraps his arms around the Indian. Holding him immobile, someone begins tying his hands behind his back. Together they throw him into the back of the wagon on a bed of hay. Before they close the tailgate someone binds his feet.

The 15-year old lies in the back of a wagon, steadily bouncing off its hard boards as the horse-drawn wagon races down the sandy road. Benquam is dumbfounded as to why this is happening to him. What would they want from me? he asks himself. Wild questions flit about in his mind as to why the men he sought to help did this to him.

The driver steadily whips the horses keeping them at a fast past for more than two hours. Suddenly, unexpectedly, the horses, now exhausted, slow. Suddenly, the wagon's ironclad wheels begin rattling over cobblestones, then abruptly come to a stop. As he lies there, listening to men talking in hushed voices, Benquam feels the push of a light breeze against the bag on his head. His nostrils flare. He senses the air is laden with salt. They are at a landing, at a dock. He hears loose lines, somewhere above him, played by the wind as they rattle against the mast of a ship. He knows where he is.

What will they do with me? he asks himself. He momentarily struggles with the ropes on his hands and feet but they are still tightly tied.

After a few minutes, he hears someone open the wagon's tailgate. Two strong hands pull him off. The next moment he is flung into the air and onto a man's shoulder. Someone else's hands steady him there. The man climbs up a ramp carrying him onto a ship. He stands there for a moment as if not knowing where to go. Benquam feels the man sway slightly as the ship gently rocks.

"Open dah hatch, damn it!"

"Dis kid's heavy," the man says quietly to someone else as he now heads for the forecastle. "I ain't gonna wait wid him all day."

He carries the boy through a hatch then down a ladder, bumping the boy's head and shoulders against the sides of the narrow passageway.

"Pud him in da back," another voice says.

Benquam is abruptly dropped onto the straw-filled mattress of a lower bunk.

His hands are untied but the sack remains on his head without the rope. He hears someone come down the ladder while rattling something metallic. As he lies in the bunk, his right leg is pulled out and clamped in a shackle. The activity's noise disturbs a man who is asleep in the upper bunk.

"Whatcha got derh?" he asks.

"Yur good luck charm," the man says as he locks the shackles to a bunk post. "You might as well git up. It's midnight. Yur watch is already mustering on deck."

"Someone will be here in the morning to look after you," one of the men who kidnapped him says to Benquam. "You'll be okay here."

This is a new voice, one that Benquam has not heard before. Was it the driver, he thinks? His voice is deep, his speech slow, reassuring.

"Don't worry, nothing bad is going to happen to you. Life could be worse. At least you're still alive. You've got a great voyage before you."

"What kind of ship is this?" Benquam asks.

"Can't you tell by the smell? I guess not," he says. "It's been a while since there's been a whale on her decks. It's a whaler."

The man finds a blanket and throws it over the boy.

"Sleep tight," he says as he climbs the ladder.

Benquam lies there without moving. He feels the boat continually rocking at the dock. He hears men snoring and activity on deck outside.

My father will wonder why I never came home. My mother will cry. She cries easily. Damn these men! He reaches for his ankle and feels the leg iron firmly gripping his leg. Somehow he falls asleep.

* * * * * * * * *

"Oh Ben, where are you, my son?" cries an elderly women. "He has never done this before. Maybe he drowned."

At first Benquam's father does not answer. Finally, he says, "There's light enough now. I will go to the crossing-over place to look for him."

Benquam's uncle also goes with him. They walk past the reservation store that is still dark inside. They reach the sandy road and turn west to the crossing-over place. The sun has just topped the horizon when the man sees a flash of light along the south edge of the road.

"What's a stringer of eels doing here?" he asks his brother. "This is not a good sign. There's his spear. This must be what Ben speared. He carried the eels and spear with him."

Lights are now on in the store as they head back. Wood smoke from a newly-started fire is pouring out the chimney. Benquam's father drops the eels next to the steps and goes inside. He smells a pot of coffee boiling on a potbellied stove as three elderly men sit around it waiting with empty cups in their hands.

"Has anyone seen my son Ben?"

They all answer no.

"He was spearing eels yesterday over at *Neish-Mimipeek* and never came home."

"Has anyone strange been here lately, yesterday?"

"No one," says one of the men.

"But Cap'n Lester, Andrew Lester, the younger one was here yesterday," says another man. "He was looking to see if any of us wanted to sail with him again. He said he needed a harponeer."

"What ship?"

"He said his brother Hiram was again in command of *Tranquility*."

"Where is she?"

"Where else would she be? At Sag Harbor."

Three days later, Benquam's father finds a horse he can borrow, and is in Sag Harbor. He goes directly to the harbormaster's shack on the long wharf.

"Any ships sail from here in past few days?" he asks.

"You missed the boat," the harbormaster says jokingly. "Yes, *Tranquility* sailed last night. There ain't another whaler going out of here that I know of. There's not likely to be one. There ain't any whales left. We killed 'em all."

CHAPTER 2

Fitting Out

Saturday, Dec. 3, 1865
Sag Harbor, L.I, N.Y.

It is mid-morning as a bright, late-fall sun floods a cloudless sky making the day appear warmer than it is. The scene is harbor side, inside a palatial house built on a hillock immediately overlooking the East Water Street docks. Beyond the inner harbor, to the east and north, is Shelter Island Sound. Water seems to be everywhere about Sag Harbor. Despite the sun, the surrounding land has a somber cast. It has already felt the heavy, frosty hand of an approaching winter. Dull browns, burnt umbers, yellows and tans have replaced the short-lived vibrant colors of fall. Only the leathery, rust-colored leaves of scrub oaks tenaciously cling to their branches to hold their positions until spring. A fresh, chill wind intermittently blows from the northwest, rattling leaves and sending ripples across the surface of the harbor's waters like cats' paws on morning dew.

The Brown House is one of a dozen grandiose structures scattered along "Blubber Row" built by the barons of sea trade--owners of ships, docks, stores and chandleries, and successful whaleship captains. The house is a typical, palatial mansion of the Federal Period in American architecture. Ephraim Brown's father, a Sag Harbor merchant, built it in 1825.

Inside the house, in a large, sun-filled living room, three men sit silently, pondering an earlier debate, momentarily immobile and engulfed in over-stuffed leather chairs. A Negro servant has just left the room, depositing a second decanter of coffee on a sideboard. For the past two hours, the three men have been debating the value of outfitting another whaleship. Suddenly the youngest, Andrew Lester, rises and moves to the sideboard and refills his cup.

"Anyone else want coffee?" he asks and stands waiting for an answer.

Without speaking, a second man, his brother Hiram, rises. He walks across the room to a large wall of many-paned windows. He stands there, looking out onto Water Street, concentrating on activity outside, just below the house. He scans his ship whose bowsprit seems to be pointing directly at him. Without turning, he waves his arm in a "no," responding to the question. "No, thank you, Andrew," he then says.

The third man, Ephraim Brown, sits motionless and unresponsive.

Smoke from their pipes has clouded the room. The rich, aromatic aroma of Latakia tobacco dominates the air. In the back of the room, opposite the wall of large, panoramic windows, is an oversized fireplace. Before the Negro left the room, he had added more oak logs to an already robust fire. They crackle, hiss and complain. Bits of ice on the wood, rain that accumulated and froze a few days ago when outside, melt in the intense heat and immediately turn to steam. Hiram Lester, in nautical garb, briefly turns to watching the activity on the docks just below the house. He turns his view again to the left and studies the lines of his ship. A slight smile spreads across his lips.

His smile quickly disappears when he sights the *Concordia*. She has been tied at the city's Long Wharf pier since early October after a rather fruitless search for whales in the South Atlantic. He remembers speaking to Alfred Rogers, the captain of the 310-ton whaler. Lester lucidly, painfully recalls Roger's words when they met: "In all of four months, we found but two whales, a small sperm and a right whale. That hardly paid for the food the crew consumed."

Her sails are gone, probably sold by now, Hiram says to himself. I guess they are slowly taking her apart. What a shame. I hate seeing a ship die; any ship.

Hiram returns to an overstuffed seat. All this is a pause in their intense discussions.

"Nearly two months," says Brown as he breaks the silence, "have passed since we three, and more than a dozen elders of the Company, met here to decide our ship's and our fortune's futures, if there is one. After nearly a day of furious debate, which ended in a one-vote majority cast by you," he says as he turns to Capt. Hiram Lester, "the Company has given you the authority to make one last sail for whale before we find a better use for *Tranquility*."

Brown pauses for a moment. "Now, cousins, how are we going to do it? Do you think it will pay for the Company's cost of outfitting the ship?"

Hiram does not immediately answer. He dislikes Brown's use of the word cousins. He feels Brown's familiarity is an attempt to pull himself closer to him because they are related.

Ephraim Brown, still sitting, is the oldest. He sports a bulging belly that puts a strain on his vest's buttons. After the diatribe he decides to stand up and walks to the window for a better look at the dockside activity. The stress of rising puts a flush on his already sanguine face. He stands there for a moment, silent, his hands clasped behind his back. He turns to look back at the two who are still seated.

"There is still time to abort this venture," he says in a voice that is shrill, irritating, and unmanly though not effete. Initially, one would expect a richer voice to emanate from such a portly body. He steps closer to the two who remain seated. He is not tall, maybe 5 feet and 3 or 4 inches. His face is round, cherubic, full. Strands of white hair sweep across the balding top of his head and heavy, white sideburns almost hide his ears. His white, bushy eyebrows partially obscure his deep-set gray eyes. He is fast approaching 60 years of age.

"You both know I am against it," he continues his harangue. "I have been from the beginning." He pauses, leaving an opening for either of the two men to respond. They don't…not at first.

Brown is a niggardly man whose greatest concern during the last 45 years of his life has been the accumulation of wealth. Some might describe him as being conservative, frugal, tight-fisted, or almost Scrooge-like. He is all of these but only niggardly succinctly and fully describes his character. And, he would be all of these even if he hadn't been an avid Quaker in his youth. He is a member of a dozen Sag Harbor Quaker whaling families who have inhabited the East End of Long Island's South Fork for the previous two-and-a-half centuries.

"We should have voted to turn the ship into a coastal trader," Brown continues. "If we had, we could make money almost from the beginning. A hunt for whales, even if successful, means that we will not realize a profit for three, four or even five years. I don't know if some of the families in the Company can last that long."

He again pauses as if hoping one of the others would contribute.

"Be honest," Capt. Lester finally asks, "why do you persist in trying to scuttle this voyage? The Company has already agreed, there will be a sail for whales and there is nothing you can do about it. We sail in three days hence. It is done!

"What is your motivation behind all this useless chatter?"

"I need money," answers Brown. "I need it now or as soon as possible. Because of the war my chandleries have suffered greatly. Their paltry marine sales have me on the verge of bankruptcy. The war has not been lucrative."

"That is no longer a prerogative we can enjoy," Capt. Hiram says as he stands up. "I cannot promise you a greasy ship; nor can anyone in these days of turmoil. However, I can promise you that I will do all that is humanly possible to ensure a successful voyage. The rest will be up to God and His will.

"We can also supplement our catch by obtaining seal skins," Hiram adds. "I know some of the islands in the South Atlantic are again filled with copious numbers of seals. Some have been overexploited but the seals recover quickly. Eight, ten years is all they need. And the market for seals in great among the Chinese."

"I never thought of that demand," says Ephraim.

In both character and form, Hiram Lester is diametrically the opposite of Ephraim. Lester is a well-weathered man of the sea. He has just passed 50, and again finds himself captain of *Tranquility*, the ship's master. He is tall for men of his era, a bit over 6 feet, lean but muscular with a prominent, square-set jaw. His lips are slight. His hair is dark black, graying only at the temples. His eyes are dark brown and guarded by a pair of bushy, black eyebrows that could use trimming. Normally, he is not especially talkative and when he does he is sparse with his words. All these characteristics command a presence in any group in which he might appear. He looks as a sea captain should. One would almost swear that in his presence there is a slight scent of sea salt in the air.

For the past month, Hiram and his younger brother Andrew have been selectively gathering a crew to outfit his vessel. Andrew, a full captain in his own right but now without a ship, has been named first mate and thus second in command on *Tranquility*. Andrew, 46, is almost as tall as his brother. His complexion is not as ruddy as Hiram's even though he has been at sea almost as many years. They are very much the same and at the same time very different. They surely are a conundrum to those who serve under them. Maybe it is the fire in Andrew's lighter brown eyes that seems ever present and sets him apart from his brother. He is equally reticent but once he begins talking one senses compassion in his voice, a quality that is missing in Hiram's. His deep voice immediately commands attention and adds to his aura as a person who can command other men. His full, dark beard masks his facial expressions and thus offers a less foreboding countenance than his brother's.

What sets them apart is Andrew's ability to make quick, often correct, decisions, a characteristic every ship captain should have but at times seems wanting in Hiram. In the past this trait had plagued Hiram in advancing his career. He knows this is one of his weaknesses but seems unable to overcome it.

"Are there any other problems to consider before we adjourn?" asks Brown. "Has the problem of an Indian been satisfied?"

"Yes," answers Andrew. "That was accomplished last night."

"We do have an immediate problem," says Hiram. "We must find two men who can qualify as 3rd and 4th mates. I find no one here to fill the bill but I know there are qualified men in the Azores. My 2nd Mate Jorge Pilla has told me of an uncle who has mated before and even commanded a whaleship. If need be, I will find them there."

An awkward silence falls upon the trio. No one speaks for the next several minutes. Andrew returns to the sideboard and leaves his cup.

"I think we should end this conversation now," says Hiram. "And, I think you," he turns to Ephraim, "should go down to the ship so that you have a first hand look at what the insides of *Tranquility* look like."

"That's a splendid idea," adds Andrew.

Chapter 3

Inside Tranquility

Huffing and puffing Brown makes it to the top of the gangway. He asks for a moment to catch his breath.

"How goes your task of filling the crew?" Brown asks hoping to delay the tour.

"Follow me," says Hiram as he begins to walk across the deck to the hatch that will take them below decks to his cabin.

"Shiphandlers aren't a problem," says Hiram. "Adrian Moore has signed on again as quartermaster; John Bellingham as bo'sun. Michael Astor, our cooper, says he still has one more trip in him and will come along as well as our sailmaker John Daily and carpenter Henry Dibble. I needed a new blacksmith preferably one who is a shipsmith. Andrew was over in Greenport last week and found Kurt Müller. He seems like a capable young man. Of course, my steward Pierre Batiste signed on for a second voyage, and more important, John Batiste, our cook, will also ship and is already ordering provisions for the trip. My worries are with filling the foremast complement."

"I hope they are successful so we can sail Wednesday night," Andrew says as he stands next to the captain's desk. "If one can believe them, the crimpers tell me they will have more men than we need.

"Excuse me for a moment. I have a matter to take care of. I will meet you two in the fo'c's'le."

Andrew scurries topside and spots the bo'sun.

"Bellingham, there's a chore I would like you to immediately take care of. There's a young man shackled to a bunk in the fo'c's'le. Free him and take him and his donkey's breakfast (straw-filled mattress) to Cook's storeroom. I believe there is still an empty bunk. Have Billy take him something to eat."

"Aye, Sir," Bo'sun replies.

"The ship has been made sound," says Hiram Lester, "and you say," addressing Brown, "a full store of provisions is onboard?"

Brown nods his head in agreement.

"Good," says Hiram. "We must catch the winter westerlies as soon as possible. If we don't, we'll lose their favorable winds."

"I've been thinking intensely about this voyage for the past two months, ever since *Tranquility* returned," says Brown. "Her last trip was hardly a financial success."

"On our last trip," says Andrew Lester who unexpectedly returns to the captain's cabin, "we were at times encumbered by the Confederate raider *Alabama* and spent more time trying to avoid her than searching for whales. I am sure it will be different now that the war is over."

Ephraim Brown has been around boats during his entire life, but he has been to sea only once, in his youth, and then for only a few months. His contribution to their whaling enterprises has always been his mastery over figures and ledgers. Accounting was a natural occupation for him. For two generations, his family operated the village's first ship's chandlery and its only ropewalk, a long building where rope is made by twisting yarn.

"There may still be a market for whale oil," Brown concedes. "Reduced, true, but there are many people who don't care to use coal oil. They complain about its odor. That's one reason why I NOW grudgingly support another whaling trip. And there is also the bounty in ambergris, no matter how slight."

"That is true," adds Hiram, "but I must be honest with you. The number of sperm whales has declined drastically in the past few years. On the last trip I found but one small glob of ambergris afloat, and that was by sheer luck. I fear it is wishful and unrewarding thinking to depend upon ambergris for profit."

"Back to what I was saying earlier," interrupts Brown. "*Tranquility* is fully provisioned for at least two years at sea. If you are frugal with its use you could possibly stretch it to three years. And, if you must stay longer at sea, if you do turn to the Pacific, you will have the money onboard to lay in new provisions for another year or possibly two, especially in some foreign port where costs are sure to be less than here. The key to a successful voyage, in addition to filling the barrels, is a tight control over the costs."

"Let us move to the bow," says Andrew as they leave his brother's quarters. "I want you to see where the Greenies will live."

"I will meet you at the gangway in a few minutes." says Hiram. "I doubt it should take more time than that."

Andrew leads Brown down into the forecastle. He quickly scans the starboard row of bunks and is relieved to see the Indian is no longer there.

At the bottom of the ladder Brown looks around. "You're right, it isn't very large," he says as he quickly turns around and climbs the ladder topside. Hiram is already at the gangway.

"I agree with some of your thinking when it comes to frugality," says Andrew as they cross the deck to the gangway, "but how are we to accomplish this? Even on a smooth voyage, there are always unexpected expenses that arise, expenses that we must endure and cannot be controlled or predicted."

"I have thought of that," says Brown. "I will, with Hiram's permission of course," as he makes a slight bow to Hiram, "sail on *Tranquility* as her disburser, as an agent, as a representative for our two families and the others who have invested heavily in her success. I can spare the time to watch the costs thereby relieving you two of this task so you are be able to devote more time searching for whales. I have already broached the idea to a few of our members. They concurred that it would be good to have a family disburser on board."

Hiram's jaw drops. For a few moments he is speechless. He is enraged by Brown's uncharacteristic audacity.

"You mean watchdog, don't you?" Hiram exclaims loudly after his composure returns.

"No, no, not at all," Brown answers immediately. "You're the captain and your word on board is always the last word."

"I will think on it," Hiram says as Brown stops at the gangway.

"Oh yes, I have one other question I would like to ask you."

Oh no, Andrew says to himself. I know what he wants.

"Have you, have you any immediate candidates for the other two mates?" he awkwardly asks Hiram.

"I already told you that there is a man in the Azores who is likely to qualify."

"I understand, from my nephew Abraham, that you have no one else in mind. Is that correct?"

Without waiting for an answer, he again speaks. "Might you not consider my nephew Abraham? He has been on two whaling trips and is reputed to be an excellent 'harponeer'."

Capt. Lester is not surprised at Ephraim Brown's petition for Abe. Rumors had filtered down, or more correctly, up to his brother Andrew, that Ephraim would "…put in a good word for his nephew." Andrew, too, feared Ephraim might raise the question but had hoped to avoid a direct answer. But that isn't about to happen. Both are familiar with Abraham Brown's past.

"He is already onboard as a harponeer and boat steerer. Isn't that enough?" asks Hiram.

Brown does not answer.

"As you know," Lester continues, "my second is Jorge Pilla, a Portygee/American. He grew up in New Bedford but spent a few years of his youth in the Azores with his relatives. He sailed with me on the previous trip. He's a good leader and has the respect of all the men who worked with him. He tells me that there are plenty of good whalers in the Azores, in his grandfather's hometown of Angra. I am taking his word that his uncle, Diogo Pilla, is one of the best. He has corresponded with him. He needs work and is reputed to be an excellent harponeer. Better, he even captained a Portygee whaler. Pilla says there are more men who can easily qualify as a fourth mate. And, they might be willing to accept a smaller lay."

Leaving the answer to Brown's question somewhat open, he continues, "But only time will tell. We will see what there is to pick from when we get to Angra. Until we do, I will let your nephew work as the acting 4th mate. He may move his gear into the mate's quarters."

Brown gleefully rattles down the gangway without turning to look back, leaving Lester and his brother on the ship.

Chapter 4

Life on the Streets of Sag Harbor

After Brown is out of sight, Hiram and Andrew leave *Tranquility* and walk the dock to Water Street.

"Do you think that was a wise thing to do?" Andrew asks his brother.

"I know his reputation," says Hiram. "But I feel I should at the least give him a chance. If I don't, I know I will be criticized by others in the Company. The leg to Angra is but three weeks. Maybe I can find fault to demote him before we get there."

"Maybe," says Andrew. "Maybe, but I doubt it. He is clever."

Hiram momentarily slows, stops and then turns around to look at his ship as *Tranquility* lies warped to several bollards in her slip. Her bowsprit partially extends over Water Street as the sun's reflection off the water dances on her bow. Her sails are all secured but a gentle breeze rattles the halyards in a rhythmic tattoo.

"Even harnessed to the dock, she's pretty," says Hiram. "What a beautiful thing is a ship."

"Even more beautiful when fully dressed in sails," adds Andrew.

"Aye, she is," seconds his brother. "Her lines are perfectly faired."

"Maybe that is why we refer to ships as she."

"Could be," adds Hiram.

"The wind is fresh from the nor'west," Andrew says as he pulls up the large collar on his heavy coat. Winds are always paramount in the concerns of men involved with the sea. "I do need another pair of gloves before we sail."

"I'm sure one of the shark's stores along the street will have them. I will accompany you," says Hiram.

The north side of Water Street parallels the water's edge. At extreme high tides, especially when coupled with a nor'east wind or a full moon, water floods part of the street. For several blocks, the wet side bristles with slips, jetties and piers. In the near-past, when Sag Harbor boasted the third largest fleet of whaleships on the East Coast, every slip on Water Street had a whaleship in it. Even more were tied to the huge dock that extended beyond Wharf Street. Now, *Tranquility* is the only working whaler in port.

The dry south side of Water Street is lined with a few seedy-looking houses. Several, with typical 1800s facades, have been converted into stores that at one time catered to the needs of hordes of whalers. Brown's house stands on a small hillock above them. Interspersed among the houses are taverns, chandleries, a few ratty-looking boarding houses and clothing shops. Only one inn is still active, the Mousetrap Tavern. Several stores are vacant and others are boarded up. Despite the poor, post-war economy, the port is alive, bustling with people, carriages, wagons and small-boat traffic in the harbor's cove. Three large coastal merchant ships are tied at the town wharf. In the corner where Water Street meets Wharf Street is a cooperage. Hundreds of empty surplus barrels are aging in the weather, waiting for a whaleship to load them. *Tranquility's* bilge is already filled.

As the Lesters walk down the cobblestone-paved street, their progress is about to be blocked by a small group of men, obviously sailors, possibly drunk even though the sun is still well below the yardarm. As the Lesters near them, in front of a clothing store, a typical shark's store, the group quickly opens a pathway for them. They have recognized Hiram's garb.

He is wearing a finger-length navy-blue tunic with two parallel rows of a half-dozen large, black buttons and a large collar that can be turned up to confront a backing wind. He wears a black, narrow-billed cap, typical of those worn by naval officers, but without any insignia. Andrew's dress is almost identical.

"Top o' the day to you, Sir," says the first man as he touches the edge of his woolen watch cap with his right index finger slightly curved. Typical to the British, this style of salute enables Hiram Lester to identify the man immediately. The man bows slightly, stepping back just enough on the narrow street to let the captain and Andrew pass.

"And the rest of the morning to yourself," Hiram says as he returns the salute.

" 'Tis a fine day to be a sailin'. Don't you think so, Sir?"

"Aye, I do," answers Hiram as he and his brother momentarily stop.

"I can see, Sir, that you are a man of the sea," says the Irishman.

"I am."

"And what may be your ship, Sir, if yea don't mind me askin'?"

"She lies off your port shoulder. Mind she doesn't poke your eye. There," Hiram says as he points to his ship.

"Glory be t' God," the man answers. "I just signed me name on the contract to sail with you. Might you be Capt. Lester?"

"That I am. And, who are you?"

"I am Egan, Sir. Patrick Egan. Pleased to make your acquaintance, Sir."

Egan immediately extends his right hand to shake Lester's. But the captain hesitates for a moment. Andrew sees this and quickly recognizes the breach of naval etiquette. To change the situation, Andrew immediately extends his right hand past his brother and shakes hands with Egan.

"I am the ship's first mate, Mr. Egan. It is a pleasure to meet you."

"And I you, Sir," answers Egan, not realizing what has just been avoided.

"What's going on here? What's the trouble?" a short, balding man asks in a surprisingly loud voice as he rushes out of the shop's door toward the group in front of his clothing store. He is in shirtsleeves and wears a black vest and chambray apron. Scissors and bobbins are in the apron's pockets and a yellow, cloth-measuring tape hangs from around the back of his neck and over his chest. A pair of black-rimmed glasses sits on the fore part of his aquiline-shaped nose.

"Is everything alright? I don't want any fighting going on in front of my store."

"Everything's fine," Egan pipes up. "Don't fret about it, old man."

"Have you been next door, drinking at the tavern?" he asks Egan. "You smell like you have."

"What concern is that of yours?" asks Andrew.

The man immediately recognizes the ship's-officer clothing worn by Andrew and his brother.

"No concern, Sir. I just don't like fights," answers the shopkeeper. "Of late, there have been too many along Water Street. That is bad for business."

"And who are you?" Hiram finally asks the merchant.

"Why, everyone here in Sag Harbor knows me. I am Solomon, Solomon Levi."

Egan and the three men with him suddenly break out into a roaring laughter, unable to contain themselves. Even Andrew begins to laugh.

"What is so funny? What is so damned funny?" Levi asks.

"Don't answer, I know," he says. "Was it you I heard singing through my store wall?"

"Was it not a melodious voice?" Egan asks.

"Baaah," scoffs Levi.

"The tavern is made of bricks and maybe our words didn't come through clear enough for you to understand them. Boys, do you think that might be this poor man's problem?"

"I do. I do," two answer in unison.

"Well then, let us fix that and not be remiss. Ready?"

...ther eye on him. And, just because we are related, don't give him any ...re leeway than you would another man.

"And where do you go now, Andrew?" Hiram asks him as they pause ...the gangway.

"To buy gloves," he answers. "And then home. Rebecca has not been ...ell of late. But you know that?"

"I must secure a room at the tavern," Hiram says. "My cabin is a mess. Henry Dibble is recaulking two of the stern windows and has them out. It is too cold to sleep there in this kind of weather."

"Why not go to Mrs. Latham's boarding house? You usually stay there when you're ashore."

"I have too much unfinished work aboard ship and have a full day of troubles to solve tomorrow. The Mousetrap is close by."

All of a sudden, in an Irish tenor's voice, Egan be[gins] the first few words, his companions join in.

> My name is Solomon Levi
> And my store's on Chatham Street;
> That's where to buy your coats and vests
> And everything else that's neat.

Without waiting to hear the next chorus, Levi puts his [hands over] his ears, turns 180 degrees and quickly runs inside his store.

"Let's be off," Hiram says to his brother. "I have business to [attend] to back on the ship."

"We'll see you onboard," Egan yells after he realizes that the[y] are underway, and waves to them.

"What do you think of Abraham Brown as a mate?" Andrew asks his brother as they cross the street to *Tranquility*.

"If it were up to me, I would not have signed him on, even a[s a] harponeer or boat steerer. I know he has a well-founded reputation f[or] being good at both tasks, but I know he can be trouble. Over the year[s] I have occasionally spoken with captains on whose ships he has sailed. He is daring in the bow of a whaleboat, almost reckless, and can lance as well as harpon. And, he is good in the rigging, but has an un-Quaker-like predilection for rum. And, he has been known to cause dissention in the fo'c's'le. He is a troubled person, a constant complainer and seems to find joy in disharmony. He is a drunkard and lecherous, and, I say again, very un-Quaker-like.

"Do you know he had been passed over as a mate on both whalers?" continues Hiram.

"No, I didn't. But I would not have doubted it. He is a malcontent," says Andrew.

"I agree with you. But brother, do me well for I ask you to keep a

Chapter 5

The Reality of Dreams

Hiram recrosses the street and momentarily stands in front of the Mousetrap Tavern. Nearly 30 years earlier, it was built as a house by Hugh Halsey. However, soon thereafter became an inn with rooms on the second floor made available to whalers by the night, week or longer. A cartoon-like image is carved in relief on a sign that hangs above the front door. A mouse rides on the back of a sperm holding onto the line of a harpoon stuck in the whale.

"Have you a room available for tonight?" Lester addresses a man washing glasses behind the small bar. "Preferably one in front."

"We do, captain," says the man as he pulls a ledger from under the bar and begins to write in it.

"What time do you serve evening meals?"

"Whenever you want. Will the room be just tonight?"

"That will depend on my carpenter."

Lester thanks him and returns to his ship.

As darkness begins to engulf *Tranquility*, and all of Water Street, Hiram Lester feels the first pangs of hunger. His steward is not expected to arrive in Sag Harbor for two more days. He closes his logbook and locks it in a drawer in the wall cabinet.

"Mr. Dibble," he asks the ship's carpenter, "when do you expect to be completed with the windows?"

"That all depends upon how cold it gets tonight," Dibble answers. "The caulking must dry out, harden, before I dare place the windows back. Possibly by the end of tomorrow. If so, I can carefully move them and we can turn on your stove to hasten the drying. Probably another two days."

"Why don't you quit now?" Hiram say to Dibble. "It's getting too dark to see anything in here unless you light all the lanterns."

"I'll see you tomorrow, Cap'n," Dibble says as he gathers his clothing and heads for the galley.

Lester is at the gangway and about to go down to the dock when he notices there is a real chill in the air. It'll make ice tonight, he says to himself and then pulls up the coat's collar and heads across the street to the tavern. As he crosses the street he hears the boisterous yelling of men inside. I hope I can get some sleep tonight, he says as he pulls a hand out of his tunic's pockets and reaches for the doorknob.

The entrance opens into the bar room, a space no more than 25 feet square. Three small tables take up most of the space and a short bar what little else remains.

"Glory be!" Patrick Egan exclaims in a loud voice. "Boys, it is our captain." They all stand and salute him.

"Remain seated. You're not in the navy now," Lester says and the four men immediately sit. On their table are four glass steins and a clutter of playing cards. On one corner there is a stack of bowls with remnants of what they had eaten.

"Can I buy my captain a glass of rum?" Egan asks Lester.

"I thank you," he responds, "but I do not drink. But, may I buy you a round of what you are drinking?"

"Why, of course," Egan says.

Lester motions to the bartender. "Add it to my bill," he tells the aproned man.

"Where shall I eat?" Lester asks the barman as he approaches Eagan's table with a freshly-draw pitcher of beer.

"Dining is in the other room. Take any table you want."

The dining room is even smaller than the barroom.

After few minutes the barman returns with a large soup dish in one hand a heavy pot in the other. He sets down the dish and begins filling it with a beef stew.

"Who owns the tavern now?" Hiram asks the barman. "Hugh Halsey has been dead for a few years now."

"Aye," says the barman. "It's his son James. He inherited it. James' two younger brothers died in the war so he got it."

"Does he stay here?"

"Never. I'll be back in a minute with bread," he says.

"What else have you to eat?" Lester asks him before he disappears. "Is there no menu?"

"This is it," answers the barman, "there's no choice here."

Lester eats in silence as the Irishmen carry on. A quartet of four other men enters the barroom and heads for an empty table. They look familiar to Lester. They must be some of the locals who have signed on, he says to himself.

The barman returns with a loaf of bread and a knife and is about to leave when he suddenly turns. "Oh yes," he says, "Here's the key to your room."

"Which room should I take?"

"Take any one you want. The key fits every door. There's no one else up there. Turn back at the top of the stairs and the room with a window on the street will be in front of you."

Still three more men come in as Lester finishes his stew.

The barroom has reached its capacity, Lester thinks to himself. Maybe that is why it is called a mousetrap. Everyone is crowded into this small hole, lured not by cheese but by rum and beer.

As Lester rises from the table, the door again opens and two giggling women enter. A gust of wind blows in with them. It is laden with the smell of a strong, cheap perfume that suddenly fills Lester's nostrils.

Oh well, he says to himself. It is more than rum that attracts men.

An exhausted Lester easily falls asleep. But isn't too long until he feels his stomach working. That damned stew was too spicy he says as he searches under the bed for a pot. He is again fast asleep but is awakened by voices in the next room. They are men's voices. He cannot make out what they are saying. Probably Egan's crew, he thinks. He tries to fall asleep but the noises bother him.

In frustration he throws off the blanket, lights the large candle on the nightstand and takes it into the hall. The voices are now louder. He knocks on the door. There is no response. He knocks again, louder and still no one answers even though the voices continue.

He opens the door and is astonished by what he sees. His candle provides barely enough light but he sees four men seated around a small table playing cards. At first he thinks it is Egan and his friends, but then he realizes that they are all dressed like ship officers, like whaling captains. They all wear beards.

Lester quickly regains his composure. "Can't you play cards without all this jibber jabber? I am trying to sleep. How can you play in the dark?"

The men continue playing cards and do not respond to Lester's plea. He takes a step closer and repeats it.

"My God!" he exclaims. "Are you all deaf?"

The man with his back to Lester slowly turns around and even in the weak light Hiram sees him glare at him. Lester believes he sees a faint smile spreading across his lips.

"Beware of a cyclone for surely it will provide a seat for you at our table."

The man turns back to the table and plays a card from his hand.

Startled, Lester bolts upright in his bed. He sees a weak daybreak light coming in through the room's window. He stops to listen. All is quiet. He gets off the bed, enters the hallway and opens the door to the next room. Only an unused bed and a small nightstand furnish the room. There is no card table nor are there four men. The room is empty.

Was this all a dream? he questions himself. It all seemed so real. And what does it mean "…that a cyclone shall provide me a seat…" A seat to what? It was the damned stew. I'll never eat stew again.

He dresses then goes to the window.

He is momentarily stunned by what he sees.

There is an unnatural stillness outside--no wind, no sun. No one walks the street. The world is covered in a light blanket of snow. The snow looks gray instead of white. Am I still asleep? he questions himself. He looks to his ship. She, too, is gray, somber. There is no activity on his ship.

How strange she looks. She looks like a ghost ship, he thinks to himself. Was it the stew or did I really see the ghosts of past whalers?

He finishes dressing and goes down to the bar to pay his bill. The barroom is empty. The barman hears him and comes out of the kitchen carrying a pot of coffee and several mugs in his hands.

Lester enters the barroom and sees portraits of four men. Strange, he thinks to himself as he pulls out his pocketbook to pay the bill, I never noticed them there last night.

Underneath each one is an engraved gold plate. He moves closer and reads the first one: "John E. Howell, master of the *France*. Killed July 1840 in an encounter with a sperm whale."

The second reads: "Stratton H. Harlow, Master of the Ship *Daniel Webster*. Died in the Pacific Ocean Oct. 31, 1838."

This is too much, he thinks to himself. Enough!

"Cap'n," asks the barman as he watches Lester read the plates, "will you be staying with us tonight?"

"One night here is more than enough," Lester says as he throws the money onto the bar and hurries outside.

"Did you have any visitors?" the barman yells.

Lester pays him no mind and slams the door.

The barman chuckles as he pours himself a cup of coffee.

CHAPTER 6

Parting Forever

As the crow flies, the settlement of Springs is 8 nautical miles due east of Sag Harbor. By water, it is 11 miles. By horse and carriage, it is almost twice as far. Andrew prefers the watery route. His gaff-rigged catboat is tied on the outboard side of *Tranquility*. He had used it two days earlier to bring his sea chest to the ship.

The whistle at the hat factory in Sag Harbor blows noon as he crosses over the deck of the ship. Seeing Abe Brown near one of the whaleboats, Andrew stops to address him, "Mr. Brown, how goes our Indian?"

"He is fine, Sir. He is still cuffed to the bunk."

"Be sure to treat him well," Andrew says, then climbs over the gunwale and drops down to his catboat.

A light southwest wind greets him as he moves the boat out of the lee created by *Tranquility*. He turns around to wave to his brother who is now watching him from the quarterdeck. The wind sets the sail with a snap. Andrew responds by pulling the tiller tighter against his waist.

On a northeast tack, Lester runs the 18-foot boat close to Mashomack Point then directly to Cedar Island Lighthouse off Cedar Point. After rounding the lighthouse on an easterly reach, he sets the boat tightly against the headlands until he approaches Lionhead Rock. He gives it a wide passage because the entire beach is strewn with glacial boulders, many of which, even at the lowest full-moon tide, never reveal their encrusted heads. Beyond the rock, he hugs the beach southward to Acabonack Harbor.

Ahead, the land is flat. Leafless trees cross the horizon obscuring most of the small village's few houses except Andrew's. Its widow's walk stands above them. He is still too far away to be certain but he thinks he sees someone rush across the open balustrade and disappear. Was it Rebecca? he thinks.

The tide is flooding through the narrow inlet into the harbor. He rides its surge west to the village. Springs is only a cluster of a dozen or so houses. His is on the water's edge. As he approaches it, he lets the sail's sheet (line) slip through his hand. The boat's momentum carries it to his dock.

Noah, his 20-year-old son, has seen him enter the harbor and comes down to the dock to help tie the catboat.

"How's your mother?"

"She's been resting most of the day. Annie was over yesterday. Her husband came to pick her up. They left about a half-hour ago."

"And how is your sister? Nearly a month has passed since I last saw her."

"She is fat and getting fatter. She said the baby must be a boy because he is so active. She says women can tell such things. Do you think they can?"

As they walk up the short path to the house, Andrew puts his right arm over his son's shoulder and temporarily pulls him closer. He is saddened by the mounting realization that he will soon be leaving him as well as Rebecca. Worse, he has no idea when he will see them again. Andrew suddenly embraces his son. He kisses him on his cheek and holds him even harder to his chest. Andrew pulls his head away from Noah's cheek and quietly says, "I love you, son. I will miss you dearly."

Andrew Lester is a successful whaleship captain but he could never have afforded such a grand house. He inherited it from his father, who along with his grandfather, both whaleship captains, were eventually able to amass enough money to build such a building. His father gave it to him rather than Hiram because Hiram already had a good, sturdy house. The house was part of his wife's dowry.

Andrew stops for a moment as he approaches the front door, letting Noah go first. Rebecca is standing at one of the front floor-length windows bracketing the entrance. He waves to her before he follows his son into the house. She responds but ever so slowly. She has been watching him and Noah walk up the path and embrace. Tears fill her eyes. Just as they enter the house, a faint smile spreads across her lips. She is pleased to see her husband. She quickly wipes her tears before Andrew enters the room.

"How are you feeling, Rebecca?" Andrew asks as he takes off his captain's long-coat and enters the living room.

"Much better today….and yesterday as well. It did me good to see Annie. I wish she would visit us more often."

"I do, too, but she has her own home and children to tend. And now, with another one on the way, getting around for her is not easy.

"Did the doctor come yesterday as he was supposed to?"

"He did."

"And…and what did he say?"

"Like always, he said it is consumption."

Just as she finishes speaking she begins to cough. Noah hears her and pours a glass of water from a pitcher on an end table next to the sofa on which she sits. She stops coughing and asks: "When do you expect to sail?"

"In two days. We're bound by the tide. The shoal off Mashomack Point has grown and the channel is nearly blocked. I sailed over it as I returned home and took its depth. There was still some tide to run-in but the water had shoaled since I was last there. We'll need a real nor'easter on a flood tide to wash it open if it closes more."

One of the Lester's two dogs begins barking in the kitchen. Noah leaves to see what troubles them.

"He must return soon to college," Rebecca says as Noah disappears. "He fears he has already fallen back in his classes."

"I would harness the horse and surrey and take him to the ferry, but I must go back to the ship tomorrow. There is still much to do and Hiram needs my help."

"I am so glad Noah will not go to sea," Rebecca says. "Yale has been expensive but it is worth the money just so some other woman does not have to wait months, no, wait for years, for her husband to return home."

"Rebecca, I know that the years of worrying about my safety at sea have been hard on you. Being a lawyer is a better way for Noah to make a living. Even if he didn't go on to college, I don't think he has the fortitude nor even the penchant to go to sea."

"In a way, I hope your voyage is not successful," says Rebecca. "That being so, the Company might turn *Tranquility* into a merchant ship. At the least, the voyages then would be of short duration. I would see you more often."

Rebecca sighs deeply after the short speech, then begins coughing. She sips on the water but it gives her no relief. She coughs until what is irritating her throat is temporarily gone.

"I have a feeling," Rebecca says as Andrew sits next to her on the sofa, "that I will never see you again."

"Pshaw," he says. "Put that silly notion out of your mind. *Tranquility* is a good, sound ship, and she has weathered many a gale and storm. I will be all right. I will come back to you."

"That is not what I fear," Rebecca says. "It is I who will not be here." She punctuates the statement with another coughing spell.

Andrew momentarily bites his lip. Silently he chastises himself for thinking of himself before his ailing wife. How callous of me, he silently says.

"Rebecca, Rebecca," he blurts out. "I am thinking of abandoning this voyage. I thought we needed it to gain enough money to buy the 200 acres behind our house. You are more important than any piece of ground. We can get along farming without it. Besides, I'm getting too old to go to sea."

"Andrew, I have lived with you long enough to know how much you love the sea. Don't do this for me.

"No, Andrew. Your brother needs you, too. We need the added money from this trip for Noah to continue attending Yale. Andrew, go."

Rebecca's eyes are again filled with tears. She pulls out a cloth to wipe them and begins coughing intensely.

"They are lasting longer and are more severe," she says. "I know I won't be here for much more time. Please, Andrew, leave while I can still say good-bye to you."

Noah returns to the living room. He has overheard most of the talk.

"Father, I know you're sailing in a few days. When Annie's husband was here, he said his father has business in Smithtown. In a few days they will be going there. Her husband said he would be willing to take me to Port Jefferson to catch the Bridgeport Ferry, if I could go then. I told him I think I would but first I wanted to speak to you."

"That sounds fine to me," says Andrew. "Maybe Annie's husband could leave Annie and her children here with mother while he is in Smithtown."

"Annie already suggested that," Rebecca says.

The two men walk outside to feed the horse. As they do, Noah asks his father what might be his first port of call. "Will there be one with an American embassy or consulate?"

"That is difficult to say because of the nature of our voyage. We might be in the Azores, or Stanley in the Falklands or even Rio, or Buenos Aires. At some time, we will probably pull into Barbados looking for a few men and provisions. However, whenever we pass an American ship homeward bound and we speak them, I will always give them a letter telling you where we are and where we are going so that you in turn can send one to a consulate, if need be."

"Father, I think there will be a need to do so. I am no physician but I have watched mother quickly deteriorating. Daily, her breathing becomes more difficult. Father, I fear her end is near. I cannot bear to leave her and return to school."

"Noah, you must. I know all this. I know it all too well. It pulls at my heart to see what is happening to her. I have thought several times of abandoning this voyage. I even proposed it to her minutes ago. She would have me do nothing of the kind

"Have you heard from your brother?"

"Like you, I have not seen Michael since he was here on the 4th of July. Manhattan seems to have swallowed him up."

The next morning Andrew faces the reality of their lives and departs quickly after kissing Rebecca. He has no choice. His character leaves him no room other than to stoically accept what is to be an unalterable destiny. If there is to be happiness it his life, he believes, it can only be gained by accepting life's ups and downs. Still, he feels he is abandoning her.

Chapter 7

Why the Kidnapping?

During the next two days, *Tranquility's* needed for a full complement to set her asail is met. The crimpers have done their job, securing the dozen men needed for the whaleboat crews. Sixteen beings, composed of a few known whalers, a scattering of local commercial fishermen, and a few desperate Long Island farmers, have signed on. There are five Black men among them, three of whom were brought North during the war by the Underground Railroad. They were set free on Long Island and eventually gravitated to the nearby Shinnecock Indian Reservation. None had ever been to sea but in a depressed post-war Long Island, they readily made their mark on the shipping contracts.

Bedlam still reigns in the forecastle on the day the ship is set to depart as 16 Greenies vie for bunks and footlocker space. Abe Brown is standing at the top of the ladder that leads into the cramped quarters listening to several men quarreling over locations. He's been told by Andrew that he is to act as temporary 4th mate. Sensing he's heard enough, that the men new to the ship are riled and that they need a leader, he drops down the ladder.

"Stop it!" Abe yells.

No one pays attention to him.

Abe jumps from the ladder and pushes two brawling men to the deck. That catches their attention.

"Damn it," he yells, "when an officer enters this hell hole an' gives an order, you do it. And do it fast."

"Who the hell are you?" one Greenies steps forward looking for an answer.

As he does, Abe punches him hard on the side of his head. The man tumbles onto another man sitting on a bottom bunk.

"Most of ya Greenies done knows me but ya will. An', yous'll regret it

"I'm 4th Mate Abe Brown. I'm in charge of yer whaleboat. I'm here tuh look over wad I can pick from dis bunch of idiots tuh make dem into whalemen. I needs four. Stan' up! Git the hell out of dose bunks. It ain't time tuh sleep.

"I done tink dere's an able-bodied whaler in dis sorry lot."

Abe walks among the men looking them over and asks a few their names. He knows he cannot choose his crew before the captain calls all the Greenies on deck once they are under way. He uses this time to see who might be his first choices.

Later that day, Abe is near the gangway when Andrew arrives from Springs.

"Good afternoon, Mr. Lester," Abe addresses the 1st mate.

Andrew responds accordingly.

"Can I have a word wid ya?" Abe asks.

"Of course." Andrew is suspicious of being greeted so formally by Abe.

"Have ya talked tuh the Indian we got dee udder night?"

"No, I haven't but I will as soon as I have all my gear on board."

"If yere too busy, I'd be glad to splain tuh him why he wuz kidnapped."

"That's quite alright," answers Andrew. "I feel it should come from me. But thank you for suggesting it."

"Aye, Sir. Tank ya," says Abe as he turns away and heads for the quarterdeck.

Damn that man, Andrew says to himself as he enters the galley. I can only imagine what he would have said to the Indian.

Andrew had Benquam taken from the forecastle by the Bo'sun and secured at a bunk in the tight food storage quarters behind the galley where Cook and his helper sleep. He sees Benquam lying on the bunk. As he approaches, Benquam sits up on the edge of the bunk.

"What is your name?" Andrew asks him.

The Indian is slow to answer.

"Benquam," he says as he tries to stand. But the chain on the shackle is too short to allow him to do that.

"That's a strange name," says Andrew. "I have been to your reservation. I even had one of your tribe in one of my whaleboats. I have never heard it before. Do you know what it means?"

"It was the name of one of my ancestors…many generations ago. I know not what it means." Benquam starts to rise as he speaks.

"Please, remain seated," says Andrew. "I am Andrew Lester. I am the 1st mate and second in command of this ship. You're going to be with us for a while. Do you mind if I call you Ben instead of Benquam?"

"Would it matter if I did?"

Andrew does not answer his question.

"I guess what has been foremost on your mind is why you were brought here against your will. The captain and I are not proud of the action but we were compelled, forced to do it. We had no choice. We are the victims of a superstition that is nearly 200 years old.

"When the first Quakers were driven out of the Massachusetts Colony and landed on Eastern Long Island it was the beginning of winter. Your ancestors helped them make it through the winter. In spring, they showed the Colonists how to utilize dead whales that regularly washed onto the beaches as food.

"After a few years, the Colonists couldn't wait for a dead whale to wash ashore and began venturing just off shore in small boats accompanied by a few Montauk and Shinnecock Indians. They all shared in a whale if it was haponed* and brought ashore. Usually the haponeer was an Indian and it quickly became a tradition to have an Indian or two onboard every large ship that went below the horizon searching for whales. In a way, they felt indebted to Indians for helping them survive and shared any success with them.

"For many years, your people gladly signed on whaling ships. But since the end of the war, they have been reluctant to do so. I even visited your reservation looking for volunteers among men who shipped with me when I was a captain. They were reluctant to sign on and believe there is now no profit in a voyage that often ends in disaster.

"There already was talk among the Greenies that the trip would not be successful without at least one Indian in the crew. There were even threats of desertion.

"Maybe you can see how desperate we were and had to kidnap you to satisfy their misguided superstition. I hope you understand.

"As soon as the ship has passed Montauk your shackle will be removed. You will start life onboard by helping Cook. However, I hope your role onboard progresses farther than that."

Ben is speechless, confused by what he has heard and doesn't respond. After a moment Andrew turns and goes topside to help ready the ship for its departure that evening.

* Whalemen have for centuries had mispronounced harpoon and call it a harpon and a harpooner is a harponeer.

CHAPTER 8

At Last, Outward Bound

Tuesday, Dec. 5, 1865

The 10th clap of the huge bell in the tower of the Old Whaler's Church quickly fades into the night as Andrew and his brother stand on the top of the ship's gangway. Both have been scanning the dock looking for familiar faces among the dockhands. There are none. Andrew thinks that maybe Noah would be there to bid him farewell. But his mother needs him now more than I do, he thinks to himself. Am I doing the right thing leaving Rebecca?

They stand silently for a few minutes. Capt. Lester turns to his brother and says in disgust, "There's no wind. We must warp the ship away from the dock. I had hoped for an easy departure but it will not be such. Order the three larboard whaleboats into the water and have them secure, in tandem, a long line to the stern. Take in the gangway. There is no one else coming with us. Damn the wind."

Lester, as do most dedicated Quakers, abhors swearing. However, out of frustration, he uses it sparingly and does not consider damning in the true sense to be swearing. And, while the left side of most ships in the 1800s was referred to as the port side, whaleship men retained the old term larboard.

Andrew is in charge of the fourth whaleboat, located aft on the starboard davit. He does not lower. Instead, he and Bo'sun oversee the other mates' launchings of their crafts. When this is completed, he signals to the captain that all is ready to haul.

Andrew Lester wears two hats on *Tranquility*. Like all 1st mates, he is the person, and not the captain, who actually runs the ship from day to night and night to day. He is not only the ship's 1st mate, and thus second in command of the ship, but he is also the sailmaster. As such, he is in charge of navigation and the actual sailing of the ship. In this capacity, the bo'sun and quartermasters are his immediate subordinates, his right-hand men. On larger ships, Andrew's jobs would be divided among several men.

Andrew Lester is more than qualified to fill the requirements of this job. There is a saying among shipmasters and owners, that a first mate is a captain in the making. Andrew, however, has already skippered two barks during the past ten years. One was a New Bedford whaleship that he returned with its hull filled with oil. The second, the *Temperance*, was one of three whaleships the Company had owned. In March 1865, he was returning to Sag Harbor, when just south of Block Island, he encountered the *CSS Shenandoah*, the Confederate raider. He tried to outrun her, but the man-o-war shot away his ship's fore- and mainmasts and began bombarding the hapless vessel. He launched her four whaleboats and the surviving crewmembers made it into Great Salt Pond on Block Island without being chased. The ship was sunk.

Capt. Lester turns to his brother, nods and says, "Time to go. Let this voyage begin."

Andrew calls to the Bo'sun John Bellingham, who is aft on the quarterdeck deck and orders him to throw off the dock lines. Bellingham's crew is split. A few rush to the bow and others to the stern. Three men scramble down the gangway and onto the wharf. Those now ashore slip the bow and stern lines off the bollards and rush back to the gangway, hauling it onto the ship. Those onboard retrieve the hawsers.

Slowly at first, the whaleboats pull the stern of *Tranquility* away from the wharf, then slightly north into Sag Harbor Cove. When she is free of Long Wharf they quickly row to the bow. The towline there is fed to the men on the bow and made fast to a huge bow cleat. As the men begin rowing they feel the remnants of the waning flood tide still thwarting their efforts.

After a half-hour remnants of the flood still remain as they reach the sandbar that could block their passage. Everyone listens intensely as *Tranquility* moves over it. There is the subtle scraping of her hull on sand. They feel it more than hear it. Andrew half-expects a jarring of the ship as she goes aground or slows temporarily as the keel bevels the sandbar's top. Neither happens. A flood of relief overtakes both captain and mates. The crews of the three whaleboats continue to bend their oars for the next two miles until they are just off Mashomack Point. There they feel the pressure against their oars ease as the ebbing tide begins to overtake the ship. A light northerly breeze has come up and adds to the ebb moving the ship faster than their boats.

"Return boats to the ship," Andrew orders the bo'sun.

Bellingham, in the bow from where he has kept watch on the boats, uses a megaphone to pass on the word.

"The ebb is making up just as we need it," Andrew says to the quartermaster who, through the ship's large wheel, now feels a mounting pressure against the rudder.

Without incident, the whaleboats are at their larboard side davits and quickly hauled out.

At first, the wind barely moves the ship. Fighting the pushing tide, the quartermaster has some difficulty keeping the ship in the unmarked channel. As they clear Cedar Island Lighthouse on their starboard side, *Tranquility* moves out of the lee of Shelter Island with the tide. Her sails now catch a northerly wind that teases her, luffing her unset sails, bringing them to life. Almost at the same moment, clouds that had obliterated the southern horizon are swept away. They expose a nearly-full moon that is already 40 degrees above the horizon. Its crisp, bright light floods the ship.

"This is a good omen." Andrew says to his brother as they stand next to Adrian Moore, the quartermaster manning the helm.

"Haul sails on fore- and main," he orders the bo'sun who stands a few yards ahead of him, below, on the main deck. "After we pass Lionhead Rock and turn due south, add the mizzens."

Bellingham repeats the orders to the mate in charge of the watch. A half-dozen men, at the ready, scurry up the ratlines to the yards and quickly reach the cross spars.

Making the eastward turn south of Acabonack Harbor is always tricky for a square-rigged ship. Immediately to larboard is the long, extended shoal, Ram Island, that emanates from the southern tip of Gardiners Island. It is difficult to clear even during the day but at night, unseen, it can abruptly end a ship's progress. As they lay close off Acabonack Harbor, Andrew moves to the ship's starboard quarter. From there he can better see a few lights in the cluster of houses in Springs.

Surely one is my house, he thinks. His mind turns again to his ill wife and the feeling of guilt rises. It is like a chill gust of winter wind rushing over his body.

"By the mark, 3 fathoms," yells the man swinging the hand lead off the bow. Bellingham repeats it.

Andrew realizes the ship is too close to the channel's eastern bank.

"Bring the helm 2 points to starboard," he commands Moore. "Lay closer to the land on the starboard," he says, "or we'll spend the next 12 hours aground on Ram Island.

"It's only an island at dead low," he says to Moore. "The rest of the time it is a menace to deep-draft ships. Three years ago, Capt. Benjamin Cartwright put his whaleship *Sunbeam* on it for nearly a week. Let's not do that."

Moore answers by turning the ship's wheel, quickly adding a few points to the compass.

"By the mark, 5 fathoms!" comes the report as the lead pulls the line down to the small piece of white cloth woven into it.

"By the mark, now 10 fathoms!" says the man as the 8-pound lead pulls the line down to a black, leather marker imbedded in the line. Deep water is now coming up fast and eases the pressure on those in the wheelhouse.

Moore looks toward Andrew, whose eyes are upon him. In the moonlight, and even in what weak light the lantern inside the wheelhouse throws forth, he sees an approving smile spread across the 1st mate's face.

The wind has freshened and a chop--small waves--now break like strings of illuminated pearls in the darkness as they crash on the remnants of Ram Island's exposed shoal. Looking south, over the sand dunes on the front, south side of the South Fork, the moon illuminates the combers crashing on the beach as they roll in from the open Atlantic. Ahead, the moonlight makes it easy to see the hazards.

Thirteen miles farther to the east they clear Long Island.

They give Shagwong's shoals on the starboard side a wide berth as the ship temporarily points east-northeast. The night is clear as *Tranquility* turns southeast and slides past Montauk Point. Now, only the black, open ocean and a star-studded sky lie ahead. The air is crisp, clean and cold, stinging the nostrils when one takes a deep breath. Moonlight bathes the tall, sand-bluff cliffs on Long Island's south side. The light seams to focus on the towering lighthouse that, even then, was a long-familiar beacon to mariners as it bid them a farewell or hello. Those on deck fix their gaze on it as the ship pass to starboard, gradually fading out-of-sight. Thirty-six souls on *Tranquility* must be wondering if they will ever again see the Light. Whaling is a risky business. Everyone onboard, excepting maybe the Greenies, knows there is always a chance they might not. And still they go. Each man has his own moment with the famous point and the steadily rotating beacon atop Turtle Hill.

Ben never sees Montauk Light. Still shackled to a bunk in Cook's storeroom, he is aware that the ship is now at sea. The power of the oncoming waves lift then drop the bow of the ship. They cause him to roll violently from one way and to the other.

I am lost, he thinks. I will never return to my home. I hate these bastards who stole me from my family, my friends. I will escape this ship when it makes a port. Somewhere. Anywhere. I will have a chance. I will be free.

Andrew orders the quartermaster to set a course to the east-southeast. They now sail seeking not only the warmth of the Gulf Stream but to escape the oncoming winter, to ride the river within the ocean toward Europe. The Stream lies a hundred miles south of Montauk. The closest it comes to land after leaving Florida is Cape Hatteras in North Carolina. The Gulf Stream flows easterly at an average speed of 4 knots. Near daybreak, as they pass to the south of Block Island, they can just make out its low silhouette on the horizon. It will be the last sight of America they will see until the voyage is over.

Hiram Lester does not go below to his cabin but remains in the wheelhouse with the quartermaster and bo'sun. Lester glances at the hourglass mounted on the foreside of the binnacle, beyond the compass, and sees that the top half is about to be empty. He waits a second or two until the last grains of sand rush through the narrow constriction. He reaches forward with his right hand and capsizes the glass. This task is always assigned to the quartermaster or his relief on the wheel but Lester momentarily usurps tradition. He then glances over to John Bellingham.

"Would you?" he asks the bo'sun, who is waiting.

Without answering, Bellingham opens the wheelhouse door, takes one step outside, and grabs the lanyard on the ship's bell. At 4 a.m. he rings it 8 times.

Two hours later, dead ahead, daylight is just a weak beginning when Capt. Lester takes the wheel from the quartermaster. He has remained in the wheelhouse to the surprise of his mates and shiphandlers.

"Stand by," he says to Moore.

Lester stares into the southeast as his hands tightly grasp the spokes on the large wheel. His mind, however, is in the throes of beginning yet another voyage, focuses on the horizon. He wonders what uncertainties might lie out of sight, beyond it. It has been nearly a year since he returned *Tranquility* to Sag Harbor with a bilge less-than-full of oil.

What a great feeling it is to be at sea again, he says to himself. To feel the force of the water against the weather side of the rudder makes me come alive. With absolute authority I challenge these swells that easily lift and drop the bow of my ship. I can feel the ocean entering me through the hull, through the timbers on the decking, through the oak wheel and its spindles, up my arms and across my shoulders. I feel as if I have total control over a great beast. For the moment, I do. I again feel as one with the ocean and my ship. Oh, what a glorious feeling it is to be at sea again, to be out-of-sight of land.

This is a must voyage for me, he continues thinking. I must make it a success not only for the Company but for myself as well. My last two voyages have been less than bountiful. Was it just bad luck or the war? But no one thinks of these when picking a captain. My reputation is at stake. I cannot let it flounder if I hope to again captain a vessel. I will win this one. I will. I will.

"Captain! Captain!" Moore startles Lester.

"Yes? Yes? What is it?"

"The course, Sir. You have moved several points to the south'ard."

Lester quickly regains his composure and looks at the compass card.

"Oh! So I have. I guess I want to get to the Stream a bit faster, but we must be easting at the same time."

Lester backs the wheel, then veers slightly until the compass card again rests on the 100-degree mark. He still holds the helm and sways automatically responding, compensating for the rise and fall of the ship. All three men in the wheelhouse move in syncopated response to the mounting heave on the sea.

A few minutes later, Andrew re-enters the wheelhouse.

"Number 1, the ship is yours," Lester says to his brother as he turns the wheel over to the quartermaster. "I'm going to my cabin."

Lester steps out of the wheelhouse and crosses the quarterdeck to the aft companionway house. In doing so, he momentarily is unsteady, as his long-unused sea legs begin their return. He pauses for a moment, his hand on the door's knob, then pulls it open and goes down the ladder to the officer's mess.

"Bo'sun," Andrew addresses Bellingham, who is in the wheelhouse with him and Quartermaster Moore at the helm, "has the patent log been set?"

"Aye, Sir. It has," Moore answers. "I heaved it off at Ram Island."

"And what was the last reading?'

"Five knots, Sir."

"The binnacle lights…have the wicks been trimmed, the lenses cleaned? I can hardly see the compass card."

"Aye, Sir. They are all in order and filled."

"Good. Now find Mr. Dibble and ask him to meet me in the bow. Also, I noticed that there are no flares in the wheelhouse. Will you see that there are four in place?"

"Aye, Sir, that I will."

Andrew leaves the wheelhouse and slowly strolls forward on the main deck, adjusting his gait as the bow of *Tranquility* now rhythmically rises and falls in response to large rollers coming from the southeast. These are the remnants of an offshore storm far, far away. Winds are light-to-moderate and have backed from north, to northwest, and have settled from the west-northwest and are now against *Tranquility's* transom. As he walks forward, Lester looks aloft, scanning the course, then the topsail, up to the topgallant and finally the royal sails. They are aglow with reddish light even though the sun's rays have not yet struck them.

How beautiful is a full sail, he says to himself. I have been ashore too long.

He stops for a moment and listens to the sounds of the ship as she comes alive. He defines the creaking of the blocks as cordage sliding in and out. Somewhere aloft, wood is riding upon wood. There is the sudden snap of a sail that comes fully taut as it catches a slight shift in the wind. The ship is alive, he thinks. He feels the wind ruffle the hair on the back of his neck and he pulls up the large collar on his coat to ward off its chill. The smell of air-borne salt fills his nostrils. I, too, am alive, like this ship, he says. How I pity the land-bound man who never knows this feeling. He again glances aloft at the sails and smiles.

They are nicely filled, he thinks. She runs sweetly before the wind. It's as fair a course as I have ever seen. Would it be this way all the way to the Azores without a tack? But I doubt that will happen. That is too much to hope for. The sea is much like a woman. For both change, change without warning is normal, to be unexpected, it is the rule. When will that next happen? He asks himself and then reviews the horizon. Not a cloud is in the sky. The sun is lazy this morning, he thinks. Maybe we can squeeze a few days out of this course. That would be nice.

Andrew's concentration again shifts aloft, to the running rigging, and pays special attention to the set of the braces on all the yardarms. They are almost square, at right angles to the longitudinal axis of the ship, he says to himself. Finally, he approaches the bow and is greeted by four pigs in a pen on the forecastle. They are grunting and rummaging through a clean pile of straw that has been placed there for them. As he nears a small coop and its fenced-in cage, a dozen white leghorn chickens rush out of the hole and down a little ramp, squawking for food.

They never seem satisfied, he thinks.

Then he reaches the gunwale, extends his right arm to steady himself on the cathead as he leans over to look at the ship's cutwater. How neatly she splits the ocean. Oh God! He says to himself as he stares immediately below, how cleanly she runs. There is not a trace of whitewater, even as she rises and falls. Her hull is magnificent. Nehemiah Hand is an artist as well as a shipwright.

"You asked for me, Sir?" says Henry Dibble, the ship's carpenter.

Lester hadn't heard him approach and is momentarily startled.

"Yes, Mr. Dibble, I know today isn't Saturday, your usual day for such things, but I noticed there is now slack in all the larboard shrouds on this reach, on the fore-, main- and mizzenmast yards. Someone did not set them properly. This also would be an opportune time to service them because we may be on this reach for quite a while, that is if the winds do not alter their course. I would like you to lower them, one at a time, and grease all the blocks.

"When we go on the other tack, I would like you to do the same to all the blocks on that side. However, before you do, please see me to make sure it can be done without altering our course by any great amount. You might need a few hands to help you do it quickly; see Mr. Pilla and tell him I said you could use two of the Greenies. They might need some fresh air."

"I'll begin immediately, Sir."

Chapter 9

The Indoctrination

Wednesday, December 6th, 1865
Somewhere Southeast of Montauk Point

Early the first morning at sea Capt. Lester tells Bellingham to muster all hands aft the foremast. Andrew emerges from the stern hatch and looks astern. His brother, on the quarterdeck, sees him. With a wave beckons him to join him.

"Good morning, Hiram," Andrew says as he climbs the short ladder to the quarterdeck.

"And to you," Hiram answers. "How was your first night at sea?"

"I always sleep better on a ship," he answers.

"Now I am ready to address the crew," Hiram says. "I have bo'sun getting all the new men on deck. Please make sure all mates are here as well."

Andrew is about to enter the hatch to the officer's mess when he sees Bellingham coming up on the ladder.

"John," Andrew addresses him, "have all the mates come up because they will be picking their crews. Oh, also make sure the Indian is there as well."

"Aye, Sir, I will," he says as he returns alow.

"I'm not yet quite sure what to do with him," Andrew says while Bellingham is still within earshot. "For now, I think he can help Cook and Billy."

"Thank you."

"Aye, sir."

"Good morning," Capt. Hiram Lester says from the railing on the edge of the quarterdeck. He pauses for a moment as he looks over the men below him on the main.

"A few of you have been to sea before. But I am sure that even fewer of you have ever been to sea on a ship, let alone a whaleship. That doesn't matter because you are not here to become seamen. Your main purpose for being here is to become whalers."

Ben stands at the rear of these men and wonders why he, too, is here.

"Running the ship is my duty, and the duty of my four mates, and the bo'sun and quartermaster. When you are not in a whaleboat or cutting-in and trying, rendering, a whale, you will be called upon to help sail this ship. There are 16 of you who will be required to climb the shrouds, man the yards, haul the lines and special ropes called sheets, and help keep us moving and afloat.

"In this capacity, you must learn the names of every bit of canvas that is aloft. And you will learn the names of the lines that control them. You have one week in which to do this. If you do not, if you make mistakes in what you are told by the mates or the bo'sun, or you do not want to learn, you will be put on short rations until you regain your memory. If you are incapable of learning these terms used on a whaleship, I will give you leave at the first port we pull into. How you get home is up to you. That port will most likely be Angra do Heroismo on the island of Terceira in the Azores. That is about three weeks hence."

I wonder if there is an American consulate there, Ben says to himself. Surely they will help me after I tell them I was kidnapped. Or, this might be my chance to escape even if they don't.

"However," continues Capt. Lester, "your principal job is to catch whales. You do this from a whaleboat. There are four on *Tranquility* — one on the starboard and three on the larboard side. It takes six men to man a whaleboat. A mate commands each whaleboat. His second in command is the boat-steerer who also acts as the harponeer when going down on a whale. The mate handles the bow oar and the boat-steerer the rudder, or steering oar, and four of you will man the other oars.

"When we have a whale on board for trying, your jobs will change to 'whale cooks'," Lester jokingly says at a rare moment. "You will boil the blubber down to its oil and begin storing it in barrels. This ship is capable of holding 24,000 barrels, or 1 million 8 hundred thousand gallons of oil. When they are filled, we will set sail for home….and not a day sooner. We may have to lower away a thousand times, and cut-in 1,200 whales to try that much oil.

"Is there anyone who doesn't understand what I have said?"

"Sir, how much oil does ya git from a whale?" asks a Greenie.

"Anywhere from 40 to 80 barrels," the captain answers, "but that depends on the kind of whale and its size."

"My two mates, Mr. Lester and Mr. Pilla, will begin dividing you into four boat crews. At the moment, we are two mates short. I hope to pick up one or two in Angra. Abe Brown, a boat steerer and harponer is temporarily acting as the fourth mate. Mr. Ephraim Brown, our disburser, will do the picking for the fourth crew. Twelve of you, composed of two boat crews, will make up the larboard watch and the other 12 the starboard watch. No others will stand watch unless I call upon them.

"Before you form your watches, a few words from Bo'sun Bellingham."

"There are three ways to perform your shipboard duties while on this vessel," Bellingham says as he addresses the gathering of Greenies, "the right way, the wrong way and my way.

"*Tranquility* is unique in its construction when compared to other whaleships. It has a quarterdeck immediately ahead of the mizzenmast. I am standing on the quarterdeck. None of you should ever be on the quarterdeck unless your duties take you there. This is officer's country.

That is, captain and mates. If I catch any of you lollygagging here I'll find something extra for you to do. And, when you must walk the main deck, you do it along the leeward gunwale, never the weather side."

There is meanness in his voice, Ben thinks to himself. He is really in charge. He is big. I am impressed.

"When it comes to eating, breakfast is at 4 bells," continues Bellingham, "that is 6 in the morning. Dinner is at noon, or 8 bells and supper is at 4 bells. You'll never hear the bell struck at odd hours on a whaleship. You will dine in your quarters. The cook or his helpers will bring the food kids, wooden tubs, to you. Most of you have been told after you signed on that you should bring onboard a tin dish and cup, and fork and spoon, if you are accustomed to using them. I suggest you put your mark on them. If you are without such instruments, tell the quartermaster. He will draw them for you from the slop chest. Of course, their cost will be deducted from your lay before you are paid off.

"The food here is not fancy. It may lack variety but it is wholesome and good. It consists of salt horse, beef to you ex-landlubbers, potatoes, beans, peas and biscuits. You'll get coffee at breakfast and tea the rest of the day. From time to time, as long as they last, you'll get eggs, until the last chicken is killed. And, that goes for hogs as well.

"Now, let's form the watches."

"When do we start seeing whales?" Ben asks John 'Cook' Batiste, as he is washes pots in the galley.

"You can speak English," a slightly startled Batiste says. "These are the first words I've heard you say. I thought you only spoke Indian."

"There has been nothing to speak about," answers Ben.

Andrew Lester is in the galley getting more coffee for the officer's mess when he overhears Ben ask the question. Before Cook can render an explanation, Andrew speaks up: "We are not looking for whales now and won't be for about three weeks. These waters are so close to ports that by now there are very few whales to be seen. Once we leave the Azores and turn to the south'ard and parallel the coast of Africa we will start the hunt. The next few weeks will be spent training new oarsmen and practicing launching the whaleboats."

Without waiting for a response, he turns and heads aft toward the officer's mess.

That's him, Ben says to himself. I now realize where I heard it before. That's the voice I heard the night I was kidnapped.

"Damn him," he says in an embittered tone. "He's the bastard who did it."

"Did what?" Cook asks.

"He kidnapped me."

"I doubt it," Cook says. "He ain't the kind of man to do that."

In a fit of temper Ben throws the pot against a bulkhead and stomps out of the galley.

"Hold on there," yells Batiste.

Ben pays him no attention.

"Crazy Indian," he says and retrieves the pot.

CHAPTER 10

Blue Whales and a Pouch of Tobacco

While en route to the Azores everything onboard *Tranquility* goes well. The Greenies turn to their chores without complaining. Ben, however, is resentful of everything Cook has him do. He especially dislikes carrying food to the forecastle feeding the "bums."

"This is squaw's work," he regularly mutters.

At first, the weather is bitter cold, even for December. Westerly winds continually push the ship southeast over a frigid Atlantic. After three days the crew begins to notice slight rises in air temperatures. Gradually the quartermaster veers farther to the south'ard and enters the Gulf Stream that here flows in a northeasterly direction. When this happens, it is as if they have crossed into another world. Water takes on a very blue cast, bluer than most onboard have ever seen. Porpoises now are everywhere ahead of the ship and flocks of strange-looking birds skim the water as if in a race with *Tranquility*. There are even small birds that seemed to walk on the water. The Portygee called them *Yehzoos Christo's* birds. Best of all, the men can now go on deck without heavy oilskins.

Now that they are well past Newfoundland the current begins to flow more easterly. At 45° W. longitude, as they move off the influence of the Stream, Andrew resets the ship's course to southeast and aims her directly at the Azores.

Winds continue to blow southeast during that first evening outside of the Stream. The next morning, as Hiram climbs the after companionway, he sees his brother, exercising his dual role now as the sailmaster by having men tuning the lines, sheets and braces. Andrew does so with his eyes constantly aloft as he gives orders to the bo'sun, who in turn passes them on to the crew on deck.

"How does she run?" Hiram asks as he comes alongside Andrew, who maintains his eyes on the rigging.

"She points especially well," he answers, "despite the wind on our nose. She runs as close-hauled as I have ever witnessed a square-rigger run. She acts more like a fore-and-aft rigged ship. I know she would give any New Bedford-built ship a run for its money. The wind has steadily risen since sunrise though it still pours out of the southeast. We may have to tack if it rises appreciably."

As they speak, the weather leeches, lines that raise or lower a sail, on the main and fore begin to shake.

"Indeed," says Lester. "She is alive and is in her element but now get to the helmsman. He's doing a poor job letting the leeches shake and is about to stall the ship."

"Aye!" says Andrew as he rushes into the wheelhouse to berate the helmsman.

Ben now spends any free time topside. His is impressed and awestruck by the power of the wind and how it bends the sails. He isn't the only one affected by what is happening aloft. The mates began taking their Greenies about the ship telling them the names of the masts, sails and lines and pointing them out. For a few it is like being back in school. Andrew sees Ben and orders him to join his crew for instruction.

"Any galley work comes later," he tells him. "If Cook has a problem tell him I told you what to do."

Ephraim Brown is a landlubber, so Andrew adds Brown's crew to his for instruction. The crew's on-water education takes place once or twice a day, when weather allows. On the sixth day at sea, Capt. Lester has the quartermaster heave *Tranquility*. In order to bring the ship to a stop he turns the ship into the wind. Mates and their crews respond by lowering their boats from the davits. They exercise by rowing around the ship for hours just to get the new men into condition for when the time to row on a whale comes.

While Andrew is lowering his boat in a drill, he sees Ben on the starboard gunwale watching the operation. He now realizes that just having an Indian on board is not enough to satisfy the crew's superstition. Once back on the ship, he has bo'sun find Ben and tell him to be ready to climb into his boat the next time rowing drills occur.

Tranquility is now ten days out of Sag Harbor and the ship's royals (sails) are stowed. The winds are down in the morning so Capt. Lester has all four crews on the water, close to the ship, teaching Greenies how to row a whaleboat. Andrew has not yet decided what to do with Ben so instead of having him take an oar he sends him with the duty watch on the foremast.

Being short a mate Hiram Lester elects to husband Ephraim's Brown's crew and mans the tiller on the fourth whaleboat. When his boat rounds the bow of *Tranquility* the watch in the foremast with Ben yells, "Whale ho! Dead ahead!"

No one needs further direction. Dead ahead is always directly ahead of the whaleship. In each craft, boat steerers point their boats' bows to where the watch is pointing. They see nothing. As the boats begin to slow a monster of a whale suddenly breaks the surface and spouts.

"Make for the whale!" Captain Lester on his boat's tiller orders everyone to bend their oars. The race is real, with each mate swearing and yelling at his crew as their boats lunge toward where the whale dove. All that remains on the ocean's disturbed surface is a glitch. A few minutes later the whale again broaches.

The captain's boat with Ephraim's crew is closest to where the big fish* was first spotted. Following whaling protocol, when more than one whaleboat goes after a whale, the senior officer is given the lead. But the captain yells for everyone to catch up. Some of the men foul their oars in their haste to dig deeper into the water. Each time the whale spouts the boats move ahead a bit faster but the whale is always a bit farther away.

"A pound of tobacco to the first crew to be on the whale," Lester yells. He has no fear of losing any tobacco. The mates know his game.

The boats are pulling at their best but the whale pulls ahead with ease. The race is taking the boats to the edge of the horizon when the captain figures that it was enough of a workout for the day. He orders the boats to return to the ship.

"We would never got close enough to that whale to plant a harpon in it," says Ephraim Brown to Capt. Lester as Brown climbs onboard from the whaleboat.

"I know that," Lester says. "I thought it would be good exercise for the Greenies. It was like a real chase."

"Wasn't that a real chase?"

"No, not really. That was a blue whale. They're the biggest and fastest of all whales. They cruise at 10 knots even when they've not been gallied. When they're scared there isn't a chance. That's why so few blues are ever rendered."

"How fast can whaleboats be rowed?" Brown asks Lester.

"Five, maybe 6 knots, about as fast as *Tranquility* can make way. Speed is something whaleships don't need, except when returning home."

* fish—*Every whaler knows whales are mammals and not fish but since early times they have been referred to as fish. The term is still in general use.*

Chapter 11

Seeds of Dissension Are Sown

The weather turns nasty for the next week so there is no rowing practice. During the week, Ben is assigned to help the cooper make barrels and spends most of the time below decks shaving staves. During mess periods, he is sent to help the steward carry food to the officers. Once they are finished, he helps clear the mess. Next, the mess feeds cooper, carpenter, shipsmith, bo'sun and quartermaster. The crew always eats in the fo'c's'le and the cook's helper and Ben continue to carry food tubs to them.

Ben quickly learns his way around the ship but goes out of the way to avoid the forecastle and the Greenies. These bums treat me like a servant, he says to himself as he feeds them. They're all unfriendly, stupid, ignorant and dirty. He recalls the second time he had to haul tubs there, when one man stuck out his foot and tripped him. The gruel poured over the deck and a few of them scooped it up with their dishes and ate it with their fingers. Who's a savage now? he said to himself as he headed forward with a tub of food.

Ben is leery of all the men in the forecastle and speaks only when spoken to. He doubts he would have much to say because he cannot understand most of the languages that dominate the talk there. At any one time one can hear American and British English, Creole, Irish, Portuguese, Spanish and French being spoken. Bedlam reigns.

At first Ben expected to be discriminated against because he is an Indian. That never occurs. Actually, many of the men look at him as somewhat of a good luck charm. In fact, Ben unknowingly gets more respect than the others because he is an Indian, even though he is considered a kid. The reputation of Indians as whalers, especially harpooners, was well established long before he came on board. There are five black men in the forecastle crew and even they are not discriminated against by the other Greenies. Ben never gets the chance to understand the men in the forecastle because he shuns them.

One day while still en route to the Azores, he goes topside after serving the fo'c's'le crew to wait until they are finished. He finds Abe Brown on deck leaning on the starboard gunwale. He has seen him occasionally in the forecastle. Ben moves to the gunwale and stands near him. Abe is smoking a cigar. From the shortness of his cigar Ben knows he has been there for a while. Abe stares not at the water moving past the ship but out to sea. He knows Abe is related to the disburser and the Lesters. Everyone knows that. And, they are all aware that his command of the starboard watch is temporary.

"Where we going?" Ben finally musters enough courage to speak.

Brown does not immediately answer. Even though Abe is a Quaker, Ben senses from casual sightings of him on the ship that he does not consider him, an Indian, his equal. Abe continues looking out to sea. Ben moves closer to him on the gunwale. As he does, Abe turns and looks at him. Ben does not like what he sees in Abe's eyes. Abe doesn't speak.

He is discontented, Ben thinks. I sense something burns inside him.

"Tuh dah Azores, stupid," he finally says. "Weren't yuh listenin' ta duh capt'n?"

"I was, but where are the Azores? Why are we going there? Are there whales there?"

"Not any more. But dere's many Portygee. They ain't workin' 'cause whales now are too damned hard tuh find."

"Why are we going there?"

"We needs men!"

"We needs one or tuh good harponeers. The captain hopes to find 'em dere."

"How old are yuh?" he asks Ben.

"Fourteen, 15 in a few months."

"Ya looks older, maybe 20. Are yah?"

"No! "

"Yur lyin'!"

Abe looks directly into Ben eyes, maybe to see if he is lying. He frowns. Ben guesses that Abe does not like what he sees. Ben is tall for his age, at least a head taller than Abe. I sense he doesn't like looking up to me, Ben thinks.

"Shouldn't ya be below washin' kids?"

"I was told to serve and that the cook and his helper would wash."

"How duz yuh likes life on a whaler?"

"I hate it," says Ben.

"It's better dan bein' on the reservation, ain't it?"

"No!"

"Whad done ya like?"

"I'm not a squaw and I am made to do women's work."

"Done braves on da reservation do women's work?"

He's stupid, Ben thinks to himself.

"Who duz ya hate most on here?"

"A man," blurts out Ben without thinking of what he has just said. He has second thoughts.

"Whad man?

"The man who kidnapped me."

"Who's dat?"

Ben doesn't answer.

"Does ya know who he is?"

"Yes."

"Who?"

Ben still doesn't answer him

"Whad are yuh gonna do 'bout it?"

"Nothing. Nothing now."

"When?"

"When the time is right. I'll get even."

"Git below an len' a hand. Ya ain't so big dat ya can't wash dishes."

Dat's two of us who hates Lester, Abe says to himself. I can use dis kid.

Ben does as he's been ordered though Abe has no authority over him.

Chapter 12

The Making of Abe Brown

Saturday, December 23, 1865
Off Angra do Heroismo on the island of Terceira

Tranquility is sailing due east, almost atop the 40th latitude line. Nineteen days after leaving Sag Harbor she is now off Graciosa, the first of nine islands that make up the Azores. The excitement of a voyage to strange lands that existed among the forecastle crew during the first few days at sea was high. However, it is fading. The Greenies expected to see whales all the way to the Azores but are disappointed.

Except for the blue whale, none of several sightings turned out to be whales. The crews of the whaleboats have become bored with the constant schooling of the ship's lines and sails. Some even long for more training exercises but the weather hasn't been cooperative. To most men brought onboard by the crimpers, it seems like a needless waste of their efforts and energies. During the last week Ben lowered twice in Andrew's boat. He temporarily replaced the waist oar and Andrew was impressed by how well Ben pulled.

Seldom is a crew happy with everything on board a ship. Dissension is a common element on even the finest-run vessel. The Lesters are not surprised that the first seeds of dissension on *Tranquility* are sown by

Abraham Brown, 26, a nephew to the disburser. At every opportunity, he slips into the forecastle and tries to prejudice the men against the 1st mate, constantly verbally challenging his authority.

Ben wonders why Abe does this. He sounds like he wants to command the ship, he says to himself after Abe boasts that he could do a better job at finding whales. There is no reason for him to say that because they all were told they would not begin whaling until they departed the Azores with a full crew. Ben becomes increasingly suspicious of Abe as Abe exerts a more open friendliness to "a savage."

At night *Tranquility* rides at anchor on a calm sea before going into Angra. After supper both Lesters remain at the table drinking coffee when Ephraim returns for another cup and joins them. In a rare initiative Hiram breaks his silence and approaches his cousin directly.

"What is wrong with Abe?" he asks. "Why does he seem to oppose everything Andrew and I do? Word does get back to me. Why does he spend so much time in the fo'c's'le?"

Ephraim is momentarily taken aback.

"I don't quite know the answer," he says.

"Throughout his short life, Abe has always been an anomaly. He seems to be a round peg trying to fit into a square hole. I realize this and often recognize his actions and shortcomings, blaming them on his childhood and his father. My wife and I eventually became unwilling surrogate parents after my brother Jonathan died. Jonathan left Abe, two older brothers and an older sister to fend for themselves. My brother was crude. We blamed him for Abe's disrespect of etiquette and the demeanor that now seems to guide him.

"Jonathan was two years older than me and preferred to farm the land or seine the sea to make a living rather than join me in our father's business. To farm efficiently and profitably, he needed a full family to help manage his 180 acres of land near Wainscot. Realizing this, he quickly began creating one as soon as he married Harriet Bennett. Three children were all born within their first four years of marriage. Two subsequent pregnancies ended in miscarriages before Abe was born. When his turn came, he never seemed especially healthy and was scraggly for a farm-raised youngster who usually had all the food he needed. To compound his father's dilemma, the land he tilled was more sand than soil and produced but little profit after the family was fed.

"As a disgruntled and disappointed father, Jonathan often took out his failure as a farmer on his wife and children. And, Abe seemed to bear the brunt of his father's shortcomings. Abe was not inherently lazy but that didn't discourage his father from taking a stick to him. After one such beating, when Abe was 9 years old, he ran away. He didn't go far but showed up at our door in Sag Harbor.

"He made such a scene when his father came to retrieve him that Jonathan told us we could have him. He challenged me to see if maybe I could get some work out of him. 'I don't want him coming back,' he said as he saw his son for the last time.

"You know Miranda and I are childless. Burdened by our Quaker morality, we felt pity for the boy and took him in. Honestly, I was never totally in agreement with the idea, at least as long as Abe's father was still alive. One night Miranda took Abe to his first Quaker meeting. When the congregation got up, 'and started acting funny,' as Abe told us, he ran out and said he was never going to another meeting of those crazy people. We enrolled him in school. That lasted two weeks. On the last day, Abe came home bloodied.

"'You should have seen what I did to him', he said. Thereafter, without us knowing, the teacher refused to let Abe back into class. Abe didn't want to return to school and wasn't about to have us vouch for him. Instead, Abe would leave the house every morning, as if he were going to school. He returned in the afternoon, as if he had just been let out. This went on for more than a month until one day, when Miranda was shopping in the village, she spotted him on the town wharf. The confrontation was not pleasant. I tried to get him back into school but was unsuccessful. We were at a loss about what to do with him.

"Abe loved to hang around our chandlery on Water Street and listen to sailors talk of their voyages to exotic lands and curse as they spoke. His vocabulary quickly expanded. He took to hanging around the docks more frequently and found new friends his age among the sons of Irish immigrants whose fathers worked as stevedores.

'One night, Abe later told us, late in the evening, when he heard the village clock strike 11 o'clock, he told his friends that: 'I better git going, home'."

'Where ya goin'?' asked one in an Irish brogue so thick that Abe said it was almost difficult for him to understand.

'Home! Done yous guys have tuh git home now?'

'You kiddin'?' one asked. 'We can get in anytime we please. Stay with us. We know where we can get all the apples you can eat. Come on?'

"Abe's friends ran down the street in the opposite direction Abe was heading. Abe paused for a moment, then ran hard to catch up with them.

"One evening, nearly two years after we inherited this wayward boy we were discussing what to do with him. One of his antics became a turning point in all our lives. Abe and several of his Irish contemporaries one afternoon stole a gallon of red wine. They consumed it under an overturned longboat on the end of Long Wharf and all became drunk. I was looking out a window in the chandlery when I saw Abe walking down Water Street. By the way he was stumbling and falling, and then slurring his speech when I challenged him, I knew what had happened."

"'I know we have failed Abraham,' my wife said. 'What are we to do with him? I know there is a good boy underneath.'

"'That might be true,' I said, 'but how do we mine it? Those undisciplined Irish ruffians are a bad influence on Abe. I knew that this was coming and have been trying to find a solution. The waterfront in Sag Harbor is not a fit place to raise someone with Abraham's penchants.'

"'Maybe we can send him to live with your older brother in Huntington. He has three sons and two daughters,' suggested Miranda. 'Even so, he has as much obligation to save his brother's son, as do we. Maybe they can pull him into their family and yet save him.'

"Little did we know that 'Little Abe,' as we often referred to him because of his somewhat diminutive size, had been sitting at the top of the stairs and heard the entire conversation. Abe decided he would have nothing to do with going to Huntington. He didn't like his cousins because they once ganged up on him when they came for a visit.

"That evening, Abe slipped out of the house and was down on Water Street, thinking of what he would do. He stopped at the foot of one dock and admired the beautiful carving of a gilded mermaid on the bow of a merchant ship. He walked farther down the dock to the stern to discover her name and hail port.

"*China Doll, Liverpool*, was painted across her transom. Abe turned and walked back to the bow, admiring the ship as he strode."

"'She's a beauty, ain't she?' a man said to Abe, so he told us. Abe hadn't noticed him until he spoke. He was standing on the ship, against the gunwale, just beyond the upper end of the gangway, looking down at the 11-year old.

"'Bet you'd like to sail on her, wouldn't you?'

"'Where's she goin'?' Abe finally asked.

"'To Bombay. On the next tide.'

"'When's dat?'

"'In about six hours. About daybreak.'

"Abe didn't respond he told us how it happened years after he returned home the first time. I can still see the picture he painted.

"He walked down the pier and back onto Water Street where he hurried his pace. Quietly he re-entered our house. We were still in the living room talking about chandlery business and didn't hear him return. Abe silently dashed up to his room, grabbed a few pieces of clothing, wrapped them into a bundle and snuck out of the house. In a few minutes, he was back at the dock. He hid in the shadow of the dockmaster's shack and watched the activity on *China Doll*. He saw the man who had spoken to him leave his position at the gangway. Now's the chance, he must have said to himself. He ran to the gangway and quietly made it to the deck. There was no one in sight. He saw two overturned longboats just aft of the foremast and slide under the closer one. After a few minutes he tucked his bundle under his head and eventually fell asleep.

"It wasn't until five years at sea that we again saw him. He told us that he was well and graduated from a cabin boy to a cargo handler. For the next ten years Abe intermittently showed up in Sag Harbor. One time he jumped ship in Angra and signed on a Sag Harbor whaler heading south. By his mid-20s he had three voyages on whaleships, the last two as a harponer.

"On each vessel, he had been passed over in becoming a mate and that bitterness has infected everything he does. I think that is still one of the main reasons for his sullenness. I might be wrong. It is no wonder that, as he was about to sail on *Tranquility*, he has not changed from the person we knew as a boy."

"His entire persona," interrupts Hiram, "is uncharacteristic of what should be that of an officer, a mate, even an acting-mate. Foremost among his faults is his habit of mixing with all boat crews in the fo'c's'le."

"There is something about gangs that must still intrigue, attract him," Ephraim says. "Maybe it is the Irish kids who still influence his thinking. The fo'c's'le crew must remind him of the gang he ran with in Sag Harbor."

Chapter 13

The Azores

Sunday, December 24, 1865, Day 20
38° 41 8" N by 27° 10' 27" W

The sighting of Graciosa caused everyone who was not on watch to crowd the gunwale for a look. When Ben came topside he saw 2nd Mate Jorge Pilla in the center of a group of Greenies telling them about the home of his ancestors. Ben was saddened by what he heard. He's going home, he thought. I wish this was Long Island and I was going home.

Abe comes up quietly from behind and asks Ben, "Whad 's dah matter, kid?"

"I'm no kid," he answers without turning.

"Maybe I can help ya."

"Help how?"

"Dere's a few more of us who wants ta git off dis ship. Wad do ya want?

"I want to go home but I want to get even before I do. You ever been here before?"

"A cupala times."

"Is there an American consulate here?"

"Yeh, but we ain't goin' derh.

"Der's nine islands here. We're goin' ta Angra an' dere's no consulate derh."

I wish I had had someone help me when I was a kid, Abe says to himself as he listens to Jorge proudly talking about his parent's home.

That evening Abe goes forward to the forecastle and throws a deck of cards on the table.

"Anyone knows how tuh play cards?" he jokingly asks.

"For fun or money?" responds Miguel Dos Santos, a Portuguese who is in 2nd Mate Jorge Pilla's crew. Adam Jackson, 29, jumps out of his bunk and grabs a three-legged stool and pulls it up to a large sea chest. Close behind him is Roger Whetstone, 22, who limps slightly as he drags the edge of a bench to the chest. His limp was caused by Rebel shrapnel at Gettysburg.

"Fer money, 'course," says Abe. "Dat is, if any of ya bums gots money."

One of the Greenies jumps out of the bunk and yells at Abe: "We ain't bums."

"You gots money?"

"No!"

"Den yur a bum. Sid down an' shut up 'fore I knocks ya down."

Half an hour later, Whetstone jumps to his feet, knocking back the bench. "You son-of-a-bitch," he yells at Abe who is dealing. "You played that king of spades just two hands ago. It was supposed to be on the bottom of the deck."

Jackson, too, jumps to his feet. Ben Jackson, a Negro in Abe's crew, in a less volatile voice, tells Whetstone to keep it down or the watch will come below to see what is going on.

Whetstone remains standing, then throws his cards at Abe. In an instant, Abe catches the younger man by his shirt and pulls him across the makeshift table.

"Ya little shit," he says, "who duz ya thinks ya are, talking like dat to a mate?" With the other hand he slaps him so hard that Whetstone falls backwards as Abe releases him. Whetstone springs to his feet, fists clutched, ready to pounce on Abe. Both Dos Santos and Jackson, in an effort to stop the noise, grab him and hold him back.

"You bastard," Whetstone yells, "you ain't no mate. You're just filling in until the captain can get a Portygee to fill the spot, someone who really knows what he's doing in a whaleboat."

In response, Abe jumps past the table and is about to punch Whetstone. Dos Santos and Jackson release their holds on Whetstone and let him defend himself when they see Abe is about to hit him.

Suddenly, the hatch to the main deck springs open. Andrew Lester, Number 1, sees what is about to happen, and yells, "Stop! What is all this about?" He needs no explanation when he sees the cards scattered on the table and deck.

As he drops onto the forecastle deck, Lester looks around, then faces Abe.

"Return to your quarters," he says.

"I don't want to see you here again unless it involves ship's business."

Abe passes Lester. As he climbs the ladder he mumbles something no one can quite hear, then slams the hatch door as he steps onto the outside deck.

Damn that man, Lester says to himself as he, too, climbs the ladder. I knew he would be trouble. I must eventually confront him.

Just after supper Captain Lester tells his brother to set *Tranquility* so she will wear ship throughout the night. As a result, she moves but little. The following morning, as the sun rises, Lester leaves his quarters, climbs the ladder onto the main deck, then takes the starboard ladder onto the quarterdeck. As he is about to step inside the wheelhouse, he stops. He stands there for a moment. With his free hand he grasps the forward railing to steady himself. His knees feel stiff, unsteady after a night's sleep, as the ship rolls slowly, gently from larboard to starboard. He views the action on deck as the watch is being set. His eyes follow the lookout climb the ratlines.

Satisfied, he moves inside and stands next to Adrian Moore. He leaves the door open because the sea air is balmy and the small house has a tendency to become stuffy. The quartermaster is manning the helm. Lester glances at the compass heading by which Moore is pointing the ship. He is on course, Lester says to himself. He is about to sip from a mug of coffee when the watch on the top crosstree of the foremast yells, "Land ho! To larboard! To larboard!"

Capt. Lester immediately sets aside the coffee and grabs the long glass from its holder and rushes outside. Almost at the same moment, Andrew comes out of the nearby companionway from his quarters below deck, also armed with a long glass. They stand side by side as they scan the island off the bark's larboard beam. After a few minutes, the captain walks back to the wheelhouse and orders the helmsman to bring the ship 3 points (33 degrees, 30 minutes) to the north.

He returns to the gunwale and continues to scan the horizon.

"Ask Number 2 to come here," he says to his brother.

Andrew turns to Bellingham, who also has come to the wheelhouse and is standing next to him. "Bo'sun, send someone to the mate's quarters and tell Mr. Pilla that he's wanted topside."

"Number 2," Capt. Lester addresses Jorge Pilla as he walks through the doorway, "we may still be a ways off for a good see but do you recognize this island?" He then hands him the glass.

"It is too far away to be certain," says Pilla, "but I think it is Graciosa. Didn't we see it last night?"

"We did," speaks up Andrew. "We were hoved-to and the current must have taken us farther north than I believed."

"Good," said Lester, "it would be if we are on course."

"We are on course," says Andrew.

Jorge Pilla, 35, is a second generation Portuguese-American. During the late 1700s and early 1800s, many Portuguese, especially those from the Azores with whaling backgrounds, immigrated to New England. They responded to the need for whalemen to man vessels in the burgeoning American whaleship fleet. They usually got to the United

States by hiring on whaleships that stopped to provision in the Azores before covering the last 900 miles to Nantucket or by hiring on those outward bound like Lester who were seeking able men.

Jorge's grandfather was one who signed on an in-bound Nantucket Whaler in 1805. He eventually settled in New Bedford and continued sailing on American whaleships as did his son Joao and now his grandson Jorge. Except for his religion, he is as American as any East End Long Islander. The Pillas still have many relatives in the city of Angra on the island of Terceira. When still a youngster, Jorge visited his grandfather's ancestral home on several occasions. On one protracted visit he was there for nearly a year. More than a dozen members of his extended family settled in the New Bedford area in the past two decades.

By mid-morning, *Tranquility* has halved the distance toward land and Jorge confirms that the island is Graciosa.

"Mr. Moore," Lester addresses the helmsman, "change course and steer south-southeast."

At noon, as on every other day when the weather permits, Lester is on deck with the sextant taking a reading of the ship's position.

"We are about 30 miles from your grandfather's house," he says to his second mate, after making an entry in his notebook. "I hope your uncle's son is still amiable to go a-whaling?"

"In his last letter, he said he was," answers Jorge. "He said his younger brother also wants to sign on. There is no work on the islands. Earlier this year he was in Lisboa for several weeks but there was even less work there than in Angra."

Pilla is excited as he leaves Capt. Lester and Andrew at the wheelhouse and drops below decks. Several years have passes since he had seen his relatives.

"I hope Pilla is right," Hiram turns to his brother as he speaks. "We are still in dire need of a 3rd mate and a good harponeer. It is good if they are related, or even if they only know each other. It makes a whaleboat crew more effective. We could even use another mate who could eventually fill the bill for 4th mate. I don't trust Abe."

"I, too, would like to replace him as soon as possible," says Andrew, "before he can further infect the crew with his insubordination."

The day is Christmas Eve and is already dark as they approach Terciera. *Tranquility* follows the south shore east until Lester recognizes the distinctive three peaks on Monte Brasil. The massive peninsula curves eastward and protects the deepwater anchorage around Angra, creating two sheltered harbors.

"It has been six years since I was last here," says Hiram. "I think we should wait until dawn before we try to find a berth on one of three long wharfs in the city. Have the crew set *Tranquility's* two anchors just outside of the eastern harbor."

"Aye, sir," answers Andrew.

The next day, Monday, Christmas Day, a customs boat greets *Tranquility* before she is able to get underway. After a perfunctory inspection and a quick conversation with Jorge, who is fluent in Portuguese, they depart and Andrew is now free to take *Tranquility* dockside. In the hands of well-experienced port personnel the docking is swift.

"I will contact my uncle and return with him as soon as possible," says Jorge. "How long will we stay in port?"

"Three days. We'll depart Thursday morning," answers Lester. "I want to give each watch a night ashore because we may not be at a dock for the next year or two. And, I want to take on a few provisions. Besides, today is Christmas."

"*Felize natal!*" Jorge says as he descends the gangway.

"What provisions?" asks Ephraim Brown who was standing at the gunwale next to the gangway.

"I want you to go ashore. See if you can get a few boxes of oranges or lemons."

"But oranges are expensive. Do we really need them? We've enough provisions. Besides, today is a big holiday here and we may not find any vendors."

"I said go into the city's market square and get a few crates of oranges. They are grown here in great numbers and exported to the continent, especially England. Mr. Brown, I may not be an accountant, but it doesn't take much understanding of costs and supply to realize that the cost of oranges here must be less than in Sag Harbor. Why? Because there are no shipping costs involved. Do you take me to be an idiot?"

"I do not, Sir!"

"Then why treat me as one? Oranges are not expensive here. Besides, they are good for the health of the crew. Brown, get them!"

Begrudgingly, a half-hour later the disburser leaves, taking his nephew and another man to help carry back oranges.

"Ephraim," says Andrew who is standing next to Lester. "Also, take Ben with you. He might like to see how people here live."

"We done need an Indian wid us," responds Abe.

"Take him I said! And make sure you bring him back!" says Andrew.

"Go find 'im," Abe orders the Greenie accompanying them.

Even on Christmas Day the streets in Angra's market place are crowded. As Ben brings up the rear he thinks that it would be easy to get lost in this crowd. *This may be my chance escape. But how could I get even with Mr. Lester?*

Ephraim haggles unsuccessfully with several vendors and pays the last one what he asks for three crates of oranges.

Burdened with a crate and a language that he has never heard, Ben's enthusiasm for Angra as a place to jump ship wanes. And, he thinks, *I have no money. Maybe a port where English is spoken is a better choice.*

"You never told me of your plan?" Ben says to Abe as they carry the oranges back to the ship.

"Ferget it. It wone work."

Near noon Pilla returns with three men. Brown and his oranges have returned just a few moments before Jorge climbs the gangway. They are being stacked for Hiram as he looks them over. He turns to the gangway as he hears Pilla arrive.

"This is my great uncle's son Diogo Pilla," Jorge Pilla says as he introduces him to Capt. Lester.

Abe looks on silently, just far enough away from the captain so as not to be introduced to another Pilla.

Lester notes that Diogo's handshake is strong and firm. His hands are rough. Obviously, he is a person familiar with hard work, Lester thinks to himself.

Diogo Pilla is not a large man, a bit above 5 feet tall and weighs no more than 150 pounds. He wears his black hair long and tied in a slight ponytail. At the temples, it shows signs of turning gray. Lester thinks he is approaching 40. He is dressed in loose-fitting pants, an unbuttoned shirt and an open vest. His sandals reveal that his feet are big and accustomed to going without shoes.

"Do you speak English?"

"Yes, not everything, but the language of a ship is universal."

"How old are you?"

"Thirty-eight."

"How many years have you been to sea?"

Diogo thinks for a moment, adding up the years in his head.

"Since I was 15. Most of them were on whaleships. I was first mate on two Portuguese ships and rose to captain on the second one. I was also second mate on one English and one American ship."

"Why did they make you captain?"

"I was first mate. The captain was drowned when a whale stove his boat. I then became captain. It was automatic."

"How long were you captain on that voyage?"

"One-and-a-half years."

"Which ship did you like the best?"

"The American ship, *Elsie*, out of Boston."

"Why?"

"The *rolos* were not so big."

"What are *rolos*?"

"Roaches, cockroaches," Jorge says as he smiles.

"What was your longest voyage?"

"The English ship. We were at sea for two years. We returned two years ago."

"Where did she sail?"

"Only in the Atlantic."

"Ah, a Plum Pudding voyage (a short trip, often less than a year), eh?" says Lester.

"Why haven't you sailed since?"

"Now, there are few whaleships that stop here."

"Was the ship greasy?" Lester sees puzzlement spread across Diogo's face.

"Was it filled with oil on the return?"

"No. Whales were hard to find. That was main reason we returned so soon."

"Wad did ya do on da English ship?" Abe interrupts the captain.

Lester scowls at him for his breach of etiquette. Diogo is silent for a moment.

"Go on," Lester says to Diogo, "answer him."

"I was the third mate."

"How many mates did she carry?" ask Abe,

"She was a whaler! She had four."

"Were da udder mates Portagees?

"No. They were English."

"Did ya git along wid 'em?" asks Abe.

"Enough of this interview," Lester interrupts Abe. "I know what you're doing. Get the oranges to Cook before they melt out here.

"As you know, I'm looking for a third mate, a man who is good with the lance as well as the harpon. But, he must also be able to command the men in his crew.

"I have commanded four whaleboat crews in my years at sea. I know what is expected of me, my men and the purpose of the voyage."

"What is that?"

"To kill and bring to ship as many whales as possible."

"I like that attitude," interrupts Ephraim Brown who is in on the interview.

"So do I," says the captain. "You're hired. Mr. Brown will get you the papers to sign. We leave Thursday. Get your gear onboard by then and be ready to sail."

"Who are these other men?" Lester addresses Jorge.

"Captain, this is Nuno Dias. He, too, is an experienced harponeer and boat steerer and has been on three whaleships and commanded two whaleboats."

Dias, 30, looks like many other Portuguese whalemen Lester has met over the years. As he interviews him he feels intuitively that he, too, is a man who can do the job demanded of him, to be placed in almost any position assigned him, and could be advanced in the whaleboat if the need arises.

Lester glances over him. "He will do."

"The other man is a cousin. He is also looking for any kind of work," says Jorge. "He is young and strong and can pull a good starboard oar."

"Why the starboard oar?" asks Ephraim out of curiosity.

"Because that oar is the longest and thus heaviest oar on a whaleboat," answers Jorge.

He is no more than 20 and unusually tall for a Portuguese/Spaniard. He is nearly six feet and weighs over 200 pounds, but is not fat. And, he has blue eyes, an anomaly among his people.

"Find room for both these men," says Hiram.

"Mr. Brown, sign them on."

"But do we really need the young man? He is an expense I did not figure on."

"Are you going to challenge all my decisions?" asks Lester. "And, in front of the crew?"

"No, Sir, I was just thinking that…"

"Don't think when it comes to this ship. I do the thinking. Are you clear on that?

"We may even need one or two extra men in this crew because a few of the bums we signed on might not make it back to sea. I have already seen signs."

"What signs?" asks Ephraim.

"They do not like the hard work they have found on a ship," Andrew answers for his brother. He does so because he, as the ship's 1st mate, has a closer working relationship with the crew than a captain.

"Several have been seasick from the moment we left Sag Harbor. I fear they will never get their sea legs. The constant nausea will drive many a man to desert just to stop the sickness. And, there are those who are bored with the routine. Life is not pleasant when cramped with 15 others in the fo'c's'le."

Brown doesn't answer but returns to the quarters he shares with the mates to get the papers for the Portuguese men to sign.

"Have all the men lay aft," Capt. Lester says to his brother.

After taking roll call, Andrew announces that everyone is present.

"As you Greenies should know by now," Capt. Lester begins, "the starboard watch is composed of the first and third whaleboat crews. The larboard watch is composed of the second and fourth crews. Tonight, there will be no liberty because there is much work to be done. Tomorrow evening, the larboard watch is on duty but may go ashore Wednesday. On Thursday, we will put to sea. When on liberty you may be ashore until 4 bells. That's 2 a.m. But, mind you what I now say. Police here are very strict. If you over imbibe, cause a ruckus and are jailed, I won't come to get you. We will sail without you. I don't think you will like spending any time in a Portygee jail. Their rats are bigger and meaner than those onboard *Tranquility*.

"Shore leave begins at the end of the last Dog Watch, at 8 bells. To you who still do not know the ways of ships and the sea, that is 8 o'clock."

That evening, as Andrew Lester lies in his bunk, his thoughts race back to the last time he saw Rebecca. It is just three weeks, he thinks, but it seems longer. The last thing he remembers before being wrapped in the arms of Morpheus is the way she looked as they said good-bye, the sad look on her face. It is indelibly burned into his memory.

Chapter 14

Shore Leave in Angra

Several transoceanic merchant vessels, as well as *Tranquility*, are tied to three long wharfs that radiate from the beach in the city's center. Two are British and one is American, from New York City.

To Captain Lester's amazement, the entire starboard watch returns unscathed by 2 a.m. Wednesday morning. To be sure, several crewmen could not have made it back to the ship under their own power, but they did return.

The night before, Andrew had been in the wheelhouse installing a new barometer he had picked up in the city and noticed Ben returning after just a few hours ashore.

In the morning, Andrew asks him why he came back so early. The young Indian, kneeling on the deck, is flaking several lines in the bow of the ship. These are used for tossing the monkey fists, small, weighted balls of knots attached to light lines that will eventually pull hawsers to waiting dock hands.

Startled by the 1st mate's appearance, he abruptly turns and stands. "Sorry, Sir, I didn't hear you coming."

"Why did you return so soon from visiting the city?" Andrew asks.

"I don't quite know," Ben says. "I didn't feel comfortable in town. I don't know the language and the men wanted to go into a *cantina* for drinks. I am not a drinker. I have seen what alcohol does to some of my people on the reservation.

" I walked around the bazaar and looked in a few shops.

"I don't have any money so I couldn't buy anything."

"I should have known that," Lester says. "The next time, I can lend you money."

"Thank you, Sir."

Why is he being so kind to me? Ben thinks. Is he trying to make up for what he did when he grabbed me at Canoe Place?

"I felt a little strange among the people." Ben continues. "They're friendly enough but they kept staring at me. I guess that I look different from other Americans from the ship.

"Maybe the next port will be different."

"Maybe," says Lester.

Later that day, in the evening, as the larboard watch goes ashore, Jorge and Diogo Pilla, Miguel Dos Santos and Egas Sanchez break away from the other men piling down the gangway and disappear into the city for a last visit with their relatives.

Abe has been to Angra three times and boasts to his watch that he knows the best taverns in the seaport city. Naturally, they gather around him because he also is the first on the dock. Five men, composed of three farmers and two ex-whalers, join him. Only two of the five Negroes onboard decide to see what Angra has hidden and go off separately from Brown's followers.

"Dere it is," Abe says after they pass several bars and round a slight bend in *Estrada Gaspar Corte Real*, a dockside street.

"Dee *Atlantico*. We can gits anythin' we wants in dis place," he says as he pushes through a set of swinging doors. Harvey Bennett, Abe's harpooner and the rest of the crew follow. Abe spots a table with a few bums from Jorge Pilla's crew and takes an empty one next to them.

"Ready for a dram of liquor?" an Irishman from another table asks Abe.

"Whalemen drinks rum!" he abruptly, loudly answers.

"Rum," he yells as he flays his arm toward a waiter approaching their table.

"How many?" the waiter asks in faltering English.

Everyone raises a hand except one farmer who asks for beer.

The tavern is filled. Unlike Sag Harbor, even a Wednesday night here seems to be an auspicious evening to be out and about in Angra. Maybe it's because of Christmas though none in the crew seem especially religious, excepting the Portuguese. The atmosphere is boisterous. Everyone in the large room seems to be talking at once. Cigar and pipe smoke creates a bluish haze that concentrates around several whale oil lanterns that fail to adequately light any part of the tavern. The pungent, rich smell of burning tobacco is second only to the caustic smell of garlic. The tavern serves food as well as drinks and every item on the menu contains fish, fish that now swim in a sea of garlic and onions.

A dozen bare, round tables are scattered around the room and a long bar, probably 50 feet in length, is against the back wall. Unlike bars in America--except for those on the frontier--there are no stools. Instead, everyone either stands at the bar or sits at tables. One of the tables next to the whalemen is filled with locals, obvious from their dress, while seamen and transients fill the others. More than a dozen Portuguese women, mostly girls no more than 20 years old, circulate among the tables. When an opportunity arises, they grab empty seats next to men. They remain there until they discover whether or not anyone is interested in their wares.

Several waiters in typical European garb for waiters are dressed in white shirts, black vests and trousers, and ankle-length white aprons. They circulate among the tables looking for orders. One is again hailed to Abe's table. After taking their order, he retreats to the bar. In minutes he returns carrying a bottle of rum, a large stein of beer and a tray of empty glasses. At the whalers' table, he places a glass before each man and fills it with rum.

The two East End farmers in Brown's crew seem ill at ease in such a place. The environment is new to them. But the whaler and two bums who fill out his boat crew are right at home. Quickly, they toss back their drinks. Almost as soon as the empty glasses hit the table, Abe yells, "More. Another round!"

The waiter, standing off a few feet, returns, and obliges him.

Bennett places his hand over his glass and the waiter skips him.

"Wads's wrong?" asks Abe. "Dones ya not likes rum?"

"Not at this pace," he answers.

The table next to them is filled with seamen off one of the English merchant ships. They have been in the tavern an hour or more before the Americans arrive and are now well lubricated. However, it doesn't take more than a round or two before the whalers catch up. The Englishmen are singing a chantey many Americans know and they join in. When it is over, one overzealous Brit staggers to his feet and proposes a toast.

"To our American brethren," he says as he raises a mug of ale, "even though they stink like rotten fish."

"Dat's whales, not fish, ya stupid Limey," responds a now tipsy Abe Brown.

"Who's stupid?"

"You an' so are all yer mates."

"Dat otta git dem," Abe quietly slurs to Bennett.

"Oh no!" says Bennett as he turns to Abe. "My nose has finally healed from the fight we had at the American."

The American Hotel is a well-known whalers' retreat in Sag Harbor.

"I ain't gettin' mixed up in this one."

He quickly rises and jumps back from his table.

"He's gettin' up," yells one Englishman. Their table explodes as they leap toward Bennett, Abe and his crew. Within minutes, punches are flying. Abe hits the man who knocked down Bennett.

"Dat'l keep yuh fer a while," he says as he momentarily sees the man motionless on the floor. A Brit pounces on Abe from behind and they are all on the floor.

"That's enough for me," Bennett says as he recovers. "I'm gettin' outa here." He springs for the swinging doors and stumbles outside.

Another table of British merchantmen join in the fight as well as a bunch of Americans from the New York merchantman. During the melee, the owner of the tavern sends one of the waiters to get the police.

Brown, however, is not so drunk that when he spots the man leave in a hurry he knows where he is going. "C'mon boys," he yells and begins gathering his crew. Let's git outa here. Duh cops is a comin'."

They slip out a side door just as police, armed with nightsticks, come through the swinging doors.

Two doors down the cobblestone street is the *Canteena Rosa*.

"In here," Abe says. The others follow on his heels.

"Let's 'ave a drink 'ere an' let tings outside settle down. Da police 'll be lookin' fer anyone runnin' down duh street.

"Wait, dere's someone missin'."

Brown senses they're a man short. He gets up from the table around which they are seated and sticks his head out the door. More police are still pouring into *Atlantico*.

"It's Bennett," Abe says as he rejoins those around the table.

The four men are served their drinks; almost to a man, they switch to beer. Brown is the exception who stays with his beloved drink--dark, spicy, rum. The evening's joviality disappears as they nurse their beers to kill time.

Unexpectedly, the doors to the tavern burst open. Then one, two, three policemen enter the cafe. The first one yells something to the man behind the bar as the others survey the men at various tables. After a short exchange, satisfied, the police turn around and leave.

"You boys look like you need cheering up," says a pretty, young, slim and over-cosmeticated girl as she approaches their table.

Behind her are two more women ready to hustle drinks. All three seem to have been cut from the same cloth. The forward one quickly sits next to Abe. She is a tad prettier than her co-workers. Her eyes are as black as coal and so are the ridiculously long eyelashes that guard them. Mascara is the last thing they need. Her nose is small, petite; her cheeks full and show just a hint of rouge. Her lips are full, generous and colored a bright crimson. All this is in stark contrast as if painted on an alabaster skin that is without blemishes, save a small mole to the left of her lips. At most, she is 20 years old.

"My god!" says Abe, "where'd ya come from?"

"Céu," she coquettishly answers.

"Where's dat," he slurs his words.

"Heaven," she says.

"Wad's yer name?"

"Caterina. And yours?"

"Abe!"

"That is a strange name. Does it come from the Bible?"

"Ya. But dere it's Abraham."

"I have not before known an Abraham."

"Ya still don't, Caterina. But I can fix dat," he says as he pulls her closer.

She responds by wrapping a bare arm around him and snuggling her ample breast against his shoulder. Seeing that there are no more empty chairs, both Fred Jolly and James Blackwell, jump up and pull two empty chairs from nearby tables. The two other girls sit without hesitation.

"Where's my harponeer?" Abe asks.

"He never came in," answers Jolly. "When we scooted from the other place he was outside. He was headed for the ship."

"Good riddance," slurs Abe.

"You buy us some drinks, yes?" asks Ilena who sits next to Jolly and encircles her arm into his. Her lips are no more than inches away from his as she speaks. Unexpectedly he lunges forward, wrapping both arms around her, and kisses her violently on her lips. She pulls back feigning anger.

"*Lentamente,*" she says, "*Lentamente, bruto.*"

The waiter, the next player in this game of fleecing sailors, is immediately behind the girls as they take seats. He stands there, waiting. He has been ready with the bottle of rum he just used to fill Abe's glass. Caterina says something to him in Portuguese. The waiter glances momentarily at Caterina and catches her blink. He spins around to return to the bar. After a few minutes the waiter returns and unloads his tray of glasses, already filled, onto the table. The girls quickly grab their drinks as he pushes one to each of them. As Caterina reaches for hers, Brown grabs it and replaces it with the drink the waiter had set before him.

Brown quickly orders another round. He is close to the waiter and grabs his free hand and slams it on the wooden table.

"If ya brings anythin' but rum dis time, I'll break yer arm. *Comprenda?*"

"*Sim, sim, mestre. Comprende!*"

By the third round, the three women are rapidly catching up with *Tranquility's* crew. A trio of musicians seated in the corner of the café have been playing throughout the evening. One now begins strumming his guitar, playing notes in a minor key and singing a *fado*.

Caterina is not immune to the song's words and their mood, as well as the affects of rum. She uncouples herself from Brown, rises from the table and walks to the corner of the room where the trio of musicians is playing and speaks to them.

She returns to the table as they began gearing up for another song. She stands there for a few moments as she, too, feels an urge rising within, an uninhibited urge to also express how she feels. The rum is working its magic.

Caterina stumbles to an area without tables, obviously where people dance. She steadies herself then throws her clasped hands into the air and holds them there for a moment, waiting for the music to catch up to her.

Flamenco, a Spanish dance, is the rage in Portugal as well as most of Europe. After but a few minutes of clapping and stomping her feet and circling around Brown, she begins to lose her balance. He catches her just as she begins to fall. He sits her down at the table.

"We go home?" she asks.

"My home's far, far away, too far," Brown mumbles aloud. He himself is not in much better shape than Caterina. Only then does he notice that Jolly and Blackwell are missing. So are the other two women. Roger Whetstone is the only one remaining.

"It's near midnight," says Whetstone, an oarsman in what will now be Diogo Pilla's boat. He had not encouraged the girl who had targeted him so she left. "I'm heading back to the ship. You comin'?"

Brown struggles as he rises, then follows Whetstone towards the door. Caterina sees him leaving and jumps up. Somehow she is able to run after him. Outside the door, she grabs his arm for support. She is about to let go when Whetstone looks back. He sees her slipping and grabs her other arm. Whetstone is not as drunk as Brown or his newly-found girlfriend. They struggle down the three blocks to the ship.

As they stand at the base of the gangway, Caterina passes out. For the moment, they hold her upright.

"What the hell are we going to do with her?" Whetstone finally says.

"How da hell do I know?"

"We can't leave her here."

"Why not?" asks Abe. "I done give a shit!"

But even he cannot bring himself to that.

"Let's carry her back to the street and let her lay there," says Whetstone.

"I done know," Abe answers, "but we better do somethin' quick. I done feel so good. Everytings spinning roun' and roun'."

"There's no one on the gangway," says Whetstone. "There's no one on watch.

"He probably went ta duh galley fer coffee.

"I know," says, Abe. "Put her in dah fo'c's'le. Dere's da Irish's bunk."

"What happens when he comes back?"

"Nuttin'. He won't. I saw him gittin' cozy wid duh Brits. I'll bet he's goin' back ta England wid dem."

They could not have managed it if they had been sober. They haul her on board, cross the foredeck to the hatchway, ease her down the ladder and somehow find Egan's empty bunk. They lay her onto it and cover her with his blanket.

Chapter 15

The Inquest

Early Thursday morning, while on the quarterdeck, Capt. Lester calls his mates together.

"Have we lost anyone, Diogo," he addresses his new 3rd mate. "You haven't had a chance to meet all the men in your crew but…"

Andrew interrupts him. "I counted all heads just a few minutes ago," he says, "and everyone in Diogo's, as well as my crew, is onboard."

"Mine, also," echoes 2nd Mate Jorge Pilla.

"Mr. Brown, how about your men?"

"I'm one shy, dat Irishman we picked up from South Street."

Abe doesn't fully remember what happened last night. He has forgotten what he and Whetstone did with the girl.

"You mean Patrick Egan?"

"Yes, Sir, Patrick Egan. He went on liberty wid us last night but he wasn't in his bunk at 2 a.m. when I tallied duh men."

"But, done worry," says Abe. "He ain't gots far tuh swim."

"What do you mean by that?"

"Ireland's a lot closer from here den Sag Harbor. Besides, one of duh English ships is leavin' tomorrow. I saw him gittin' really friendly wid dem Limeys when we first wuz at a café.

"Den he wuz gone."

Capt. Lester doesn't respond. He doesn't like the tone of Brown's flippant response.

"Mr. Lester," he addresses Andrew, "get the quartermaster and bo'sun topside and have them make ready to sail. The winds are favorable and we should be able to leave the wharf without lowering whaleboats.

"Oh yes, that young man who came onboard with you Diogo, what is his name?"

"Sanchez," answered Diogo Pilla, "Egas Sanchez."

"Mr. Brown, seeing that you're now a man short in your crew, put him in your boat."

"He wuzn't in my crew. He wuz in da 3rd mate's crew. No," he corrects himself, in Mr. Diogo's crew.

As soon as he and his brother are alone, Andrew pulls Hiram aside and says: "This is strange. I was in the fo'c's'le this morning and counted heads. It was a full count."

"Did you see Egan?" asks Lester. "Maybe he returned after Brown took a count."

"Maybe," he says. "I better go forward to make sure."

A few minutes later, Number 1 returns to the wheelhouse. Lester is standing outside the door talking to the bo'sun.

"You won't believe it. You must come to the fo'c's'le and see this for yourself."

"What is it? Damn it! Andrew, you have a ship to tend. Lines are already being loosened from the dock."

Capt. Lester hurriedly follows his brother forward, then down the companionway ladder to the foremast's quarters. He approaches Egan's bunk as Andrew begins shaking the body that is still asleep under the covers. There is no response.

He pulls back the blanket and a fully-clothed woman unexpectedly sits up.

"My God!" Lester exclaims. "What in all tarnation is she doing onboard?

"Go topside and hope we can still toss a line to the dock. There'll be hell to pay for this.

"Have you any idea who brought her on board?"

"I have an idea," Number 1 says as he rushes up the ladder, "but I can't prove it."

"Hold the warp," Number 1 yells to the bo'sun. "Toss a monkey fist to the stern side and see if you can have them haul a warp to the bollard. We are not leaving quite this minute."

The crew on deck rushes to the forward line that is still fast to the dockside bollard and several men begin hauling in the slack and bringing the bow of *Tranquility* back to the dock. A second line aft is also caught; a hawser is being pulled off the ship and eventually is made fast to another bollard. Slowly, the ship is warped back to the wharf.

"Haul the gangway back in place," Andrew orders the deck hands. "We have a stowaway going ashore."

In the meantime, Capt. Lester, with the aid of Jorge, questions the woman as to how she got on board. She still seems to be drunk and constantly repeats in Portuguese that she doesn't know. When asked with whom she was drinking, the answers are the same.

"Get rid of her," orders Capt. Lester. "Prepare to get off the wharf."

As Caterina staggers down the gangway, helped by Andrew, men watching the event begin to cheer and whistle. Andrew stops, turns and scowls at the men. They immediately become silent.

"Number 1," says Hiram to his brother, "as soon as we have cleared the harbor and are underway, have all mates and boat steerers in the lounge."

Half-an-hour later, they assemble in the captain's lounge and wait for him to enter from his cabin. Ephraim sees all the activity topside and follows the mates into the captain's lounge.

"What's this about?" Joshua Edwards, Andrew Lester's harpooner asks.

"It's pretty evident," says Andrew. "Didn't you see us off-load the woman?"

"Is that all?" says Edwards. "I thought it was something serious."

As Capt. Lester walks though the doorway he hears what Edwards says.

"This is serious, damned serious!" he says.

"I won't have someone turn this ship into a hen frigate. I want to know who's responsible for bringing the woman onboard!"

Lester pauses, waiting several minutes before speaking again.

"Number 1, do you know?"

"No, Sir."

"Number 2, do you know?"

"No, Captain."

"Number 3, do you know?"

"No, Sir, I do not know."

"Mr. Brown?"

"No, Sir, nutin', Sir!" answers Abe.

"Somebody must know and I will know before anyone leaves this lounge. Who had the Middle Watch?"

"It was mine," says Diogo.

"Who did you have on the gangway?"

Diogo hesitates for a moment, not to stall the questioning but to try to remember names of his crew that were still new to him.

"Ahh, ahh," he says. "I believe it was Newman."

"His name is Norman," interrupts Andrew.

"I'm sorry," said Pilla. "Yes, it was Norman, Sir. Paolo Norman.

"Paul Norman," corrects Lester.

"Get him now," Hiram orders and momentarily returns his cabin.

Norman is aloft, on the mainmast. It takes him a few minutes to come alow.

He follows Pilla into the captain's lounge and is surprised by the array of officers and steerers who are assembled. He knows he is in trouble.

"Get the captain," Andrew says to Jorge who was sitting closest to the door to the captain's cabin. He knocks and instantly Lester opens the door.

"Mr. Norman, did you have the Second Watch this morning?" asks Hiram Lester.

Norman hesitates then sheepishly answers that he did.

"Did you see who brought the woman on board during your watch?"

"No, I didn't…Sir."

"Did you ever leave your post at the gangway during your watch?"

"No, Sir," he said instantly without thinking because it was the answer that might keep him out of trouble.

"A woman was brought on board during your watch. I ask again, did you ever leave your watch?"

This time, Norman is slow to answer.

"Maybe," he says. "Yes, just once, but just for a few minutes."

"Why?"

"It was cold, Sir. Cook's boy Billy was supposed to bring coffee to the watch at 1 o'clock, but he never showed. I waited an hour and when he didn't come topside, I quickly went to the galley and got a cup. But, Sir, I did it so quickly that no one could have come on board. I listened…you know how noisy the gangway is. It rattles. I would have heard someone come aboard, if they did."

"Obviously you didn't," comments Lester.

"Did you see any of the crew come onboard during your watch?"

"No, Sir."

"Did you see anyone on deck during your watch?"

He starts to say no but stops and then thinks of the repercussions if he is shown to be a liar.

"Yes Sir, I did."

"Who was it?"

Norman pauses for a moment as he scans the faces of the men assembled in the lounge. His eyes abruptly stop at Abe Brown. Brown glares at him, fixing his eyes directly on Norman's. They emit an easily-understood message. Norman has feared Brown because of his unpredictability but now is even more frightened of Capt. Lester. He has never seen him so angry. He pauses too long and finally answers.

"It was Mr. Brown."

"Which Brown?"

"Abe Brown, Sir."

"What was he doing topside."

"He was at the larboard gunwale, Sir, relieving himself."

"Did you hail him?"

"I did, Sir. He said something that I didn't understand. I think he was drunk."

"Where did he go after you spoke to him?"

"He went aft, Sir. To this companionway," Norman says and turns aside, pointing to the ladder just ahead of the wheelhouse that leads to the captain's and mates' quarters.

"That's interesting," Captain Lester says aloud as he strokes his chin.

"And when you saw him, from which companionway did he emerge on deck?"

"Why, the crew's Sir, the one before the foremast."

"Mr. Brown, what were you doing in the fo'c's'le?"

Brown is slow in answering because he, too, is formulating a response that he hopes will satisfy Lester.

"I went… I went dere to see if'n all my crew returned."

"And did they?"

"Aye, Sir, dey wuz all dere, 'cepting of course, da one dat I already tol' ya, dat damned Irishman wuz missing."

"Why did you not come aft to your quarters using the second deck?

"I 'ad ta piss, Sir. Pardon my English."

"When did you come aboard?"

"I'm not sure, Sir. I tink I wuz drunk an' can't quite remember."

"Who had the First Watch?"

"I did," says Andrew Lester.

"Who was posted on the gangway?"

"It was Joshua Edwards. I stood most of the watch with him because earlier that evening, there was a lot of activity on the wharf. There had been a commotion on one of the English merchantmen."

"Did you see Mr. Brown come aboard?"

"No, Sir."

"Mr. Edwards, did you see Mr. Brown come aboard."

"No, Sir."

"Mr. Brown, how did you happen to come aboard without anyone seeing you?"

"I done knows, Sir. I mus' admit, Sir, maybe I had a wee bit too much rum. It makes me mind go blank. Which it does dat at times. I guess da Portygee rum is right powerful stuff…Sir."

"Did anyone come onboard with you?"

"I done 'member dat, too, Sir. As I said, I guess I kinda blanks out."

Lester realizes that he has been checkmated with a lie. There is nothing more he can do. He crosses his hands behind his back then walks around the table. He stops in front of Abe Brown and looks him directly in the eyes. Brown stares back and the faintest smile spreads across his lips. Only Lester could have seen it. Brown knows that he has out-maneuvered the captain.

Stupid bastard, Abe says to himself, as he continues to look into Lester's eyes.

Lester walks away, knowing that he will eventually have the last word. But for now, it is a draw. All the men leave except Andrew. Hiram motions him to follow him into his cabin.

"Close the door," he says.

"I'm sorry we didn't find a fourth mate in Angra," he says to Andrew. Is there anyone we might consider who is onboard?"

"No one has the experience he has," answers Andrew. "I talked at length about it with both Jorge and Diogo. They said there were other men who could but we didn't have enough time in port to go after them."

"Too bad," says Hiram. I guess we are forced to make do with what we have."

"How is your Indian doing?"

"He is smart. I think he will surprise us."

Later, when Abe is alone topside, his uncle approaches him.

"That was stupid," he says. "You have just blown any chance you might have had to be named 4th mate. I cannot believe your stupidity."

"He can't do a damn ting," Abe says.

"You really are stupid," his uncle reiterates. "He can do almost anything he wants. He is in command of everything on *Tranquility*."

"Maybe he wone always be."

"Don't ever let anyone hear you say that again. He could stretch your neck on the yardarm if he heard you say that. And, it would all be perfectly legal to do so."

"Wad could I say to 'im?"

"You should have told the truth. He might have understood the predicament you were in. You are stupid, really stupid. I cannot believe you are a Brown. Maybe I should question your mother when we get back to discern if my brother really was your father. It would explain a lot!"

Suddenly enraged, Abe grabs his uncle by the throat. He is about to clasp the other hand on him when he realizes what he is doing. Instead, he releases his grip, turns around, and walks to the bow.

Chapter 16

The Search for Whales Finally Begins

Thursday, December 28, 1865, Day 23

Delayed, *Tranquility* clears Angra's harbor by noon. Now, nothing but the open Atlantic lies before her. Winds, fair out of the northwest, fill her sails and blow about the hair on Capt. Lester's bare head as he stands next to the open door of the wheelhouse.

"A perfect day for sailing," he says to his new 3rd Mate Diogo Pilla who stands immediately behind the quartermaster on the wheel. "Have the helmsman set the course at 120 degrees, south-by-east." After he sees that it is done, he walks the main deck to the bow, then returns to his cabin.

At supper that evening, with his officers around him at the table, Hiram reveals his sailing plans.

"I intend to hunt the Brazil Banks," he says to his three mates and Abe Brown, the boat steerer who is still acting as 4th mate. "While we were in Angra I spoke at length with Capt. Livingston from the *Emerald*. He told me they had spotted whales there, along the coast, as they came north.

"Before we can seriously hope to bring in a whale, we must spend a few more days training the whaleboat crews. We must work them until each man knows what is expected of him as well as the man next to him. There may well come a time when he will be required to perform both jobs.

"Right now the winds are fair on our transom. We'll continue on this course as long as we make progress to the south'ard. I believe it will take us about 12 days to reach the Cape Verde Islands. We will pass between them and the coast of Africa, off Dakar. Whenever the weather en route slackens, we'll hold a few more drills."

A few minutes after the meeting ends, Joshua Edwards, Andrew Lester's harpooner, climbs the ladder onto the main deck, crosses over to the starboard side of *Tranquility*, then works his way aft to his whaleboat. He sees John Adams, that boat's waist-oarsman and tells him to follow. Edwards climbs inside his boat and emerges with several harpoons and lances. After examining their cutting edges, he hands them all to Adams.

"Follow me," he says to Adams, letting him carry the bundle.

Kurt Müller is already at the grindstone, a large sandstone wheel. "Here's some work for you," he says to the ship's blacksmith.

"Can you do them now, or should I come back?" Edwards asks.

"Hang around," Müller answers. "These mincing knives are almost done."

The next morning Ben is topside, watching the sun rise just a bit ahead of the larboard beam. The weather continues to warm, getting a bit hotter each day as *Tranquility* reaches farther and farther to the south'ard.

Long Island summers are hot, he thinks, *but I have never been in such awful heat. Thank God we can sleep on deck. Maybe it is the heat*, he continues, *but the seas have taken on a different color. They look especially blue as we ride up and over the backs of following waves. In a way, it's kinda fun.*

Ben looks aft, down the gunwale he has been leaning upon, and sees John Adams, one of the farmers in Andrew's crew.

He is vomiting over the side.

I feel sorry for him, he thinks to himself. He is always seasick.

Most Greenies eventually recover but Adams hasn't. On the first training launch after they left the Azores, Andrew tells Ben to take Adams' place in his crew, as the waist oar. Even though he has never rowed a boat before he feels it seems easy enough. He has been watching other crews work and doesn't believe he will have difficulty bending the oar. In fact he has an advantage that Andrew plans to capitalize upon. Ben is taller than either of the two Negroes or John Adams, in his crew. He performs so well that on the second practice launch Andrew makes Ben permanent waist oar.

"Congratulations," he says to Ben as they leave the whaleboat in the davits and jump onto the main deck. "I knew you would do well. Oh, by the way. You don't have to work any longer with Cook."

"Thank you," says Ben. "That was fun to do."

"That's just the beginning," says Andrew before going aft.

I wonder what he meant by that? thinks Ben.

After that move, Ben's life on the ship drastically changes. He has been sleeping with Cook and Billy on the second deck behind the cooking area. Andrew later tells him to gather his gear and move permanently to the forecastle. Ben is suspicious of the men there but he almost immediately senses that he is no longer looked upon as the mess boy or someone everyone can order about. He had received some meager respect from them just because he is an Indian. Now it is because he has become a part of a whaleboat crew. He now has a position of which he can be proud. And, because he can read and write, some of the Greenies now ask him to write letters for them.

Tranquility makes good progress to the south'ard. In two weeks she is just northeast of the first Cape Verde Islands. There, 37 days out of Sag Harbor, the crew sees their first good whale, a humpback. But before the ship can be brought about and whaleboats launched, the whale sounds and never resurfaces.

"The rough seas hides it," says Capt. Hiram Lester.

No other whales are seen that day. Lester tells the crew that this area was always a good spot to locate humpbacks. However, he cautioned that was years ago. Even so, he offers a pound of tobacco for the one who first spots the next whale.

Late that day, the lookout sees a sail on the horizon.

"She's headed in our direction," he yells alow to the men on the main deck. As the sun sets, a concerned Capt. Lester orders an extra man on each mast. He doesn't want a collision in the dark. Seldom are men atop the sticks after dark.

Andrew sends his crew aloft. Ben has been relieved of his kitchen duties and now is a part of the watch. That includes time aloft. This is the first time he's been atop the main. And, it is the first time he must negotiate the yards after the sun has set. Josh Edwards, Andrew's harpooner and thus second in command of the watch, goes up while Andrew remains below at a mate's meeting.

"I'm not afraid to climb the rat lines in the darkness, but I am concerned," Ben tells Edwards as they start the climb.

"And well you should be," Edwards answers. "It takes practice. I don't think you have been aloft very many times even during the day. Go ahead of me. Take your time. There is no hurry. I will be right behind you."

He watches Ben take slow, measured steps, making sure his weight is on each line before he takes the next step upward.

"It takes practice," Edwards says again. "After a dozen or so times, you'll be able to climb with your eyes closed."

Not me, Ben thinks. But Edwards is right.

No one sees the ship pass in the dark.

The next morning the winds fall off so Lester orders the watch to wear ship. All four crews practice on the ocean until late in the morning, when winds again freshen.

"Now that we are in the vicinity of whales," Lester says while on deck with his three mates and Abe Brown, "after the whaleboats are hoisted, we will switch to four-man lookouts. Between sunrise and sunset, post two crewmen on the foremast's topgallant yards. On the mainmast, I want a mate and his boat steerer.

"As you all are aware," Lester continues, "Andrew is this ship's sailmaster as well as second in command of this vessel. You will take orders directly from him in affairs of running and standing rigging, as well as other matters. He is an excellent sailor and I have placed all my trust in him, as well as you three, to make this a right ship. He will further instruct you."

"Also," says Andrew after his brother goes below, "we will shorten the length of a watch and switch to four, 3-hour watches during days. Correspondingly, at sunset, I want all sails lightened. I want *Tranquility* to heave-to as much as possible. This amount of sail should allow us to drift without a lot of rolling. There is no profit in sailing over waters that may contain whales we cannot see in the dark.

"We still have a few hours of daylight remaining, so set the lookouts. Mr. Brown," Andrew Lester addresses Abe as the mates and their seconds are beginning to disassemble. "It is your watch. Send two of your crew aloft on the foremast and you and a third man take the main. I want the head of each watch, either a mate or his boat steerer, on the main whenever the four-man watches are posted. Now be done with it," he orders, then goes below.

Just before sunset Andrew is again topside checking to see how well his instructions are being carried out. The bo'sun is in the wheelhouse and when he sees the 1st mate appear on deck, he joins him.

"Good evening, Bo'sun," Andrew says while still looking aloft and studying the rigging.

"Good evening, Mr. Lester," Bellingham answers.

"The furled sails are flapping a bit in this wind," Andrew says. "Send two of your men aloft to frap the sails and remove the slack. I just checked the barometer. It is falling and I fear we are in for some heavy weather this evening. I don't care to ruin the sails so early in our journey."

Late the next day the winds swing to the southeast and scattered clouds move in with exceptional speed. They are dark and getting darker and seem to lower more each furlong *Tranquility* makes to windward. Minutes after the sun sets, Abe and his boat crew climb out of the forecastle. Andrew is still on deck and watches as Brown instructs his watch. Spray has been intermittently pelting them since they came on deck. The crew is about to go aloft when a strong gust of wind hits the larboard side of the ship and carries the top of a wave over the foredeck.

"Git below and git yur oilskins," Abe yells at his men. He waits on deck as each man returns. He sends two to the foremast shrouds and watches them climb the ratlines. They are about a dozen feet above the deck when the spray from another wave breaks over the foredeck. Andrew watches as one man momentarily losses his grip but regains it before he can fall.

"Hold on there!" he yells loudly as he rushes forward to Abe.

"You men, come down."

The men stop climbing.

Brown turns and sarcastically asks, "Wad's it now?"

"What kind of mate are you, who would send his men aloft on the leeward shrouds in weather like this?"

"I'm not really a mate, tanks ta yer brudder," Abe contemptuously responds, "sos I can't answer ya rightly."

"Rightly, what?"

Abe is slow to respond.

"Rightly......Sir."

"You two, come alow," Lester again orders.

"Jolly," Andrew speaks to Fred Jolly as he sets foot on deck, "are you some kind of dunce? This isn't your first time going aloft. You should know better than to climb the leeward shroud in weather like this. You've been on whaleships before."

"What's your name?" Lester addresses the second man.

"Jackson, Sir. Adam Jackson."

"I can understand your move, being a Greenie. But don't you have any common sense? Always climb aloft on the weather side of the ship. In case you lose your grip, the wind will push you into the shrouds and you can regain it. On the leeward side, if you fall you'll fall into the sea. Now get aloft, there's still enough light to see."

The men climb the ratlines and move higher into the standing rigging. On deck, Abe approaches Lester.

"You had no right addressin' me likes ya did afore my men," he says. "They'd a learned der own whad ta do in dis kinda weather. It's the best way ta learn."

"As you said before, you're not a mate so they cannot be **your** men. I had every right to call you down. I have every right to address you whenever and wherever I see fit!"

"But, didn't ya see how fast dat monkey climbs da shrouds?" Brown asks.

"Are you calling Jackson a monkey?"

"Well, he looks like one, done he? He's black like one."

"What if he fell overboard?"

"Dere's damned more where he comes from."

"You're disgusting," Lester says.

"And you're not da cap'n. Leastwise on this ship you ain't."

"In regard to you, I might as well be. But I am the 1st mate and you will treat me as such. Now get your ass aloft."

"Yu'll pay fer dis," Abe says and turns his back on Lester as he, too, scampers up the weather ratlines.

"I'll pay! What do you mean?"

Brown continues climbing the shroud and ignores Andrew. He stops for a moment then looks down. A faint smile spreads across his lips but it is already too dark to see it.

"You're time 'ill come," he says.

"Is that a threat?" Andrew yells above the wind.

Abe turns and continues climbing aloft.

The spray from another wave is carried across the entire foredeck, pelting Andrew who automatically turns his back to its sting.

Damn that man, Andrew says to himself as he makes for the aft ladder to the quarterdeck.

"Bo'sun," Andrew says to Bellingham as he returns to the wheelhouse. "The weather's worsening. Call down the watches aloft. Before they go below, have them string jack lines 3 feet above the deck between the mizzen and main and another between the main and foremast."

Near the end of the evening meal the ship shudders so violently that Jorge is almost thrown off his seat in the officer's mess. A few seconds later, a very wet Bellingham appears, clambering down the after-ladder. He is followed by a gush of seawater.

"That was a damned big rogue wave," he says, as he pulls off his hat, opens his slicker, and reaches for a mug. "They're getting bigger," he says as he pours coffee from the ever-present pot on the small charcoal heating stove. "I think we should double the men on the wheel and retire the two watches on the bow."

Turning to and addressing Andrew directly, he says, "Might it not be a good idea, Mr. Lester, a bit easier on the ship, if we veered a few degrees to starboard so we wouldn't take the waves head on?"

"You might be right," Lester answers. "Let me get my gear and I'll join you topside."

Andrew is directly behind Bellingham as he clears the small housing that shelters the entry to the companionway. They both just make it into the wheelhouse as another wave, though not as big as the monster that hit the ship earlier, sweeps a wall of water over the larboard bow and floods the entire foredeck.

"What's that clanging?" Andrew says and opens the wheelhouse door to better locate the source of the sound. Bellingham is immediately behind him.

"It's the try pots. Sounds like one of the cooling tubs is loose and banging between the two pots," the bo'sun says.

"You're right," says Andrew. "Go forward and find two men on watch. Have them secure the cooling tub and then tell them they are off watch after that."

Bellingham disappears down the after companionway and goes forward through steerage and eventually reaches the forecastle.

"Jackson and Dos Santos," he orders, "get on your oils. Take two light lines and go topside to secure the cooling tub that's come loose. It's shitty out there so stay close together. If you can find them, tell the two men on the bow watch that they may end the watch."

From the forward window of the wheelhouse, Lester watches as two foremast men emerge from the housing that protects the companionway ladder. Though it is getting dark, he can just see the men working their way toward the try pots. They are holding onto anything they can find. The ship's bow plunges into the back of a wave. On the way up, a large wall of water sweeps over the bow, inundating the two men. They seem frozen to the safety jacklines as another wave slaps against the larboard quarter. A river of water washes across the decks and pours off the gangway break in the starboard gunwale.

"I think they're afraid to move," Andrew says to Adrian Moore, the quartermaster on the wheel. "There they go."

Ben Johnson, one of the two men clinging to the safety line, is a large, powerful man, a Negro. This is the first time he has ever been on a sailing vessel. However, he is imbued with a fair degree of common sense.

"You go first," he says to Dos Santos. "I'll be right behind you."

As they inch their way toward the overturned try pots, yet another wave sweeps over the larboard quarter and escapes off the starboard side. They see the two men on watch huddle against the gunwale at the bow and tell them to go below.

"I don't think I can make it," Dos Santos says as he sputters and spits water.

"Sure you can," Johnson says.

No sooner do the words escape Johnson's mouth than they are engulfed by yet another wave. Johnson later said he felt Dos Santo's body brush against his as the wave hit. When the water cleared, Dos Santos was missing.

"He is against the life lines on the gangway," Andrew yells.

"He's clutching the lower rope."

The winds become so strong that they begin to push the ship

downwind onto the backs of the rollers ahead of *Tranquility*. To reduce the surfing and lack of control, the helmsman brings the stern around a few degrees, but the bow still plunges into the backs of waves. As another wave batters the larboard bow, it defies the wind and sweeps over the gunwale. When it clears, Andrew is surprised to see that Dos Santos is still there.

"I don't think he will take many more before he lets go," says Moore.

"You're right. I'm going out," Andrew says.

"Bring the bow another point to starboard; it may lessen the force of the waves."

The move has no affect. Waves now are so big that the bow is under water more often than it is clear.

Between waves, Andrew dashes out of the wheelhouse and grabs the lifeline that had been strung between the mizzen and main mast. Holding on to it, he works his way to the main. He unties the lifeline from the mainmast that leads to the foremast.

I hope whoever tied it to the fore knew what he was doing, Andrew thinks to himself. Damn it, I hope this works.

Lester takes three steps in front of the mainmast and grabs the slack in the line to tie himself around the waist. Then he begins, hand-over-hand, pulling himself toward the foremast. As another wave brakes over the transom Andrew is washed across the deck toward the bow. When the water disappears over the side, he is momentarily able to stand upright in the melee. Dos Santos still clings to the lifeline stretched across the gangway opening, but his feet dangle off the ship. Andrew hears his plaintive cry for help as yet another wave clears the larboard side of the bow. The water comes down so heavily that it smashes him onto the deck.

The wave knocks the wind out of him and he lies prostrate on his belly. Water rushing off the deck carries him sideways, toward the starboard edge. His face rubs against the deck, unprotected because he needs two hands to maintain his grip on the lifeline. He is washed toward Dos Santos and stops just short of colliding with him. Lester is able to brace one foot against a stanchion through which the lifelines run. He stretches his right hand towards Dos Santos.

"Give me your hand!" he yells. "Give me your hand!"

Dos Santos is unresponsive as a gush of water again sweeps over them.

Lester sees Dos Santos let one hand go.

Andrew again yells to him.

Lester both feels and hears the next wave hit the ship's larboard quarter. Seconds later it is on top of him. He feels the ship shudder in response through his ribs on the wet deck. Then he experiences an excruciatingly sharp pain across the left side of his chest. That wave felt bigger than the others, he thinks, and then remembers Dos Santo's plight.

In desperation, he reaches for Dos Santo's hair, grabs it between his fingers and pulls him back from the ship's edge as still more water sweeps over them.

For a long moment, Lester lies there, breathing heavily. The pain in his chest intensifies with each gasp for air.

What the hell do I do next? he says to himself as the pain increases. He knows that he has broken a rib, possibly two, when the wave knocked him to the deck.

Unexpectedly, he feels a tug on the line he has wrapped around his left arm and is still firmly holding. Then it comes again. Slowly, he is pulled across the deck, toward the foremast with Dos Santos' hair still in his right hand.

"I thought you two needed a little help," Johnson says to Lester as the remnants of a wave sweeps over their backs. At the cubby leading to the companionway, two men are waiting until Johnson has Lester within their reach. Then they pull a water-logged Dos Santos and Lester into the forecastle.

The next morning, as the foremast crew is eating breakfast on their trunks, Lester's actions from the previous night are the center of conversation.

"That Mr. Lester is some mate," Roger Whetstone says. "He risked his ass for one of us. Hell, the Portygee ain't even part of his boat."

"Do you think Abe would have done that for one of his crew?" asks James Blackwell.

"Hell no," he says, answering his own question.

Later that day, Cook finds some muslin cloth and binds Andrew's chest.

"Damn it, cook, do I need to be bound so tightly that I cannot breathe?"

"That's the whole idea, Mr. Lester. When you fill your lungs don't the ribs hurt like hell?"

"Well, they do."

"If you can't inflate your chest all the way, the ribs won't hurt as bad. Also, by not being able to move them they are likely to grow together a lot faster…if they do."

"You sound like a doctor," says Andrew.

"Did you learn this in school or somewhere?"

"No Sir, I learned the hard way."

"How was that?"

"In my younger days I was in a fight and a real doctor bandaged me."

"How long did you wear the bandages?"

"Three or four months. Don't quite remember. But I was lucky. The guy who beat me broke only one rib. I think you have two ribs broken."

After that, Andrew is looked upon with a lot of respect from everyone, from everyone, that is, except Abe Brown. He even gets a halfhearted salute as he passes some of the forecastle Greenies.

Jan. 21, 1866, Day 48

A few weeks later, the captain tells the crew that they are passing through the middle of the narrowest part of the Atlantic Ocean.

"Only 1800 miles separate Africa from South America," says Lester. "It also will be the hottest."

And, each day *Tranquility* sails south the winds seem to die a little more.

It is now nearly a month since she left Angra and the crew has spotted only one whale. It broke the surface twice but never again. Launching the whaleboats would have been useless. The men are becoming discontented and restless. The make-ready work they are doing onboard is seen as a waste of time and their energy. They all know it is only something to keep them busy. They even look forward to days when the winds slow and whaleboats are lowered for drill. At least it is something to do.

Standing on the quarterdeck and watching the men on deck below lethargically moving about the make-busy work, Capt. Lester senses the men's frustrations. At that moment, Andrew emerges from the after companionway.

"No. 1," he calls to him, "find the bo'sun and have him join us at the taffrail."

In a few minutes Bellingham and Andrew join Capt. Lester who, for the moment, is staring into the wake of his ship as it slowly plods along under light winds. The wake of any ship seems to have a mesmerizing affect on anyone who gazes into it.

"I guess it is time to begin building the try works," says Lester. "Have two watches do it at one time, three-hour shifts, then replace them with the other watches. I want all the crews to take part in its construction. Andrew, make sure that enough of the casks are filled with water to replace the weight of the bricks. I don't want our center of gravity to rise."

The entire day is spent hauling bricks topside from the bilge. The 250-gallon try pots, huge iron kettles that had been stored upside down on deck, are righted. Their insides are covered with rust. Two buckets of sand are hauled from storage and dumped into each pot. With worn strips of sailcloth men inside the pots begin scouring the rust.

"That will take another few days of work," Andrew says to his brother as they watch the progress from the quarterdeck.

"How are your ribs?"

"They are extremely painful. I don't think I can handle my whaleboat's rudder.

Under the mate's supervision, the crews build the firebox around the kettles on three layers of bricks that will keep the deck from becoming scorched. The men sense that this is not busy work and they appear to actually enjoy what they are doing.

"Just tink," Abe says, as he watches over the crew laying bricks, "wad would we 'ave done wid a whale if we'd killed one? Duh works ain't even set."

"The 1st mate said it wouldn't take but a day to build this if we were pushed for time," said Obie Jones, a Negro in Ben's boat.

Jones is one of three men kneeling on deck setting the bricks in mortar for the two trypots. Nonchalantly, Abe walks over to Jones and stops next to him. For a moment, with his hands on his hips, he watches Jones as he works, then looks up at the quarterdeck to see if anyone is watching. He sees no one who matters and kicks Jones in the ass.

"Keep yer mouth shut, nigger! No one spoke ta ya," he says as he bends down and speaks directly into Jones' ear.

Ben, next to Jones, stands up quickly because his back has cramped. Abe, thinking he is going to do something, rushes over to him.

"You gots a problem, Indian?"

Ben doesn't answer him but bends down again on the deck and moves some bricks.

There are many ways to be sick, Ben thinks to himself. His is the worst kind. Why is he like this? Abe stirs up the whaleboat crews whenever he can. He does it just to create trouble. I know the captain and his brother are aware of this but they don't do anything to stop him.

"Dis damn, stupid captain doesn't know wad he's doin'," Abe later says to a few men in the fo'c's'le. "It's been a month an' a half since we left Sag an' we ain't put an ounce of oil in a barrel. Hell, we ain't earned even a cent for all our work. Dah kettles are rustin' faster than we can scrape 'em clean. We ain't got a lay ta show for our work. If I was captain of this scow I'd show ya how ta fine whales."

Seeing that no one responds Abe gets up and leaves.

"What's a lay?" Ben asks Harvey Bennett sitting next to him.

"Whalemen," he answers, "ain't never paid by the day or week, but get their due only after they return to port. Even then we gotta wait 'til after the oil and bones bin sold an' only after the ship's owners takes their shares. If there's anythin' left over it is split up according to the lay, or shares you signed on for when the trip started. The captain gets the biggest lay then the mates and on down the line to us. But first, they figure what you took out of the slop chest and sometimes you can even owe them money. That's where Abe's uncle gets his due before you.

"How'd ya like it now dat yur in da fo'c's'le?" Bennett asks Ben.

"It's changed. When I was first hauled onboard I hated the job I was given….helping the steward, Cook, or any other job that needed doing. It is squaw's work. But most of all it was cleaning up. Everyone was my boss. The crew looked at me more as a servant rather than a shipmate. That didn't bother me. I was used to that. That was often the way I was treated by people when I went off the reservation.

"But that Portygee Nuno Dias was different. When he came onboard in Angra he said hello to me without knowing what I did on the ship. I was surprised how good he spoke English. I remember the first time we talked.

"You Indian?" he asked one day when I was sitting on the bow windlass.

"Yes."

"Then why you no harponeer? All Indian I know are harponeer."

"I don't know how to handle a harpon. No one has shown me how. Maybe they think I'm too small, too young."

"You big boy. You no have trouble with harpon. Go in my boat and get harpon. Is okay. You go, get harpon. I show you how."

"I was in Pilla's boat untying one of the harpons when Andrew saw me.

"What are you doing?" he asked me. "You are not supposed to be there!"

"Nuno Dias, Mr. Pilla's harponeer, told me to get a harpon from his boat."

"Why would he have told you that?"

"He said he was going to show me how to handle a harpon."

"Is okay," Dias yells to Andrew when he sees him questioning me. "I tell him get harpon."

"Here," Mr. Lester said, "hand it to me. I don't want you to fall overboard. The harpon is too valuable to lose.

"Do you want to become a harponeer?" Andrew asks with a slight smile.

"I would, Sir."

"Good."

After that I began to see him in a different light. I found it more difficult to hate him for the kidnapping. Nuno, too, was always friendly to me. There were now two people that I think I can talk to.

Chapter 17

Confessions

After Ben is made a permanent member of Andrew Lester's whaleboat crew, he begins looking forward to each time the boats were lowered, even for practice. Andrew has his crew launch their boat, primarily for Ben's practice. He even has them launch several times in one day. After the exhausted crew hauled the boat to its davit, Andrew takes Ben aside as the crew disperses.

"Have you any skills?" Lester asks.

"I am not skilled at anything."

"Did you attend school?"

"We had to. We were forced to. All children on the reservation attended the State School."

"See! There! You do have skills. You can read and write; can you not?"

"I can."

"Do you know how few others on this ship can do that? Probably not one in ten. How long did you stay in school?"

"I liked school. I stayed in until the 8 grade. No one in my family had ever gone that high in school. Most of my friends quit when they left 6 grade. I remember that it was unusual for anyone, Indian or White, to stay in school much longer than that. They all left to find work. So did

I, but I worked after school, on Saturdays and Sundays, and during the summer when there was no school."

"What kind of work did you do?"

"Most of the time, I worked on the fish docks at Moriches Inlet, cleaning, salting and packing fish. But that wasn't very steady and the fishermen didn't pay me as much as they did a White who worked next to me, doing the same work, maybe even less than I did. But I also worked in a dry goods store in the village, in Good Grounds."

"What did you do there?"

"At first, I swept floors but then Mr. Bernstein had me unpacking boxes and stocking shelves. I also helped him do inventory when that time of the year came around. He said I was good with figures."

"You speak quite well, your English that is."

"Why shouldn't I?" says Ben. "After all, you Europeans have now been living among my people for more than 200 years. To many Indians, especially those of my age, English has become our first language."

"Do you know your native language?" asks Andrew.

"I can speak some. My parents and grandparents speak it as well as English. When they don't want us to hear something they are saying, they use our native tongue. Younger people on the reservation use mostly English. That is because of school. And my grandfather, who was a very wise man, said I should learn to speak the language of the Whites because he said my future lays among them."

"You're an interesting young man."

"So are you," says Ben.

"How so?"

"No one, especially a White man, has ever asked me what I did for a living or cared who I am."

Even though Ben is beginning to change his mind about Lester, he still has reservations. He now believes that Andrew is inherently a good person. And, he senses that Lester wants him to learn everything that is possible about the ship and boat.

But why? He asks himself.

"What do you have planned for me?" he asks Andrew.

Andrew is only mildly startled when Ben asked him. He suspected that Ben had a feeling that he was being groomed.

"Just having you row a whaleboat seems to have satisfied those on board who felt this voyage for whales was doomed unless we had an Indian, an Indian harponeer in our crew. I think the next step in your maturation is to let you try to stick a whale. True, we have not had many chances to do that, but it will come. I know that. Are you amiable to the idea?"

"Yes, without hesitation."

Changing the subject, Andrew asks: "Do you and others on the reservation celebrate Christmas?"

Somewhat startled by the abruptness of the question, Ben hesitates at first to answer. "Some do and some kind of don't."

"What do you mean by that?"

"Oh, we do have our share of preachers. Some White and some Indian. They tell us of the good to come but few see it happening. The Blacks among us seem more prone to believe them."

"How about you? Do you consider yourself a Christian?"

"There are many among us who do but they don't do it completely."

"How is that?"

"Manitou is still believed by most Indians on the reservation. They mix their old beliefs with that of Christianity."

"What is Manitou?"

"Correctly, you should ask WHO is Manitou? He is both a good and bad spirit. Most look at him as being good. He is our strongest spirit. In the past, before Europeans came to our land, we believed that everything--trees, animals and everything alive--has a spirit. Our sachems were able to talk with them. Today, some Indians fear to give this up to believe in only one god.

"I am one of those with mixed feelings."

The first Christmas at sea comes and goes and is hardly noticed on the ship. For Indians on the reservation the most celebrated holiday is the 4th of July. Nor do Quakers make a big event of Christmas, but Catholics, especially the Portuguese, do. While the ship was in Angra, the captain asked the cook to kill a few extra chickens that day and everyone ate well, Christians or not. New Year's Day came and the captain issued a short ration of rum for anyone who wanted it.

Neither event replaces, even for a while, the returning restlessness of the crew as *Tranquility* continually moves father to the south'ard. And, as if conditions onboard aren't bad enough, they gradually worsen as the crew encounters the first really trying period in the voyage, The Doldrums. The phenomenon occurs is an area in the mid-Atlantic where there are no currents or winds.

The course Capt. Lester has Andrew set takes them too close to Africa and rather than catching a westward-moving current and winds, they become trapped. Literally they must launch the whaleboats and row their way out of them. If they don't, there is the possibility of running out of both food and water before the first winds catch their sagging sails or the currents move the boat westerly.

For five days the crews row both day and night, two hours on and two hours off switching with watches. Only when they can sense *Tranquility* moves faster than they are rowing will it be over. This occurs just in time because the 16 men bending the oars are near total exhaustion.

On the fifth day of rowing, Capt. Lester looks aloft and then back at the boats. "There's no wind," he says to Bellingham who has joined him. "It is the current that is moving us. Call the boats back."

He calls both boats back to the davits. Tired men trice the davits and haul on the gripes (the lashings which hold a boat laterally to the cranes, after hoisting). They had towed the ship far enough to the west, Lester later tells them, to pick up the edge of the South Equatorial Current. One of the mates told his crew that the captain told him they had rowed the ship nearly 50 miles in those five days. The next morning, as the ship still drifts westward, the few sails set on the foremast begin to respond to gentle puffs of the Southwest Trade Winds. By mid-morning, all the sails are set and the captain orders Jorge to unlock the water casks.

Chapter 18

At Last, Underway Again

Friday, February 17, 1866, Day 74

The winds are light and don't come fresh enough to create a real wake. When they do, they came with rain and in the middle of the night. Sleeping on deck ends as everyone scurries below. The forecastle is like an oven and the air foul. But, at last, they are again underway!

"Once again I can control *Tranquility*," Capt. Lester writes in the ship's log. "We are now 74 days out of Sag Harbor. Four days ago, I was finally able to set her on a southwest course. I held her on that course until nearing the archipelago of Fernando de Noronha. Then I turned the ship due west toward Atol das Rocas. Four lookouts are again posted and day watches are reduced to three hours. I even reminded lookouts of the tobacco reward."

"Andrew," Lester says to his brother as he leaves his cabin and takes his seat at the head of the mess table. "I believe that we are approaching the realm of the humpback. I can almost feel the presence of whales. It may all be because of a dream I had last night. I dreamt that whales were everywhere about the ship. Or, it may only be the change in the weather that has me thinking in such a bizarre manner. I hope for a change in our luck. God only knows, we need it."

Different whale species prefer different habitats in the ocean. Lester had learned early in his whaling career that humpbacks prefer to feed and linger around small islands. This collection of islands and rocks, just off the heel of Brazil, is the perfect place for them. He is led here by past success, but that is no guarantee for finding whales now.

After passing the last of the das Rocas Islands he alters course to a west-northwest direction. Every evening just after sunset, he has the watch heave-to, bracing the fore and striking all other sails. With the remaining sail set, the ship is hoved close to the wind. Lester doesn't want to move any distance.

Thus the ship, the following morning, is in a position close to the place where she was the night before. This move is also used to give the crew a chance to rest. The goal is not to pass over grounds in the dark that might contain whales. Though most of the depths over which *Tranquility* is now cruising range from 1,000 to 2,000 fathoms there are enough rises and shoals off the bottom to interest any feeding whales.

During daylight hours on these whaling grounds the ship is put into a cruise mode. Under somewhat shortened sail, she is tacked back and forth across the grounds, heading west in the mornings when possible, then easterly in the afternoons. This is so that a spout would be made more visible in the respective light.

Five weeks later (*Feb. 27, Day 85*), late in the morning, ship continues on course. *Tranquility* is moving along well, steadily, but not more than 3 knots, when the lookout on the foremast's topgallant crosstrees, yells he has spotted a spout.

"Keep your eyes skinned," Number 1, who was on deck, yells aloft. "It may breach again."

"He's gone," Nuno Dias," yells alow to Mr. Lester. "I see nothing more."

Tranquility moves on for another hour when the lookout repeats the alarm. A few minutes later he yells, "There are two, maybe three whales spouting."

"Where away?" asks Andrew Lester.

"Five! Off the bow! Off the starboard bow," the lookout yells alow.

Lester passes on a new heading to the helm and the quartermaster backs the ship 15 degrees farther to larboard.

"There they are," Lester says, "a pod of whales spouting regularly at will. Strike the royals, then the gallants," he orders. The ship heaves-to and almost immediately comes to a stop. Before issuing the next order, Lester waits a few minutes until the momentum of the ship slows to a complete stop. While this is happening, his brother comes on deck.

"They're humpbacks," Capt. Lester says as he studies the pod of whales through his glass.

"They're humpbacks," he repeats himself. "They blow two streams to larboard. No other whales blow like that. They're a mixed pod," he says after a pause, "mostly bulls with but one or two cows."

"Lower the boats," Andrew finally orders.

"Cast off the gripes," the 1st mate orders. "See that all line-tubs are onboard; clear the boat falls (the lines between tackle blocks) and remove the stops from all whalecraft and sails."

Responding, the four crews come alive. They had expected the order to come as they, too, watched the whales spouting.

"It is done, Sir," answers Number 1.

"Then lower away and clear away," says Capt. Lester.

"Take care," Andrew says to the crew in each boat as it comes free of the davit lines, "they're humpbacks. Don't let them jump on your boat. And, be aware of their flippers. Now, get over the gunwale and down. Be ready to jump into your boats as soon as they touch water."

Second Mate Diogo Pilla and his crew are the first to harpoon a whale but it breaks free.

Andrew Lester's whaleboat crew works especially well and has mastered the technique of harpooning a whale. Much of this is due to Andrew's attitude toward his men. They pull for him because they want to and not because they must. John Adams, the farmer in Andrew Lester's crew who has been constantly seasick is replaced. Because Lester is a fair man, Joshua Edwards, his boat steerer and harpooner, follows his style. Edwards is related to Andrew, but not closely. There are two Long Island Negroes on *Tranquility*, Obadiah Jones and Ezekiel Jones. They have the same last names but are not related. 'Obie,' came North on the Underground Railroad and mans the tub oar. His oar is the stroke (pacing) oar. Paul Hicks, another Long Island farmer, is on the thwart seat just ahead of Ben. Ben handles the waist oar, the boat's longest and heaviest oar.

Andrew steers his boat toward the nearest spout. Josh is on the harpoon oar with the iron handy at his side. The boat quickly cuts the distance to where the whale had last shown and Lester stops the stroke. They drift silently for nearly 10 minutes. Then birds, little birds that seem able to walk on the water, and gooney birds began circling and squawking frantically.

"Get ready," Andrew says.

In a gush of water, the whale broaches, nearly clearing the surface just a hundred yards ahead of the boat. The behemoth lands with a tremendous splash. Huge flippers, a third the length of its body, slap violently on the water. It remains on top spouting its wet, odorous breath. She it lies almost motionless, breathing heavily and seemingly daring the boat to come closer.

Flawlessly, silently, the boat moves toward the whale.

"Quietly peak your oars," Andrew says in a loud whisper. "And no noise! Thrum your paddles or you'll gallie the fish."

Responding to Andrew's orders, the crew raise their oars then take the paddles from under their seats. Their handles have been wrapped in old canvas. Andrew silently sculls the steering oar and the boat glides onto the unsuspecting whale.

The whale still lingers on top replacing more of its water-logged breath with fresh air. Slowly, on the surface, it begins swimming forward, rising, spouting, lowering and raising its body at a leisurely pace. She arches her back just enough to get her monstrously large head under the surface, then straightens out.

The boat is now directly downwind of the huge beast and its foul breath consumes the crew. The boat is 3 fathoms from going onto the whale. Josh lays aside his paddle and grasps the heavy harpoon in both hands. The boat continues to slide effortlessly through the water. The monster is big, at least half again the length of the whaleboat.

"It is a cow," Andrew confirms in a whispers. "Males are smaller. She's big."

"Now!" he yells.

Josh stands up with his left knee solidly braced against the clumsy cleat on the thwart behind his seat. He raises it as high above the whale as he can. With his arms momentarily extended he holds the harpoon above his head with the point aimed just ahead of its lateral fin. The boat is now but a foot away from going onto the behemoth. With a great effort Josh plunges the full length of the harpoon's iron shaft into the spot between its eye and the fin. Only the harpoon's wooden shaft stops it from going deeper. He doesn't intend to kill the whale, that's the mate's job. His job is to drive the iron as deeply as possible, through its thin, black skin, through its thick layer of blubber and into its flesh where its toggle tip opens when the whale moves against it.

The world about the whaleboat explodes!

The whale bolts, then rounds out, arching its back to dive. The boat is violently jerked ahead and the bow takes on water. As the whale begins its dive its huge flukes rise out of the water carrying much ocean with it. When it comes down it misses the bow of the frail craft by just a few feet.

"Stern all! Stern all," Andrew yells. At the same time, he springs to the after oar to pull on it as the after oarsman, Jones, pushes on it.

The cascade of water the flukes created floods over the gunwale and for a moment the Greenies think it will fill the boat. But the boat responds quickly and rises as most of the wave passes beneath.

At the same time the boat is being lifted Josh rushes aft as Andrew jumps off the cuddy board seat and clambers forward to the bow. Josh then takes control of the great steering oar as the boat moves faster and faster across the water. The warp (line) attached to the iron leaps out of the main tub as it is pulled and pours through the bow-chock and into the water. The main tub carries 225 fathoms (1,350 feet) of line. The warp loosely whirs around the loggerhead as Jones pours water on it to keep it from catching fire.

The main tub is almost emptied of line when the whale slows enough so Josh can take a second turn on the line and snubs it fast around the loggerhead. It makes the boat jump, then move quickly because the line is now fully fast to the whale. The humpback does not sound, as do sperm whales, but dives just under the surface and begins a mad rush forward. The boat and its crew are at the whale's mercy. The course it takes is over a wide circle that brings the boat near the stern of *Tranquility*. Shiphandlers onboard cheer as it is hauled past at a frightening speed. It is a real Nantucket sleigh ride.

After 15 minutes the whale begins to slow, then stops. The crew immediately begin retrieving line when they are able. Obie Jones, on the tub oar, carefully coils it in the tub in case it is again called upon if the whale takes off. The spare tub holds 100 fathoms of towline but the bottom of the ocean is far deeper than all the line in the boat. If the end becomes exposed where it was secured to the boat, the mate must chop the line free. If he doesn't act fast enough, the whaleboat and its contents could be carried into the deep by the whale. This time, it didn't happen because humpbacks don't sound when harpooned.

The whale stops on the surface, as if to catch its breath. This allows the crew to retrieve more towline. They haul it at a rapid pace and when the slack is aboard they slowly pull the boat closer and closer to the whale. Andrew looks around and sees that Abe Brown's boat is fast to a whale. The other two whale crews are watching the water, watching the birds.

Slowly the whale comes alive. Its flukes rise and fall unhurriedly as the boat is sculled forward. Edwards loosens a turn on the loggerhead, expecting the whale to make another rush. She doesn't but slows as if it is mortally wounded. Andrew doubts that the iron fatally hurt the whale.

At a snail's pace, more line is cautiously retrieved as the whale is approached on its right side. Andrew slowly takes a lance from its holder on the boat's starboard gunwale and readies himself for the kill.

Putting an iron (harpoon) into a whale is dangerous but driving a lance into the lungs or heart is many times more perilous because the lance is not thrown, nor is the harpoon. Instead, the boat must be brought alongside the whale, "wood to black skin," often brushing its side. Now the mate plunges the lance again and again, with all his might, into vital places on the animal. The man who does this must be strong and fearless. Not every man can manage the lance.

Ben has turned his head and watches Andrew. He wonders if he could do it.

Even if the lancing is successful, the danger is not over. The danger to the boat and the rest of the crew becomes even greater because the whale is now usually gallied. In its death throes it flurries, thrashing around with head and flukes and at this point many a whaleboat has been stove. The humpback is dangerous, but a sperm is the worst.

Andrew orders the oarsmen to back off. They do just as the humpback's flukes smash on the water next to the bow. The whale goes mad as it flays about.

"She's into her flurry," Andrew yells. "Back off more! Back off more!"

The enraged whale begins swimming in tighter and tighter circles on the surface but at no great speed. Everyone senses the whale is dying. She rapidly weakens and begins listing to one side. As if making a last effort to escape, she lifts her head above the water, summoning every last bit of strength. Her entire body begins to quiver, to shake, to vibrate and she violently smashes her flukes on the water.

"She spouts red," Joshua yells. "The cow's chimney's afire."

Everyone knows it is over; it is now just a matter of time until all movement ends. It stops almost the way it started. The whale quits abruptly and lies motionless on top of the water.

"Fin out! Fin out!" yells Lester. "The whale is dead.

"Hurry on, let's lay another iron on her before she can sink."

After the second iron, they manage to wrap a chain around the flukes and attach a line to the chain. Andrew pays out 20 feet of line as the oarsmen begin rowing the whaleboat back to the ship. He runs the line through the bow chock and quickly passes the line back to Josh who is on the steering oar. Josh grabs the line and secures it with two turns on the loggerhead.

"She's secure," he yells back to Andrew.

The 2nd mate's boat is now close at hand. As he brings it along side Andrew waves him in.

"Jorge!" he yells to Pilla, "quickly take a turn on the chain. She is barely afloat. She's a heavy one and I fear she might sink on us."

Pilla's crew quickly adds a second towline to the chain. With two boats fast to the cow, she will surely stay afloat. Towing the humpback is almost as much work as towing the ship and they are 3 or 4 miles off. Andrew raises the mast on the fore-and-aft sail the whaleboat carries. Pilla does the same.

With no encumbrance, Abe's boat passes them en-route to the ship.

"What happened?" Josh asks as his passes close by. "I saw you were into a whale."

"Da iron pulled," he disappointedly yells back. "Damned luck. I 'ave a Jonah in my boat."

At the time, Ben has no idea what Abe means.

Capt. Lester, through the long glass, sees the sails go up in the whaleboats and orders the bo'sun to crowd all sails. *Tranquility* responds and begins to bear down upon the two boats. Now, the real business of gathering oil begins. From here on it is work, all work, the hardest work whalers must perform. This is the job they were hired to do.

Chapter 19

Cutting-In and Trying-Out

By the time the whale reaches the ship, it is too dark and too late to begin the dangerous job of cutting-in. As Andrew's boat comes alongside, Joshua reaches up and passes the towline to the bo'sun. He has a man take it forward, pulling it through the anchor hawse pipe, and secures it on a large deck cleat used to tie the ship to a dock.

"Well start this one tomorrow," yells the bo'sun on the stage to Andrew's crew still in the whaleboat.

The whale is secured to the starboard side of the ship. The boat crews are exhausted and even slow to climb onto the ship.

Standing next to Capt. Lester on the starboard gunwale, bo'sun comments on their tiredness.

"They'll get used to it," Lester says. "They may have more than a thousand launchings before we fill the ship with oil."

"All hands lay aft for we're to splice the main brace," Captain Lester announces as the last man climbs on board. "Tis a fitting way to celebrate our first whale."

He immediately gets a cheer from those on deck who are within earshot. The last boat is secured in the davit in record time.

"At last, we are whalers," Ben says to Andrew as they climb onto the ship's deck. Yes," he agrees, "we are whalers."

Ben knows this is an important occasion but he tells Edwards that it is strange to hear the captain address the crew. "He seems he does that only when it is important," Ben says. "He always keeps to himself. I guess this is important."

"If he has something to say," Edwards responds to Ben, "it usually comes through one of the officers. Most of the time it's Mr. Lester."

"That's because it is really Andrew who runs the ship, He is responsible for almost everything. But he does it, like any 1st mate, only with the captain's orders, with his approval.

"I guess Capt. Lester is no different from other captains, at least that is what some of the mates say who have been to sea under other captains."

"That's what some in the fo'c's'le believe," says Ben. "The captains kinda keep to themselves, Bennett once told us. That is so they get more respect from us. I never did agree with him. I think it is something else. Something deeper. Who knows for sure?"

Monday, February 27, 1866, Day 84

"We brought onboard our first whale today," Lester writes that night in the logbook. "It seems a long time coming but I thank God for answering our prayers."

The next day, men are on the cutting-in stage even before the sun rises. These are experienced whalemen, usually harpooners, who have many times before stripped the blubber from the body meat and bones of a whale. Officers, the mates, and harpooners control the try pots and are working on the stage with a few deck hands while whaleboat crews are manning the blocks and hauling blubber. Many jobs temporarily change onboard the ship when cutting-in a whale. Everyone is either a butcher or cook.

Andrew has divided the four crews into two shifts of eight hours on and eight hours off. But that doesn't really matter. There is so much work to do and so much new to learn that most of the time, everyone is working somewhere. The only jobs that do not change are those of the quartermaster and the lookouts. There is always a chance that more whales might be around while the crew is trying out a whale.

As Ben climbs out the forecastle he is given a flensing spade by Josh Edwards and told to take a position on the stage with three harpooners.

"Just follow what the others are doing," he tells him.

Sharks, in great numbers, are about the whale. From the looks of tears in the whale's sides, thinks Ben as he looks down at the melee in the water, they have been there most of the night. Some sharks are bleeding from cuts made by the long-handled spades the crewmen use to free the blubber from the meat or bones. Stabbing them does little to scare them off the carcass because blood in the water excites them into a wild, crazy feeding frenzy.

The weather is not cooperating with the rendering of the whale and has turned squally overnight. Winds have risen enough to where they now are bothersome to men on the stage. The quartermaster is having a difficult time keeping the ship to windward even though *Tranquility* is still light on sails. Only by keeping the weather, the wind, on the ship's larboard side can the body of the whale be held tight against the starboard side. This is where the whale is always worked. The wind pushes the boat against the whale.

The whale rises and falls as if keeping to a beat as the ship slowly rocks from side-to-side. Edwards, at the bulwarks, has a fit as he tries from there to get the blubber hook into a hole cut through the blubber just ahead of the fin. Capt. Lester is next to him. To his vexation, the heavy block and tackle holding the monstrous iron blubber hook bangs repeatedly, furiously against the ship's hull.

"Do something else," Lester yells at Edwards, "before the ship is damaged."

Edwards curses the sea and the winds that now cause water to rise and fall nearly 6 feet along side of the ship every time a wave hits.

"Who'll go over?" a frustrated Edwards asks the crew gathered behind him and Lester. "Who here is man enough to set the hook?"

"A pound of tobacco," the captain interrupts. "A pound of tobacco to the man who sets the blubber hook."

A pound of tobacco at that time was worth about $11, or what an infantry soldier was paid each month while in the war.

No one volunteers.

"Damn you all," yells Lester, "will we be here all day deciding?"

"I'll do it," Adam Jackson finally says. Jackson is a Negro in Abe Brown's crew and just relieved Abe on the cutting stage.

"Good," yells Edwards. "Get the monkey belt," he yells to a crewman on deck.

In a few minutes, the man returns from the locker with a stout rope that has a bowline bent on one end. Jackson leaves the cutting stage and is back on the ship, slips the loop over his shoulders and goes over the side, jumping onto the whale. The crewman on the other end allows just enough slack in the line so Jackson can work his way to where the hole is cut.

Unexpectedly, the larboard side of the ship is heaved upward by a strong gust of wind. In the reverse movement, the whale is covered by two feet of water as the starboard side falls and the line holding Jackson slackens. For a moment, a shark is atop the whale but retreats as the water falls away when the ship again rises. This continues for several minutes as Jackson cautiously works closer toward the hole, carrying the hook in his right hand and with the other balancing himself against the hull of the ship. During half of the time, he is knee-deep in water on the whale's back.

Another rogue gust of wind lays the ship hard on its starboard side. Water rushes over the whale and causes a bare-footed Jackson to slip off the carcass and into the water. Before crewman can take up slack on the monkey rope, Jackson is surrounded by sharks.

He screams in pain as one, then two sharks are upon him. The startled crewman hauls on the line and then runs backwards across the deck to take up the slack at a faster pace. Others seeing what has happened quickly rush to aid him. Jackson is pulled back onto the whale but the sharks have bitten him badly. He is writhing in pain, bleeding freely, as he is dragged up the side of the ship and onto the deck.

"Get the cook," Captain Lester yells, "and the medicine box."

Cook is as close to being a nurse or doctor that is on board *Tranquility*. His medical knowledge at best is rudimentary. He wraps Jackson's leg with a white shirt and ties it tightly by its sleeves above the missing thigh flesh. Blood continues to spill onto the deck as Jackson cries aloud. Slowly, the bleeding stops. Cook grimaces. It is already too late.

"Get him a donkey's breakfast," Edwards orders. Someone runs into the forecastle and in minutes returns with a straw-filled mattress. "Put it under the spare whaleboat," Edwards says. "Give me a hand. Let's get him there."

Back on deck, Edwards again dangles the blubber hook on the end of the tackle, swinging it back and forth across the whale whenever it rises out of the water. It is fruitless and he curses in disgust.

All eyes are shift to Ben as he unexpectedly runs off the platform and jumps onto the ship. He drops his flensing iron and picks up the bloodied monkey belt that has been taken off Jackson. As he slips it over his shoulder he yells to the crewman on deck to grab the line. He then waits for a wave to lift the whale. When it is at its highest he jumps onto the whale and grabs the dangling chain attached to the hook to steady himself. He spots the hole cut in the slab of whale blubber. Before it can disappear under a rising wave he dashes to it and slips the hook into the opening. Even more quickly, as water begins covering the whale, he jumps up grabbing the large lines on the tackle that will haul the blubber blanket. He lifts himself off the whale and climbs up the lines to a point even with the deck. Edwards, now armed with a gaff, pulls the tackle to the deck and Ben jumps on. As he does, he turns to an astonished captain and asks: "Where's my pound of tobacco?"

Watching from the far side of the gangway opening is Andrew. There's more to this boy than meets the eye, he says to himself.

"Son-of-a-bitch," says Abe who also watched the performance from the stage. "Did ya see dat Indian move?" he asks the mate next to him.

Edwards yells at the men to quickly take up the slack so the hook won't swing free the next time a wave lifts the whale.

"Haul," Edwards yells to five men on the bitter end of the line. Slowly the line is pulled through one of three cutting-in blocks (pulleys). The cutting-in tackle is guyed out from the mainmast and the cutting-fall runs from three blocks just off the guyed block.

Once all the slack disappears, the line goes taut. Men on the stage, with their long-handled spades and flensing irons, begin to cut the shape of a narrow blanket from the exposed carcass. Ben looks for his iron, finds it against the gunwale and scampers back to the cutting stage. As the blubber is cut free of the meat, the hook is continually under pressure lifting the freed blanket as it begins to peel off, like someone skinning an apple.

"That's a fat one," Edwards says. "Its blanket was almost 12 inches thick."

"Board ho!" Edwards shouts from the gangway as the blanket-piece is about to be swung onboard. Edwards turns to Ben and tells him to come back to the ship.

"There are enough lancers on the whale. I just wanted you to see how it is done," says Edwards. "Now I know what they mean when someone says 'crazy Indian'." He pats Ben on the back. "Good job," he says.

"I'm not crazy," Ben answers. "All you have to do is watch the timing of the waves. Of course, you have to move fast. Besides, Jackson's an old man compared to me."

"He's only 29," says Edwards.

"Maybe, being a little bit crazy does help," says Ben.

Edwards laughs and then puts his arm over Ben's back.

"Maybe next you'll want to harpon a whale. Huh?"

"This is an unusually big humpback," Hiram says as he watches men on the stage flense the behemoth. He turns away from the gunwale upon which he has been leaning and addresses those on deck. "I believe it's an occasion when we might splice the main brace. Andrew, will you see to it?"

"What does 'splice the main brace'," mean? Ben asks Abe.

"I done knows," he answers, "but it sure do taste good. Ask yer buddy Andrew. He knows everythin'."

"No one quite knows what it originally meant," Andrew tells Ben. "The Brits started it about a hundred years ago. It has nothing to do with splicing or tying together lines or braces. It's a celebration, a reward, often rum, for successfully completing a difficult mission."

The following evening during supper Jorge Pilla, the 2nd mate, vents his disappointment because the humpback didn't yield as much oil as a sperm or right whale might. And, it took long to render.

"The trouble getting the blubber hook into the whale on the first day caused much delay," rationalized Andrew. "The crew is inexperienced. I'm sure they'll get better. And, the weather was not in our favor. The next cutting in will be easier for the Greenies."

"Mr. Brown," asks Jorge Pilla, "how much did she yield?"

"We filled 47 barrels," Ephraim says. "That's about $1/50^{th}$ of what we need before we can see Sag Harbor again."

You could hear the men around the table moan after being told by Brown of how much more was needed before they could think of going home.

Chapter 20

Up the Brazil Banks

Saturday, March 3rd, 1867
88 days out of Sag Harbor

"Killing our first whale, for a while, raised the crew's spirits," Lester writes in the logbook, "but that jubilation does not include the Negroes in the fo'c's'le."

Adam Jackson lost consciousness after being sequestered under the spare whaleboat. While Cook attended him, everyone else went about the business of cutting-in. But even he had a job that must be performed. Cook left Jackson and returned to the galley to prepare the evening meal. During a break he revisited him only to find him immobile. He had bled to death.

Believing that his brother is the most compassionate of his officers, Hiram puts Andrew in charge of the burial detail. That evening, while everyone is still at work cutting-in, he tells Abe to have the two Negroes wrap Jackson in his mattress cover. This is done on the larboard side of the ship, away from the cutting-in activity.

Andrew fiddles through his tunic looking for the small seaman's Bible he retrieved earlier from his footlocker. Abe and the Negroes lift Jackson's body to the gunwale. Abe is about to launch the body but is resisted by the two men who see Andrew opening the Bible. Andrew begins a prayer and stops for a moment to clear his throat. As he resumes, Abe pushes the body off the ship.

"I didn't tell you to let him go," Andrew yells at Abe.

Abe hesitates for a moment then says, "I taut ya wuz tru."

"No, you didn't," Andrew says.

After the burial, rather than return to the stage area and oversee the dismantling of the flensing stage and cleaning the deck and trypots, Abe decides to drop down the nearby ladder into the crew's quarters. Three men from his boat crew are off watch and resting in their bunks.

"What now?" asks Harvey Bennett as he swings his feet off the bunk and onto the deck and sits up.

"I just tru Jackson off da ship," Abe says. "Ifen I'd had my way I'd trow a few more off.....including you. You bastard," he addresses Bennett, "ya cost me a whale. I taut ya knew somethin' about harponing."

"I did it right. As right as any man can."

"Ya didn't set da iron right. Ya didn't burying it into da fish.

"You're full of shit! It was done right. It went in up to the hitches. It couldn't go in any deeper."

Bennett, 26, like Abe, is also an East Ender. Until the incident they had been friends on the ship and ashore. Abe's mother is Harriet Bennett and Harvey is her nephew. They often drank together while in Sag Harbor at the American Hotel, a favorite watering hole for whalers between trips. Abe chose him first above the others for his boat crew and made him the harpooner. Bennett is not a greenhorn. He is an accomplished whaleman. This is his second trip on a whalership. He had risen to harpooner and boat steerer status on his first voyage, which also was with Capt. Hiram Lester. On this trip, when Bennett shipped on *Tranquility*, he had looked up to Abe. But he has became disillusioned with him after Brown tried to cast the blame on him for the pulled iron and lost whale.

"The iron drew," Bennett now heatedly yells back. "The damned iron pulled. That was it. It happens. It just happened. You know I don't like Sag Harbor irons. You don't either. Their toggles are too small. We should have Temple Toggle irons like other whalers use."

"Bullshit," Brown yells. "Ya muxed da job. Dat's all."

"I buried it to the hitches. It was in a solid spot. I did what I was supposed to do. I did it right!"

Abe doesn't answer. He looks around the quarters. When sees no one is paying attention to him, he turns in a huff and climbs the ladder back on deck.

Sunday, March 4th, 1866, Day 90

The following morning cruising sails are set after a hurried breakfast and lookouts posted as *Tranquility* again turns northward. Most of the Greenies are put to work using holystones on the deck. Once underway, the episode between Brown and Bennett would have been quickly forgotten, especially if they had spotted whales the next day, or the day after that. Neither happened. It did, however, cause Abe to seek out Capt. Lester. After breakfast, Abe is slow to leave the mess and is alone with Lester.

"Can I 'ave a word wid ya, Sir?"

"Yes, Brown, what is it?" asks Lester.

"Sir, I am surprised dat we're still using dem old Sag Harbor style irons," he says. "I had one draw out yesterday. I'm sure it wuz well placed. I believed dat we had Temple Toggles on board."

"So do I," a surprised Lester replies. He hesitates, then says: "Bring me your irons, I want to see them."

"Here are two," Brown says, slightly out of breath, as he returns. "An', I took one from yer brudder's boat. See."

Lester looks over each harpoon, flicking toggles on each to see that they work.

"Thank you, Mr. Brown. "Return these for now. Then go forward and find Müller. Tell him I want to see him immediately."

Within a few minutes, the shipsmith is alone with Lester. He begins pouring a second cup of coffee from the decanter Pierre brought in from the galley.

"Some coffee, Mr. Müller?" Lester asks before the smith can speak.

"Of course, Sir."

"Sit down, please."

"I know I ordered a goodly supply of Temple Toggles before we sailed. Did you not get them?"

"Aye, Sir, I did."

"Then why are we still using Sag Harbor irons?"

"Mr. Brown told me not to use them until all the old irons were gone."

"Since when did you start taking orders from the 4th Mate?"

"Oh no, Sir. Not Abe Brown. I mean his uncle, the disburser."

"Damn him," Lester says loudly.

"Go back and see the bo'sun," Lester says. "Tell him I gave you an order for him to have his men go into all the whaleboats and retrieve any iron that is not a Temple Toggle iron. You will then replace them with the Temple heads. And, then take all the old irons down into the bilge and store them among the barrels. But, be sure they are not in any water. We might have use for them someday."

"Thank you, Mr. Müller."

"Oh yes. Find Disburser Brown on your way aft, tell him I want to see him immediately."

"Aye, Sir."

"Ephraim, you're an idiot. A goddamned idiot!" Lester yells at Brown as he enters the captain's salon. Brown is shocked by Lester's language. He has often heard him say damn but never the full curse. Damn is hardly looked upon as cursing by even the most devout Quaker, especially those involved in whaling.

"I have half-a-mind to have the bo'sun take you into the bilge, clamp leg irons on you and chain you to a post. That is what I should do because I think it is the only way I can stop you from meddling in ship's business and frustrating what I hope to accomplish.

A flabbergasted Brown is momentarily speechless. Brown quickly regains his composure and blurts out, "If I have done something contrary to your wishes it is only because I want what is best for the people of the Company, and you as well."

"That's bullshit," Lester answers.

"Do you know what your ill-conceived frugality has cost us? Do you realize the dollar value of the whale Abe lost yesterday? Why do you think I ordered the Temple Irons when you still saw a surplus of the old irons in the hold?"

"I have no idea," Brown sheepishly answers.

"Because we lose whales with old irons. Now, do you see why we have them?"

"I. I. I guess so."

"Get out of my sight before I call the bo'sun."

Brown immediately returns to steerage.

Lester climbs the ladder topside and continues onto the quarterdeck and takes a stance in the wheelhouse. *I must alter our course*, he says to himself as he glances at the compass.

Pushed by the Southeast Trade Winds, Lester plans to take the ship on a course that parallels the coast of Brazil, but about 300 miles off shore. The area, known as the Brazil Banks, 50 years earlier was a haven for sperm whales. Though without physical boundaries and thus ill-defined, the Brazil Banks extend approximately 1,500 miles, beginning near the heel of Brazil and stretching in a northwesterly direction to about French Guiana.

Friday, March 16, 1866, Day 101

Now underway only during daytime hours, *Tranquility* sails nearly 500 miles up the Brazil Banks. Two weeks have passed since the crew has seen a whale of any species. It is an ocean bare of whales. Lester feels the whaleboat crews are now good enough and no longer makes them practice. Only on one day did he set all four boats on the water for what turned out to be a false sighting. Hiram thinks the lookouts are beginning to imagine they see spouts.

It is mid-March, still in the ship's first year at sea, when one morning the foremast lookout sees a sail on the horizon, sailing up *Tranquility's* wake. It was the first sail the crew has seen since leaving the Azores. By late afternoon, they are overtaken by the *Nancy Ann*, a coastal trader out of New York heading home. They spoke the vessel and its captain suggests a gam. Along with mail, Capt. Lester takes the seasick farmer, John Adams, with him to the vessel. Lester tells him he can find his own way back from New York to Sag Harbor.

After Lester returns from the gam, just after the sun sets, he orders the ship hove-to for the night. "There is no sense covering waters that might contain a whale," he says to Bo'sun.

"I got no useful information from her captain," Hiram tells his mates during supper. "Stopping was a waste of time. However, I did give him our mail."

No sun rises the next morning. The winds have turned more easterly and even though they are light, *Tranquility* moves at a brisk pace. Hiram Lester is up early and studies the ship's wake before he enters the wheelhouse.

"What reads the log?" Asks Hiram.

"Sir," answers Adrian Moore the quartermaster on duty, "I just returned the log. She's running at 7 knots. With a fair wind on our transom I think we are in the Guiana Current."

"I believe you to be correct," says Lester.

By early afternoon, the weather turns squally, nasty, causing Andrew to cancel the lookouts and lighten sails. Only the course sail on the foremast and the jibs are working. It rains heavily and for the next four days a gale wind blows without let-up. When it eases and the skies clear, Lester takes a noon sighting.

"We have moved nearly 500 miles in four days," he says to Andrew who temporarily shares the larboard gunwale with his brother.

"We must have been going at 10 knots or better. Astounding!"

With light winds, Andrew orders the four lookouts back into the rigging. Just as the sun is setting, and the lookouts are about to come down, Diogo, the 3rd mate in charge of the watch, spots a whale spouting.

"Too late to order the whaleboats lowered," says Andrew.

"They'll be there in the morning," adds Diogo.

March 22nd, Day 107

"Today is a significant day," Capt. Lester says to his three mates and Ephraim Brown, who again regularly joins them in the officer's mess for breakfast. "We've been at sea for 107 days and have but one whale to show for our efforts. I have never been to sea and seen such poor sightings or the oceans so barren. This must change soon. Maybe we should continue on north, catch the Gulf Stream, and make for Sag Harbor."

"We shouldn't do that," speaks up Brown. "We already have too much invested in this voyage. Nor do I think the fo'c's'le men will accept it. Their lay from one whale is impossible to figure out. It's nothing. We must continue the search."

"The fo'c's'le crew has nothing to say about what decisions I make," Lester answers Brown.

Two mates, however, mumbled in agreement with what Brown said.

"It is still too soon," adds 2nd Mate Jorge Pilla. "I know it has been poor but there is still a lot of ocean between us and Long Island that we haven't seen."

"Actually, I agree with you," says Capt. Lester to their surprise. "I wanted to fathom your feelings. I have no intention of quitting. But I feel I must have your support. I do think the fo'c's'le is getting restless. I sense the dissention mounting and must find a way to thwart it."

Just as he finishes his last word, he hears "Whale ho," drift down the hatch opening. It seems ironic. Everyone rushes topside to see if it is a real sighting. Abe is on the mainmast with Harvey Bennett. They both confirm what the lookout in the foremast has seen.

"Where away?" asks Andrew as he looks to the top of the mainmast for direction from Abe. "Where away?"

"A half-mile astern," Brown yells back.

"We must have sailed over him. It's a sperm. I had the glass on him. He spouts forward and to the left as only sperms do. The spout rises above 50 feet. It is a big one. There! There! He is up again. And…there is another spout just beyond him."

"Number 1, order the shiphandlers to bring us about," Lester says to his brother. "Haul up all sails on mizzen and mainmasts. That should turn us sprightly into what little wind that is out. That will be enough."

At first, *Tranquility* responds slowly to the helm but gradually builds momentum as she turns on her foremast. Her wake is clean, white and strong as she continues turning toward where the whales spouted.

"Mates, ready the crew to their davits," Andrew orders. "I think you all will soon be in the water."

Tranquility bears down on the whales that continue spouting, unaware that a force is soon to be upon them. Their spouting is an easy guidon. *Tranquility* is but a quarter mile from them when Andrew gives the order to heave-to. Seconds later, he calls for all four whaleboats to be lowered then heads for his craft.

"There were but two whales spouting," Andrew says as he and his crew enter their boat. "The bigger one is really big, over two whaleboats long, over 60 feet. That is a big bull, a bull whale," he says to Edwards his harpooner standing next to him. The smaller one is half that size, probably a young cow, a female."

The pair now moves together just under the surface and rise only to spout, then dally on top for a few minutes before again going under.

All four boats race for the bigger whale. Andrew's boat is the fastest but leads the 2nd and 3rd mates' boats only by a boat length. Abe Brown's boat is three or four lengths behind. In respect to his rank, Jorge, the 2nd mate, gives way to Andrew as they near the whale. The 3rd mate sees the move and he and Abe move off toward the smaller whale.

Edwards is in the bow as the crew sets aside the oars for paddles and the boat glides toward the whale. The crew knows, because they have been told many times, that the sperm is the most dangerous because it has no blind side like right whales. The behemoth sinks but Edwards has sight of him just under the water. When he comes on top, the boat is next to him.

"Lay the boat on," Edwards yells back to Andrew.

With a single sweep of his steering oar, Andrew turns the bow onto the whale and the men all feel it hit.

Edwards is in a position to strike and strike he does. The iron shaft disappears into the whale and quickly the mate and harpooner switch positions.

The whale dives and instantly disappears. The bull sounds, heading for the bottom. Line in the main tub empties quickly and begins pulling line out of the spare tub. Smoke rises from the loggerhead as the line rattles around it. Andrew is ready with the hatchet in case the line is not long enough. All fear the whale might pull the boat under. Suddenly, the line stops running.

"It must have reached bottom," Andrew yells. This gives Joshua just enough time to take another turn around the post and secure the line.

Jorge, the 2nd mate, has pulled his boat to a spot ahead of Andrew's and waits in case his help is needed to rescue the men.

Seeing the line racing toward the surface, Andrew yells, "He rises! He rises!"

The whale breaks the surface, leaps across the water, then comes down with a tremendous crash 30 feet from Jorge's boat. It stays there for the longest time, as if trying to make up its mind about what to do next. Maybe it hasn't felt the pain of the iron. Then suddenly it begins lobtailing, thrashing the water with its huge flukes. It is a wild thing.

The time on the surface is enough for Jorge's boat to come alongside the whale.

"I see your iron," yells his harpooner as he, too, plunges his harpoon into the whale. The sperm immediately reacts, not by sounding but by turning around and lashing, smashing the water with its huge flukes. It almost upends Pilla's boat. Then the whale begins to race away, dragging both whaleboats. The whale acts as if it isn't even bothered, tearing straight away from *Tranquility*. Ben glances back and watches as the ship grows smaller and smaller. What next, he thinks to himself. Could this be the end?

Before losing sight of *Tranquility* Andrew takes a quick bearing on the whaleboat's compass as the ship disappears under the horizon. As he does, the crew senses that the whale is slowing. A few minutes later, both crews begin retrieving line. Because Andrew's boat has a shorter line on the harpoon they are first onto the whale. He plunges his lance several times into the whale. Blood immediately begins spouting, a sure sign the lance has pierced the lungs. As the whale thrashes about, its tail strikes a glancing blow, banging hard against the boat. Andrew, who is standing, and Obie Jones are thrown into the water.

While the whale was still thrashing wildly, Jorge had his crew put him onto the other side of the whale. Now he, too, buries a lance into the monster. The whale suddenly turns on him, lifting its huge head out of the water and begins snapping its narrow, tooth-lined lower jaw. He is just feet away from their boat when it stops. Gasping for air, the whale lies there a moment, then rolls onto its side.

That Mr. Pilla is one brave man, Ben thinks.

"Fin out! Fin out!" yells Pilla as Andrew's crew is busy retrieving him and Obie.

"Where's the ship now?" Andrew asks his men after Pilla's crew bends their line to the chain on the whale's tail and begins rowing. He again unboxes the compass and takes a heading. He knows where the ship should be. There is a fair wind on their faces and both boats raise their fore-and-aft sails.

"There she be!" Jorge yells after they have moved a mile or so to windward.

They see *Tranquility's* sails break above the horizon and grow rapidly. She is underway toward them. Captain Lester, seeing the two boats being towed away by the whale, had the sails raised and is heading in their direction. The whaleboats are making good way in the direction of the ship when they see *Tranquility* has stopped.

"Don't fret," Andrew says to his crew. "Our two sails now handily haul the whale. It would have been a long, tiresome row back to the ship if the wind had not come up.

As they near *Tranquility,* they see the 3rd mate's boat is fast to the smaller whale and is now hauling it to the ship from a different direction. At first, Abe's boat is nowhere to be seen. As they draw near to the ship, they see his sail on the far side of *Tranquility*. He later tells them they had spotted a third whale and had taken off after it. The shiphandlers said they saw no third whale.

Chapter 21

Finally a Greasy Ship

March 22, 23 & 24, 1866
Days 107-09

Tranquility continues heading northwest along the Brazil Banks while moving only during daylight, and only at cruising speeds, 3 to 4 knots. Again, they find the ocean barren and no whales are sighted. Lester has bo'sun ship-shape *Tranquility*. The deck and cutting gear are cleaned again until all traces of whale oil disappear. It isn't the make-work tasks the crew had been assigned before a whale was rendered. All this now has purpose, a meaning which the crew can visualize. No one of them complains.

Thursday, April 26th, 1866 Day 142

Not until the ship has covered nearly 1,300 miles, and is off the coast of French Guiana more than a month later, that another whale is spotted.

"We have another sperm to contend with," Capt. Lester says as he peers through his glass, watching intently where the whale had been sighted.

"We'll lower only three boats," he says to his mates as they surrounded him. "Brown," he addresses Abe Brown, "you're short one oar with the loss of Jackson. Your crew did not fare well on the last lowering because of this. Have you thought of anyone to replace him?"

"Aye, Captain," he answers respectfully. "How 'bout da Indian in yur brudder's crew? He's young, but he's big, an' can sprightly bend da oar."

"Wouldn't that leave Andrew's crew short? Anyone else?"

"Maybe one of duh shipkeepers. Dey aren't all needed when we ain't makin' way an' are after a fish."

"Have you approached any of them?"

"No!"

"Don't do it now. Do it after the boats are back. Don't lower this time."

"Shit!" Abe says in disgust as he walks away from the open gangway, then crosses the deck to the larboard side to his whaleboat. His crew is there, waiting.

"Do we go?" asks Fred Jolly as Abe reaches for a gripe and begins re-securing the boat to the davit. Brown doesn't answer. Others in his crew begin pitching in.

"Damn it. Even wid one man short we can still kill a whale," Abe says somewhat under his breath so only his immediate crew can hear. "Dat damned man duzen't want us ta earn our lays (share of profit). See how he favors his brudder?"

"So what?" says Bennett, Abe's harpooner. "We still gets a share of what oil is sold when it is all divvied up back in Sag. And we ain't gotta go out there and risk our asses. Besides, his brother is 1st mate."

"Dat duzen't give 'im privilege over us," says Abe. "He needs ta be showed a ting or two."

Jorge Pilla's boat is the first to fasten to the sperm. The whale sounds, then comes up for air and rises almost under Diago Pilla's boat. His harpooner, Nuno Dias is ready and a second iron is planted in the whale. The sperm is large, taking three days to cut-in. To everyone's delight, renders 50 barrels of oil, not counting the spermaceti.

Chapter 22

Barbados Rum

Sunday, April 29th 1866, Day 145

Tranquility is again underway. Lester is taking her in a northwesterly direction. He has her cruising during the day and hoving-to at night. Winds are light out of the southwest. They are all Andrew needs to hold the ship in position overnight. It is slow progress. They are not interested in speed, but spouts.

After two days of no sightings, Capt. Lester, his three mates, and Abe and Ephraim Brown are sitting at supper when he announces his next move.

"We are three days off Barbados Island," he says. "I plan to pull in there for one day for some fresh stores. More important, we are also in need of a new hand for the fourth whaleboat. We should also have two extra men in case such things happen again."

"Aaah," Brown says after deliberating a moment. "Yes…two, or even three men won't be too much," he says. "But their lay must be less than the other Negroes on board. They will have missed a part of the voyage."

"Who says they must be Negroes? Aren't there other inhabitants on Barbados? We'll see," said Lester. There was little doubt that the new men would not be Negroes.

That night, Capt. Lester isn't quite ready for bed and climbs the companionway to the topside deck. He nods to the quartermaster on the wheel as he passes aft to the transom. He stands against the taffrail that tops the stern gunwale, grasping it with both hands to steady himself. The night is a dark even though the sky is ablaze with millions of stars. It seems especially dark to Lester as his eyes slowly adjust to the lack of light.

Lester turns and stares aft at the wake *Tranquility* creates as she moves toward Barbados at flank speed. She looks like a comet he thinks, with her wake aglow. He is mesmerized by its radiance until he hears footsteps.

"I couldn't sleep either," says Andrew. "What bothers you?"

"It is Abe Brown."

"He is disturbed and unpredictable," says Andrew. He respects no one, not even his uncle. He has no respect, not even for himself. I can offer you no solutions. I have been closer to him that you and can see how he gets his men to perform. It is out of fear."

"Maybe there aren't any solutions," Hiram says. "I think I will go below and ponder it further, if needs be. Good night, Andrew."

Andrew is taken back by his brother's short stay. He remains. At times like these I wonder how well I do know him, he thinks. Do I really know him? He's not the brother I remember when we were younger. He has been unreachable ever since Isabella died. That's a long time ago. Surely he should have adjusted to life now.

Lester has been a widower for the past 30 years. His wife Isabella Edwards-Lester died in childbirth. Some, like Andrew, believe that Hiram never fully recovered from his wife's death. When he returned from that voyage and discovered that she had died, he openly blamed himself for not being by her side. Thereafter, Lester carried the burden in the back of his mind. His brother, often seeing him standing alone against the gunwale of the ship looking off toward the horizon, would try to engage him in conversation. He knew where his brother's thoughts must have been.

May 3rd, 1866 Day 149
13° 10'N, 059°32'W

Light is already brightening the southeastern horizon when the lookout spots Barbados and calls the sighting. Throughout the last three nights the winds held fair against *Tranquilty's* transom from the southeast and continues so into the day. Captain Lester is awake before sunrise and is now on deck, armed with a cup of coffee. He orders Andrew to spread all sails to hasten their approach into Carlisle Bay.

The anchor is lowered in the bay just off the mouth of Constitution River, really a tidal finger-like extension of the bay within sight of the bridge that gives the island's capital its name, Bridgetown. Small craft are already hustling among several other ships anchored close to shore as 1st Mate Andrew Lester lowers his boat and is ready to make for the river and its docks. Before he does, his brother approaches him.

"Andrew, I want you to go to the American embassy as soon as possible, drop off any letters the crew may have written, and find out where we might pick up two or three able men. Hopefully you can find enough men wanting to sign on. We'll be gone the next morning. There won't be any shore leave. I don't want to lose anyone."

At almost the same time, Jorge, in company with Ephraim, also lowers and heads for the market to buy fresh fruit, vegetables and chickens. Capt. Lester orders him to acquire a few large flagons of rum, one of the local industries on Barbados.

Just after 8 bells (noon) are sounded, Andrew's whaleboat is back to davit and is ready to be hauled up.

"I see you have been successful," Capt. Lester says to his brother as he leans on his elbows on the starboard gunwale. "Three men and they all look fine."

"Have any of you ever sailed before?" Capt. Lester asks once they are on deck.

"No," replies one, "we are not sailors, but we are fishermen who have been over the horizon more than once."

"What do you do for work?"

"When fishing is poor we find work on sugar plantations," he answers in a clipped British accent. "We know hard work if that is what you are asking about."

"Yes, I am," says Lester.

"Number 1, take them to the fo'c's'le and see to their needs. Assign them later to where you want them to work. When Mr. Brown returns, see that they sign their papers."

After berthing the men, Andrew returns to the quarterdeck. The captain is nowhere to be seen. He goes down the companionway ladder to his brother's cabin. The door is open and he sees him at his desk.

"What is it?" Hiram asks. "Did you find space for the men in the fo'c's'le?"

"I have sad news," Andrew says without answering his brother's question. "There was a letter at the embassy from Noah. Rebecca has died."

Hiram immediately rises, dashes in front of his desk and hugs his brother.

"Dear God! When was it?"

"A month after we departed Sag Harbor. He wrote that her breathing became progressively more difficult. The doctor gave her laudanum to ease her pain. She is buried in our family plot. He wrote that no one was able to locate Michael. He still doesn't know. But this letter is now months old."

"It is a blow," says Hiram. "It always is whenever someone close dies. Knowing that it might happen still does not prepare one for the event. I am saddened. Andrew, I don't have to tell you. You know how I feel."

Hiram looks at his brother then again embraces him. Tears are in Hiram's eyes.

Before Jorge has his boat alongside, it is mid-afternoon *Tranquility*.

Capt. Lester watched him return, seeing the difficulty they had in the short run to the ship. The bay's waters were covered with whitecaps and made the rowing laborious. Thinking that the weather might be about to change, he returns to his cabin to check the barometer. He doesn't like what he sees. It is too early for hurricanes but not for a whole gale (winds 55 to 63 mph).

Once again on deck he greets Pilla and Ephraim.

"I see you had no difficulty finding rum. Was it at a price to your liking?"

"That is was, Sir. Just in case, I picked up an extra flagon."

"Mr. Pilla, find the other mates and meet me in the mess," said Lester.

"Gentlemen, I had hoped to be underway tomorrow but am changing my plan. The barometer is especially low. This is too early in the season for a hurricane but there is a storm afoot and I don't want to test it here. Make ready as soon as possible and we will ride out the weather in a slip in Bridgetown."

"But that will incur a fee," speaks up Ephraim. "Is it really necessary?"

Lester looks sternly at Brown. Without speaking, he turns and begins climbing the ladder topside. "We should be here at least two days," says Lester. "The starboard watch will have liberty tonight at 6 bells and larboard tomorrow. However, I want each mate to accompany his crew. He will be responsible for bringing them back….alive, drunk or dead. Liberty ends at 8 bells. The winds are quickly picking up. Now see to it!"

Chapter 23

A Decision: Move North or Homeward?

After departing Barbados *Tranquility* resumes sailing northwest along the east side of the Lesser Antilles, riding on the back of the North Equatorial Current. Off Haiti Lester turns his ship and makes directly for the Bahamas. He passes just seaward of Nassau Island. From there he takes *Tranquility* due west and picks up the north-flowing Gulf Stream. The ship passes along the east coast of Florida and, from time-to-time, the men sight glimpses of land. However, the humidity in the air is so dense that they are not sure if it is land or a mirage. The number of sails they spot increases to one or two a day. These waters are the main north-south shipping lanes off the East Coast on the United States. None of the vessels have blackened sails.

By June 2nd they are off Cape Hatteras. They've been on the move for a month, having covered 2,500 miles and are now 194 days out of homeport. In that stretch they have tried only five whales and have not seen another whaleship. Most of the crew now believe this all bodes ill for any future success. Talk in the forecastle about getting home increases daily. Abe is pleased to hear others now talking of jumping ship in the next port if the ship doesn't make for Sag Harbor.

Hiram Lester is on the quarterdeck leaning on the taffrail and looking down at the water. He sees scattered bits of grass floating past. They are now on the edge of the Sargasso Sea.

"This might alarm some of the men, especially the Greenies," Andrew says as he approaches his brother and sees where he is looking.

"The weeds are becoming more numerous," Hiram answers without turning around. "I don't need a crew at this point that might become needlessly fearful of the Sargasso Sea. And, there are those on board who would surely create an unwarranted fear among the Greenies. The ocean to the west is clear."

To the east, growing amounts of seaweed, Sargasso plants that were blown off the stagnant Sargasso Sea, clutter the water's surface. All first-time seamen fear it, thinking they will become trapped and becalmed as in the Doldrums.

To avoid having the southern edge of the Gulf Stream pull the ship into any more grass, before he leaves the quarterdeck Lester instructs the quartermaster to back the ship 5 degrees. *Tranquility* now sails so she will catch the faster part of the Gulf Stream. After two days Lester turns her slowly to the northeast, then due east, leaving Hatteras in her wake and Bermuda ahead. A week later, June 9th, they pass north of Bermuda.

Saturday, June 9th, 1866, Day 201

Capt. Lester writes in the ship's logbook: "We are now 201 days out of Sag Harbor and the prospect of a full ship grows dimmer every day we are at sea. There are real grumblings in the fo'c's'le. I know A. B. is stirring them."

He lays aside the pen, turns in his seat, and stares out the stern windows. The three Negroes we picked up in Barbados, he thinks to himself, according to Andrew are working well but the two who signed on in Sag Harbor in Mr. Pilla's crew are slacking off. I know how to correct that but at this time such discipline might work against me. I fear they will infect the other blacks with their attitude. If their hands were busied more often with blubber I'm sure the problem would ease. We are at a critical point in this voyage. We have spun around the Atlantic and have found but five whales. Daily, I ask myself, should we go on or turn back? I will tomorrow again test my mate's dedication.

Lester heads topside and as he steps on deck, he hears loud voices coming from the forecastle. He sees a Negro being thrown out of the forecastle hatch and Bellingham is immediately behind him.

Lester rushes forward.

"What's going on?"

Bo'sun, with one arm, lifts the man to his feet.

"He and two of the Bajans were fighting."

"Fighting over what?"

"It seems one of them stole this man's cup."

Just then, one of the Barbados men steps onto the deck.

"It's not our fault," he says. "None of us have cups or plates, or even forks to eat with. We must eat like animals."

"Weren't you told to bring them on board when you signed on?"

"No, Sir. No one told us."

"Bo'sun get them what they need out of the slop chest," Lester says as he turns aft for the quarterdeck. "Charge it to me."

"Aye, Sir."

Just when their future seems the darkest, a right whale is spotted, harpooned and brought aboard. Morale on the ship is akin to the antics of a spring barometer. Spirits rise and fall with the various events. Abe and his crew harpoon the whale and have an easy time towing it in because right whales, unlike all others, float.

New hopes rise after the whale is cut-in but weeks again pass without the sighting of another whale and morale quickly returns to the state that existed before the whale was killed.

"That's six whales we have killed," Ben says to Bennett, who shares the starboard gunwale with him. "That's not many. I wonder what the captain will do now."

Chapter 24

The Decision to Hunt South of the Equator

The taking of the whale puts off Lester's plan to address the future of the voyage with his mates but now he must face the inevitable. The evening after trying the whale, while all are still in the mess having coffee, he confronts them.

"We have circled the mid-Atlantic," he says, "and our efforts have been dearly wasted. I am trying to decide, should we go around again? I tend not to think so nor do I want to. I know it might be six whales less than what we have seen. We are wasting time cruising hereabouts and should try searching deeper into the south Atlantic.

"Should we cut our losses and return home, or should we make take a second trip around. I think the former might be the best plan."

"What say yea?"

As Lester expects, Ephraim Brown is the first to respond. "As you are aware, Hiram, I was against this voyage from the beginning. But now that we have so much invested I think it would be wrong, foolish if we are to head home."

"I expected that would be your decision," says Hiram.

"We have been at sea for just five months," continues Ephraim. "That is not a long whaling time. It is only natural that the northern half of the Atlantic be scant of whales. They once offered the closest voyages for Long Islanders and New Englander whalers. There is a time when it is appropriate to cut one's losses but I don't think it is now."

"I think Mr. Brown is right," says Jorge Pilla. "It is too soon to turn back. We have invested nearly a half-year of time as well as effort. Besides, the southern Atlantic always did produce more whales than the northern half."

"I, too, agree with Mr. Brown and Jorge," says Diogo Pilla. "What else could we do if we returned? All I know is whaling. Do we become farmers?"

A long silence follows as everyone ponders their futures if they now return.

"Dis voyage never 'ad a chance," Abe Brown speaks up. "We all knows dat whalin's over. Look at duh few whalers we've seen. Duh others are smarter dan us. I agree with Capt. Lester. Let's git dah hell outa here. Duh faster duh better."

No one speaks for a while as the choices rattle about in everyone's mind. Everyone's, that is, except Hiram Lester's.

"A ship is not a democratic society," Lester finally breaks he silence. "I do not need your approval but I do need your cooperation to run this vessel efficiently. Therefore, out of deference to you I would like a show of hands. And, you, too, have a vote," Hiram says to Ephraim.

"How now? To the south'ard?"

Jorge, Diogo and Ephraim raise their hands.

Quickly seeing a tie is in the making, Andrew raises his hand.

"Four for and two against," says Hiram. "We sail to the south'ard immediately.

"How do you think the fo'c's'le and shiphandlers will take this decision?" Andrew asks the group. "There's been talk among the crew that we are homeward bound."

"How could that have started?" Hiram asks.

"It started right here," says Andrew.

"I had two from my crew approach me to ask if we were heading for Sag Harbor. When I asked them who told them, they said it was a mate."

"Which mate?"

"Abe Brown!"

"Yur a lying son-of-a-bitch. Ya just made dat up," Abe says as he rises from his seat with a clenched fist and spills his coffee.

"Sit down or I'll call the bo'sun," yells Capt. Lester.

"Not true. Andrew did not make that up," Jorge says as his rises from his seat. "One of my men, Egas Sanchez, asked me the same question. He said Abe told them that we were going home two weeks ago when he was gambling with them in the fo'c's'le."

"I never said dat," claims Abe.

"Your brudder is saying dis," says Abe, " 'cause he dozen't want ya ta make me 4th mate. Yur all agin me. Even my uncle.

"I have petitioned for you," a heated Ephraim yells at Abe. "You've done the most damage to your not becoming 4th mate. You haven't changed since you ran away from my home."

"Everyone, take your seats," says Hiram. "In trying to be fair, I asked for a vote. This is your decision and I will abide by it."

A deafening silence overcomes the mess. For the longest time, only the creaking of the ship's tackle topside is heard.

"Steward, bring us more coffee," Hiram Lester says to change the mood. Then he disappears into his cabin and quickly reappears with a bottle of Barbados rum in his hand.

"I have a drink better for the moment than coffee. I think it is worth a toast to the future."

Even the three Quakers fill their tumblers.

"To blubber," says Capt. Lester. "To a greasy ship."

"To blubber," the officers echo.

"Bottoms up," says the captain.

"Or da rest in yur hair!" adds Abe Brown. He throws his tumbler to the deck without toasting and walks rapidly through the shiphandlers' quarters, the galley and disappears into steerage.

The mates then leave. Only Andrew stays behind.

"Why did you vote to continue the voyage?" Hiram asks.

"Do you think I don't know you? I knew you didn't want to return. You figured it would be a tie and I would have to override the men. I just saved you that problem."

"Thank you, Andrew."

Monday, June 11, 1866, Day 210

"210 days out of S.H.," Lester writes in his logbook. "This morning we spoke the *Annabelle K* out of Port Jefferson, Long Island, a coastal trader burdened with rum and molasses. Last night I offered the mates and E.B. the chance to null this voyage and return to Sag Harbor. By a vote of 4 to 2 they elected to try another turn around he Atlantic. That problem is solved."

"I had hoped the rumors of going home were true," Ben says to Andrew as they share the gunwale outside the forecastle hatch. For some reason I miss my mother and father more than before."

"It's just the false hope that the scuttlebutt started you thinking that way," says Andrew. "I would think that by now you would have learned to take everything Abe says with a grain of salt."

"I don't have much to do with him," says Ben. "From the first time I met him I could tell he was a strange person, that he has something inside that is bothering him.

"I never thought I would miss my home so much. The bay outside our house is now probably filled with weakfish. I used to spear them in great numbers. My mother and aunts would smoke them. They always tasted so good on a cold April day."

"What of the other men in the fo'c's'le?" asks Andrew. "How do they feel?"

"Abe told them it was the captain who said we were going south and not home."

"No it wasn't," said Andrew. "The captain even asked the mates to vote on what we would do. The even vote included Abe's uncle. It was 4 to 2 in favor of the South Atlantic.

"But how did the crews react?"

The Portagees don't seem to mind. It's hard to know what they are thinking because when they are together they always speak in their own tongue. But I don't think they mind. Long Island is not their home. The men the crimpers brought on board do not like the decision. They don't like hard work and they all seem to like strong rum."

"But what about you?"

"I hated it when I came onboard. I didn't like carrying food tubs. But since you permanently moved me to your boat, things have changed a lot."

"I know some of the men think differently about you after you jumped on the whale's back and set the hook," said Andrew. "They respect you now even though they might not show it."

"You, too, have gained respect from everyone on the fo'c's'le. It was a daring thing you did to risk your life to save Dos Santos."

"I don't think it was that daring" says Andrew. "I was safe as long as the line held me. But, my ribs do hurt."

Chapter 25

Below The Line, The South Atlantic

Captain Lester sets a course directly for Ascension Island. This allows him to continue skirting the northern edges of the Sargasso Sea to avoid even the slightest possibility of encountering the masses of floating weeds. He drives *Tranquility* southeast, using the southern edge of the Gulf Stream. When it turns south and then west, he follows it and then slips off the merry-go-round onto the Canary Current. This takes the ship on a more easterly course and he follows it to Guinea hugging the coast of West Africa. In just 31 days, after passing north of Bermuda, he brings *Tranquility* to a position off Liberia. He continues this southeast course as long as the currents stay alive. In a bit more than three days, he crosses the Equator at exactly 10° longitude, the same imagined vertical line that also passes just outside of Lisbon. Off Liberia the Guinea Current does a hard westerly turn, almost 180 degrees, and leads *Tranquility* onto the South Equatorial Current.

Doldrums are not unique to the northern side of the Equator, or even to the Atlantic Ocean. A similar phenomenon occurs on the south side of The Line. Fortunately, this time, Capt. Lester is able to move *Tranquility* just south of their precinct. He takes advantage of the west-flowing South Equatorial Current. After three days on this current, they still fail to spot a single whale, but an island now looms ahead. Lester rides the current west to Ascension Island, mid-way between Africa and South America. They are off Ascension Island on July 14th.

Sunday, July 14, 1866, Day 222
Georgetown, Ascension Island, South Atlantic
007 ° 55 ' S, 014° 19' W

With the aid of two whaleboats, *Tranquility* is slowly brought alongside the only wharf in Clarence Bay, in the city of Georgetown. It is a tight fit because five other vessels are also tied at the dock and two are at anchor in the bay. All except *Tranquility* fly British colors.

British customs officials began boarding the ship.

"We need only water. Our stock is running low," Capt. Lester says to the first of three men who climb the ship's Jacob's Ladder, a ladder made of rope and wooden steps, onto the main deck.

"Water is always at a premium here," he answers. "Surely you must know that we have no natural fresh water. All our water is collected from rainfall and stored in cisterns about the island. Didn't you come through some heavy showers off West Africa? You should have collected water there. It's been rainy here, too. However, for that reason, you should be able to buy water rather cheaply at this time for I hear the cisterns are all full, even over-flowing."

"What? Buy water? Are you crazy?" says Ephraim, who had hurried topside as the ship was being secured to the wharf. "I'm against it."

"Number 1, go below and check the state of our water casks," orders Hiram.

A few minutes later, Andrew returns. "We're down a bit more than half."

"That should see us through another month," says Brown.

"More like two weeks," corrects Number 1.

"We'll depart tomorrow at daybreak," Capt. Lester says to his brother. "Let the other mates know my intent!"

The next day, as planned, they tow *Tranquility* off the wharf shortly after what would have been sunrise on a clear day, and move westward.

As they stand out of Clarence Harbor and turn to the south'ard, well off Tartar Rock and the city of Georgetown, and begin the task of raising more canvas, it begins to rain. Without letup, it rains for the next three days. From the onset, water casks are set up under the clews of the coarse sails and quickly fill with slightly smoke-flavored fresh water.

August 9, 1866 Day 247

In 23 days *Tranquility* crosses the thousand miles to where they can pick up the south-flowing Brazil Current, just south of the Heel of South America. They do it at a cruising pace, 3 knots, and make way only during daylight hours. When *Tranquility* is put on a southerly course, Capt. Lester senses a new direction to the current. The next day, after more than two months, the lookout spots the first spout. As whaleboats are lowered, the lookout yells alow that two more spouts are at work.

"I see three, all at once," he says. "They're right whales."

By day's end, three whales are tied off the bow of *Tranquility*. Two days later, while they are still cutting-in, a fourth whale is spotted. Everyone's been working day and night, not only trying whales but also fending off sharks in squally weather.

Ben is delighted when he hears Capt. Lester tell Number 1 to lower away. His crew has not set an iron on the other whales and Hiram must have felt it was Andrew's turn. Ben is glad to get off the cutting stage.

As they lower, Ben is about to jump into the whaleboat when Andrew, already in the boat, calls to him.

"I want you to take Joshua's place in the bow," Andrew says. "He is running the cutting-in and the captain doesn't want him to leave. LeRoy will take your oar. I don't think you'll have any trouble placing an iron, will you?"

"What?" asks Ben. "You really want me to harpon a whale? I have never done that before."

"There's always has to be a first time. You've now seen it done a few times. Haven't you?"

"Yes, Sir. But watching is a lot different than handling the iron. I'm not sure I can do it."

"You've speared fish in the bay, haven't you?"

"Yes. But that was easy. And if I missed there were always other fish nearby."

"A whale is a lot bigger than a fish and harder to miss."

"And whales sometimes fight back."

"Ben, just think of it as another fish. A big fish but still a fish, as some of the old-timers still call a whale. Do it. I have confidence in you."

Seas are running 2 to 3 feet but the whaleboat easily cuts through the waves. Andrew, on the rudder oar, sees the whale spout to larboard and turns the boat to starboard. As they near, it is making only shallow dives, just under the water. The men pull the boat into its wake. A right whale cannot see forward because of the position of its huge head and mouth. Because of this, Lester again warns the crew that its tail is its only defense. The tail is to be feared if it senses something approaching from behind and is easily gallied. As they draw closer, Ben lays his oar aside and picks up the iron. He remembers how Edwards sets his knee into the clumsy cleat.

In a few minutes they are alongside, passing its flukes. Andrew watches as Ben rises, his right arm lifting the harpoon as high as possible. For a moment, Ben seems frozen, looking much more like a statue than a man about to kill a whale.

"Put wood to skin. Wood to skin," yells Andrew.

In a burst of energy, Ben drives the heavy harpoon down. Through his arm he feels the harpoon break the skin then stop with a jolt as it is buried to the harpoon's wooden shaft.

"Now," Lester yells as he starts forward. "Come back and grab the tiller."

"The iron stopped at the hitches," Ben yells to Andrew as they pass directions. "It was easier than I thought it would be."

Ben reaches the tiller oar and abruptly turns around to see Andrew steadying himself in the bow. He sees the powerful flukes of the whale thrash from left to right. They could crush anything they touched.

"Back off! Back off!" Lester yells to the crew.

He didn't have to say that; the crew knows exactly what happens next and unpeak their oars (oars held vertically). The boat slides off to one side, away from the flukes.

"Well done," Lester says to Ben as they again reverse their positions in the boat. "Just hold on. There is nothing more you can do until we begin taking back line."

The iron holds as Gerald LeRoy, the Barbados Negro who replaced John Adams, takes a turn on the loggerhead. A half-hour later, the whale stops running. The crew reacts by hauls in line at a fast pace. The whale comes so easily that at first Ben thinks the iron has pulled. As the boat nears the whale's flukes, Ben steers the boat to one side and the line again comes taut.

"In closer," Lester yells to Ben while still facing the fish.

He is standing with the lance raised, poised, ready to find the whale's heart or lungs. He does. Again and again. In a few minutes the whale is finished.

Ben starts to go forward to let Lester steer when Andrew holds up his hand.

"Stay there," he says. "Now you can learn to steer a boat."

The whale isn't an especially big. Not even quite as big as the other three, but it is a whale. It is Ben's first whale and that sets him above his crew and even above other crews in other whaleboats. Ben has just been graduated.

There is now an Indian with a harpoon in his hand on board *Tranquility*, Andrew says to himself. The superstition is satisfied.

As they approach *Tranquility* hauling Ben's whale they see another whale is already being maneuvered to be cut-in. Now there were two.

"Seems like a good time, a very good time, to splice the main brace," Andrew says to his brother at the bulkhead as his boat is lifted up to its davit. "One man at a time come aft," said Hiram. "Ben, this time, you're first."

As Ben and Andrew walk closely together aft across the main deck Lester says to him: "That was a fine job. I knew you could do it. But don't let it go to your head. Edwards is still the harponeer in our boat. But, things could change."

Ben does not speak but a smile spreads across his normally reticent face.

CHAPTER 26

On the Verge of Mutiny

Friday, October 25, 1866, Day 295
37° 5' S, 12° 15' W

October's end is approaching. *Tranquility* and her crew are down to the 20th degree line of latitude, south of the Equator. They are nearing Trindade Island, about 600 miles off Bahia, Brazil. Nearly two months of hunting off the coast of Brazil produced one sperm and one right whale. The polarization between dissident members of the crew and the captain and his officers, that began after Lester decided not to head home but to the South Atlantic, is again growing. It is spurred on by their lack of regular success.

"I wish I'd never signed on," Fred Jolly says as he and men in his watch gather in the forecastle after darkness engulfs their ship. "We ain't going ta make a cent on this trip. It was doomed from the beginning."

"Ya shoulda knowd better," adds Abe, who follows his watch into the forecastle and mingles with members of his boat. He is well aware that the 1st mate has repeatedly told him not to fraternize with his men or others in their sleeping/living quarters. He does so knowingly, in open defiance of Andrew, almost hoping to provoke him.

Jolly is an experienced whaler, one of the very few in *Tranquility's* boat crews. This is his third whaleship but only the second time under Capt. Lester's command.

"He's wandering all over this ocean, like a chicken with its head cut off," Jolly continues. "Hell, who ever gave him command? I shoulda gotten off in Barbados."

"Pipe down," cautions Abe, who is lying on an empty bunk with his arms folded behind his head, "or someone might hear ya bitchin'. When I came down here his brudder wuz in da bow, sitting on da win'lass."

"I know the next time we put ashore, I ain't coming back," Jolly says.

"We're gittin' close tuh Trindade Island. Ya can git off dere," suggests Abe.

"I've been there before," responds Jolly. "It's not the kinda place I like.

"Besides, there ain't much traffic there, mostly Portygee (Brazilian) fishermen. What boats there is, is always goin' back and forth tuh Brazil. Those Portygee, they're a mean bunch."

"Maybe it's you and not the Portygee," pipes up Egas Sanchez, a Portuguese who joined the ship in the Azores and was assigned to Brown's crew. "It's gotta be you, you're such an ass."

Jolly turns around and faces Sanchez while making a fist. Sanchez quickly stands up. Jolly runs into Sanchez's fist and is knocked to the deck. Abe jumps off the bunk and is about to rush to Sanchez then stops. On second thought, he surmises, dat fuckin' Portygee is a lot bigger dan me. Besides, Lester's gotta hear wad's goin' on.

Jolly returns to the bunk and sits. He regains his composure. I'll get even with that bastard, he says to himself, but not now.

"Yur best bet's da Cunha, Tristan da Cunha," Abe suggests to Jolly, who is wiping blood from his face. "Dere's always traffic headin' fer Europe, some even fer duh States. But, if dey knows ya jumped ship dey'll lock ya up. Dem Brits don't take to mutiny or jumpers."

"We could take over the ship," says James Blackwell.

Several others in the forecastle openly agree with him.

Abe makes a mental note of them.

"I'm fed up wid tings here," says Abe. "I thought we'd take over duh ship."

"What would we then do?" asks Jolly.

"We'd be pirates 'cause dah Navy's got a new squadron in duh South Atlantic. We could head back ta duh Caribbean, sell da oil an' whatever's on dis tub, even sell duh boat. I knows a few islands where it could be done. I been dere. Dere ain't no law."

"There aren't enough men willing to do it," says Jolly.

"Dere may be some who 'aven't spoken up," says Abe. " But I thinks yur right. Mutiny's too risky. Jumpin' ship's a better idea."

"When do we do that? The next port?" asks Blackwell.

"Dats stupid," says Abe.

"I'd rather we returned home instead of jumping ship," says Paul Norman, the tub oarsmen in Diogo Pilla's crew. "Maybe if someone went to the captain and let him know how we feel, he might consider it."

"No one here's got the balls to knock on his door," says Roger Whetstone. "Not me, anyways. Maybe someone should talk to his brother. He's a lot easier to talk to than the skipper. And, he's always been fair with me and others in this crew."

Unexpectedly, Ephraim Brown appears in the deck hatch and stops on the first step. Momentarily, all conversation ends.

"Abe, I'd like to talk to you," Ephraim says to his nephew. "Come outside."

Abe springs from the bunk and follows his uncle onto the deck.

The forecastle is silent. Abe sees that Andrew is no longer there. After a few minutes, Fred Jolly, who thinks Brown is out of earshot, speaks. "Maybe we should ask Abe to do it."

Abe is back at the hatch and coming down the ladder. "Do wad?" he snarls, indicating that he overheard part of their conversation.

They tell him what they had been discussing but skip the part involving the 1st mate.

"We'd like you to speak for us," Jolly says even though you does not represent all of the forecastle crew. "We want you to tell the 1st mate how we feel."

"Not da 1st mate but da cap'n!" says Abe. "I'd be glad ta do dat."

The men agree. It is a leadership role and Abe likes that. It is a role Hiram Lester has denied him. Now he can confront Hiram directly. But first, he thinks to himself as he climbs the ladder back onto the deck, I should ask my uncle's advice.

Abe sees his uncle is still topside, just below the quarterdeck. He is talking with Andrew. They stop talking as they see Abe approach. In reality, their conversation has just ended and had nothing to do with Abe. Lester turns, climbs up the quarterdeck ladder without acknowledging Abe's appearance, and crosses the quarterdeck to the weatherside.

Abe tells his uncle what the forecastle crew wants him to do.

"You knew from the beginning" Ephraim answers his nephew, "that this voyage had less chance of success than previous ventures. The Company undertook it as a last resort. Surely we must see it through with the captain or I will lose everything I own. You, too, Abraham. I don't like the role you're playing. You should be helping both Lesters keep the crew under control. Instead you seem to fire them up at every opportunity, at every perceived weakness you think Hiram Lester possesses. He is not a weak man. Do not be misguided by his reticence. You are only hurting your chances of him permanently making you 4th mate."

Unsuccessful in obtaining his uncle's endorsement and unheeding his advice, Abe later that afternoon sees Capt. Lester at the transom. Lester is against the taffrail, staring at the feeble wake his ship is creating.

"Sir, can I speak tuh you? Can I speak openly?"

Momentarily, Lester is surprised.

"Don't you always?"

"My crew's discouraged," Abe says. "Dey wants tuh return home. We can jus' make it back fer Christmas if we spread more sail."

"Are you also a navigator?"

"I thinks I could if needs be!

Sir, it's nearly a year since we left Montauk. Worst of all, we gots little more dan gittin' old tuh show fer it. Dere seems no future in whaling."

"You seem to be in a strange position," Lester tells Abe.

"How so…Sir?"

"You tread my ship with one foot in the officer's quarters and one in the fo'c's'le. How do you manage to do that?"

"I done knows wad ya means, Captain."

"You know damned well what I mean. Are you an officer or a foremast man?"

"I done know, not fer certain. It's yous whose put me betwixt. Maybe if'n I were made 4th mate I could see my position more clearly."

"Being my 4th mate would not change you a bit. You are a malcontent and a new rank would not change your personality. If it hadn't been for your uncle's intervention, I would not have signed you on. Now, be away!"

When the foremast crew hears that Lester refused Abe's request, there is a flurry of complaining and grumbling in the forecastle. In the heat of the moment even open rebellion is suggested.

"We gots two choices," says Fred Jolly. "We can jump ship at the next port we pull into or…."

"Da skipper's not goin' to do dat," James Blackwell interrupts. "He knows dat might happen the longer we's at sea. Dat's why whalers don't make port unless dere's a problem with da ship."

"Or," continues Jolly, "we could take over the ship and sail her into a port, or some island where we can get off. Just like Abe said."

"That's stupid," says Harvey Bennett." The authorities in the port would arrest all of you for mutiny the minute you stepped foot on the dock. Why not even fly the skull and crossbones? Besides, who would skipper the boat?"

"Abe could," says Jolly. "He's always sayin' he can, better than the Cap'n."

"That's a lot of crap," answers Bennett. "Sayin's easy. Doin's a lot tougher. Besides, all the mates and shiphandlers would be against us. I don't want to go up against that fuckin' bo'sun. He's one tough son-of-a-bitch."

"But there's 20 of us…against maybe 10 of dem," says Jolly.

"This be bullshit, all bullshit," says John Coachman, one of the Negroes added to the crew in Barbados. He rises from his bunk and climbs the ladder. So do two others from Barbados. Behind them rise Obie and Zeke Jones. Sanchez and Kinder join them.

"What? No one else?" asks Jolly. We don't need dem Niggers anyway."

Surprisingly, Harvey Bennett gets off his locker and climbs the ladder.

"You just lost half your mutiny," Blackwell says from his bunk. He turns and faces the bulkhead and asks, "You finished? I gotta get some sleep before I go on watch."

While a possible uprising is in the making in the forecastle, Ben, with Andrew Lester on the mainmast yard, spots a whale. He yells alow of the sighting, and as he looks down, is surprised by the number of men already pouring out of the forecastle. Curious, he thinks, they're mostly Negroes. Why?

"Thank God," Hiram Lester says aloud as he steps out of the wheelhouse. "Where away?"

The sighting is a right whale. The crew's disposition immediately backs 180 degrees. Excitedly, they fall into the routine of whaling. Before day's end, two more small whales are spotted and harpooned. In the evening, spirits are again elevated; for the moment, they have forgotten Long Island, abandoned the thought of mutiny and again are whalers.

Chapter 27

Anything for a Greasy Dollar

Tuesday, October 29, 1866 Day 299

"We're dropping down to the 40s. We'll ride the Brazil Current southeasterly until it peters out, then head easterly," Hiram Lester says to his 2nd and 3rd mates and Joshua Edwards, who are with him as he shoots the sun. "There's money to be made here in more ways than whaling. On my last voyage I skirted several islands along the 40-line. We're headed for the Tristan Islands. Damn the whales. That is for now, anyway."

"Are you talking about seal skins and oil?" asks 3rd Mate Diogo Pilla.

"Precisely," answers Capt. Lester.

"I was there eight years ago," adds Joshua Edwards, "when I was on the *Daisy*. We spoke a New Bedford ship, the *Resolute*. She was a whaleship but was on a mixed voyage. Her captain said she was burdened with seal and walrus pelts and their oil, as well as whale oil and bone."

Ephraim exits the forward hatch and sees what appears to be a meeting around the captain on the quarterdeck. He quickly joins them asking what is happening. Lester repeats what he told the others.

"This sounds good," Brown quickly adds. "I know the Chinese are always in the market for sealskins. We may yet save this voyage from ruin. I hear there are also many penguins there. Are not these birds also a source of oil? I have heard other ships take them and render them with the seal oil."

"We are still a whaleship," Capt. Lester abruptly reminds the ad hoc bursar, "and as such we will cruise, not race to the islands. Mr. Pilla, make sure that we maintain four men on the lookouts."

"Sealin's a greasy business," Jolly says as he sits on the windlass and with several of the foremast crew. "I hates it!"

"What's so bad about it?"

"If you thinks whale blubber stinks, you ain't smelled nottin' yet."

"How far's the next port?" asks a Greenie.

"Quit thinkin' about that," says Jolly. "There's a couple seal islands in the way."

"Shit," the bum says and heads for the forecastle hatch.

November 5th, 1866, Day 304

"If I didn't have a calendar," Capt. Lester writes in *Tranquility's* logbook, "I wouldn't have known what today signifies. Exactly 11 months ago we left Montauk in our wake. It took my brother Andrew to remind me of its importance. I made a ration of grog available to everyone. At one point, I wished I hadn't because it reminded the men of home. It was a stupid thing for me to have done.

We have been underway for 20 days since leaving Trindade," Lester says to himself as he writes in the ship's log., and have failed to raise a single whale. Our success, has been worse than I had anticipated. Far worse. So far we have tried only thirteen whales and stowed 510 barrels of oil. That won't even begin to approach covering the cost of fitting out this ship. This must be done even before we can think of dividing the lays.

"The Pacific has got to be a better ocean than this ocean," he says quietly as looks at the water through the rear windows. "I had hoped not to attempt the passage to the Pacific. I don't have a choice," he says to himself as he turns and closes the logbook.

For the last 10 days slight, barely perceptible, but still noticeable changes in the weather begin to take place. Every day at noon, when Lester shoots the sun, it is a degree or so closer to the horizon. Air temperatures are slowly falling and the nights are chilly. No longer does anyone sleep topside. Water temperatures are also chilling. This is a sure indication that they have left the Brazil Current and are now riding the remnants of an easterly flowing current.

Saturday, November 24, 1866
Inaccessible Island
037° 15' S by 012°45' W
Day 424, the longest day of summer here.

At sunset the evening on the day before they go ashore, the entire starboard watch is mustered on deck. Andrew Lester turns to the bo'sun and orders: "Brace the yards to starboard and spill the wind from the sails."

Bellingham passes on the order to the deck crew to shorten sail. *Tranquility* now comes about into a cool, dying, southwesterly breeze. Men aloft quickly shorten her sails while in the bow the anchor detail is getting ready.

"Bo'sun," says Andrew, "use the short lead line and have your man call out the depths loudly and clearly."

As the ship slowly drifts toward the island, a man on the bow begins swinging the lead.

"By the mark, 7 fathoms," he yells back after retrieving the lead's line and counting slips of colored leather or cloth woven into the line at every fathom.

"By the mark, 7 fathoms."

"By the mark, 6 fathoms."

"By the mark, 5 fathoms."

"By the mark, 4 fathoms."

After the man yells 4 fathoms, Hiram says quietly to his brother without releasing his gaze on the island, "Now, Number 1, let it go."

A few seconds later, the anchor is released and immediately takes hold. The ship swings smartly about on the hook, then weathercocks. Capt. Lester, through his glass, studies the rocky shore on Inaccessible Island. In the fading light he isn't sure if the beach is covered with small boulders or seals. He does know, however, that there are a lot of strange noises emanating from shore. That night, *Tranquility* calmly rides in 20 feet of water, 200 feet off the northwest corner of Inaccessible Island, one of five islands in the Tristan da Cunha Group.

The next morning in the growing light of daybreak, there is no doubt that a great horde of seals covers the beach. They are a mixture of Antarctic fur seals and the much bigger elephant seals. The island is one of several breeding grounds both species use. Their constant barking floods over the water and fills the ears of everyone on the ship as a low-pitched roar. Higher up the gravel beach the crew see penguins nesting. They mix their high-pitched chatter with the baritone bark of thousands of seals.

"The light air carries a chill, the kind the men haven't felt in nearly a year, not since we left Sag Harbor," Andrew says to Bellingham as they stand outside the wheelhouse. The chill rides on a fair wind, blowing down from the southeast.

Even though the edge of permanent ice is some 1,500 miles farther to the south, its chill is far-reaching and noticeable. It is a hint of weather to come but few, if any, of the crew are looking that far into their futures.

Inaccessible is one of five volcanic islands in a collection known as the Tristan da Cunha Group. They include Tristan, Nightingale, Middle and Stoltenhof islands. One hundred ninety-two miles to the south is another group with Gough Island the largest. Lester looks at all these islands as work sites for his long-stagnant crewmen. Brown looks at them as a source of hides and oil, and eventually money. Fur seals yield the hides and each adult elephant seal the oil, about 25 gallons.

The island was discovered in 1652 by the Dutch ship *Nachtglas* and named after it. However, in that ship's log, after the name, in parentheses is (Inaccessible), because the sailors were unable to get farther inland than the base of the high cliff that perpendicularly ends on the beach. Ever since it has been known by its latter name. It is still as uninhabited by humans in 1866 as it was in 1652.

"Mr. Pilla," says Capt. Lester, addressing his 2nd mate, "after breakfast, be prepared to lower your boat. I will accompany you. We will go ashore for a looksee."

"Head directly for shore, then swing to starboard," Lester orders as they move away from *Tranquility*.

A southwest wind comes fresh as the day progresses and creates a surf that roars as it crashes on shore and rolls both seals and gravel back and forth, and up and down the high-pitched, ramp-like beach. Seals are playing everywhere in the surf. Hundreds of heads bob up and down in the water as the boat comes within 25 feet of the breakers.

"Close enough," Lester orders. "Swing off to starboard and parallel the beach."

As they move along, hordes of seal heads disappear before them only to reappear in the boat's wake.

"There are hundreds," says Jorge. "No, thousands. I have seen seals on islands before, but never so many."

The whaleboat moves about a mile down the beach before Capt. Lester tells Pilla it is far enough and to return to the ship.

"Make ready to sail," Lester says to Number 1, as he climbs off the boat before it is lifted completely into the davits. "We will circumvent the island to see where there is any place suitable to land a boat and build a camp."

The 7-mile counter-clockwise trip around Inaccessible Island is short-lived. In two hours they cross over the previous night's anchorage but continue on to the island's south side. There, they had spotted a small hook or peninsula about a thousand yards long that created a small lee on its east side. A small hillock, South Hill, rises more than 1,000 feet from the beach and adds to the shelter.

"This place will do," says Hiram, "Let's return."

"Steady on the helm," Andrew Lester cautions the man on the wheel as the ship is being hove-to.

"We have five fathoms," the man on the bow wielding the lead yells back. The ship's momentum causes it to inch farther in, closer and closer to the beach.

"Now we have 4 fathoms."

"That's close enough. Release the anchor!" Andrew orders.

The ship already faces to windward. The anchor drags but a few feet and then takes hold. The wind pushes the ship back and the cable gradually snaps taut.

"We are secured," the man on the lead line yells aft.

"I think we have more than enough room to swing on the anchor," Ephraim inserts into the conversation.

"There's no fear of swinging at this latitude," Andrew corrects him. "It will be a rare moment when the winds here don't blow from the southwest. They are that constant.

"The beach here looks good for a landing. There seem to be even more seals than on the west side. Don't you agree, Mr. Brown?"

"Indeed I do," he says as if Andrew really values what the disburser thinks. "This seems a bountiful place to begin our quest."

"Jorge," says Capt. Lester, who has been within earshot of his brother and Brown but never enters the discussion, "on your way forward, stop in steerage and tell Daily and Dibble to be in my lounge at 8 bells. And, see that all boat steerers are there as well. Oh yes, also make sure that Blackwell is among them."

"Aye, Sir."

"Gentlemen," Lester begins again, "here is what I propose to do. If we are to derive any lays from this voyage we must find a source for making money. Obviously, whaling has been slow, too slow. However, all that noise you hear outside is another source, and for a while at least, we are to become sealers. A few of you have had that experience and found it distasteful, but most will be new to it. You, too, will eventually strongly dislike it. That's no excuse.

"I am putting ashore a semi-permanent party whose goal will be to harvest as many hides and oil as possible and render them ashore.

"Number 1, since you have been on a mixed-voyage, you will go ashore and be in charge of establishing a camp for this venture. Before we launch it, however, we must pay heed to accommodations. I want Mr. Dibble, our carpenter to begin constructing two rigid frames for tents. John Daily, our sailmaker, is to cover them in as much old sail as possible. Begin your construction on board but hold off assembling it 'till you go ashore. Jorge, pick as many men as might be needed to aid Mr. Lester in setting up camp.

"Number 1, I want you to draw an oarsmen from each of the four crews to take ashore with you. They will kill, skin, stretch the hides and render the seal's blubber. Chips, you will be responsible for taking barrels ashore and bringing full ones back to the ship. Mr. Pilla will assign two crewmembers to regularly aid you.

"Mr. Brown," Lester says to Abe Brown, "you will go ashore with your boat and three of your men. There you will begin assembling the try works. Use as many suitable stones as you find on the beach. This will require fewer trips to the bilge to retrieve bricks. Of course, take the spare try-pot stored on the second deck. They are smaller and will thus be not too cumbersome to take ashore.

"Steward, bring out the box. Mr. Blackwell, give him a hand; it's heavy."

A few minutes later the pair returns with a long wooden box and proceed to pry open its lid.

"As you all know, Blackwell was in the Union Army and is an experienced rifleman, a sniper. He will be responsible for this ordnance and the training of three men to shoot. Blackwell, can you do that?"

"Aye Captain, I can do that!"

"What do you think of our rifles?"

The steward hands Blackwell a cloth as he lifts one of four rifles from the box. The firearm is covered in a heavy coat of grease, designed to protect it from salt air.

"These are rather recent issue," Blackwell says as he puts the butt of one to his shoulder. "It's a Model 1864, Type II, 58 caliber. It was issued to infantrymen during the last two years of the war. It was made at the Springfield (Mass.) Armory.

"I guess you got them pretty cheap, didn't you?"

"Why, yes," an amazed Ephraim says. "But how did you know that?"

"These were used for only two years, until the end of the war. They are the last of the army's rifled muzzleloaders. Since then, they've been replaced by breech-loading rifles. Still, they are a good gun and fairly accurate. But then again, I don't think seals will require a long shot."

"Day may not need shootin' at all," interrupts Abe.

"How is that?" the captain asks.

"I ain't never been tuh sea after seals," says Abe. "But I talked to captains in Sag Harbor who 'ave an' who've saved deir trips wid seal furs. Dey says dat in some places, seals are so tick dat dere men went among dem clubbing 'em."

"Using that technique," interrupts his uncle, "we can save the cost of powder and balls. Anticipating that we might hunt seals, I took it upon myself to equip us with half a dozen iron belaying pins, bigger than the wooden ones used here. I would have preferred the cheaper wooden pins but they weren't available until after we sailed."

"I agree with Mr. Brown," says Hiram Lester. "We have no intention of shooting the fur seals, clubbing will do. However, the elephant seals are much bigger and a quicker disposal of them by shooting is more humane. Make sure the men on the beach know this. I personally do not take delight in clubbing seals but that is of no matter now."

The next day Andrew, along with his crew, goes ashore searching for a tent site. They find several rectangular formations of bigger rocks on the beach, under the cliff's footing, as well as several fire-ring stones.

"Looks," says Andrew, "like someone has camped here before,".

Upper areas of the beach are pocked by nesting penguins and dozens of fur seals are in the process of giving birth. Hordes of young pups, almost shoulder-to-shoulder, are everywhere about. The pups quickly make room for the party as the men wade through them.

Abe and his crew are the first sent ashore to begin the harvest. After landing, Blackwell goes inside the tent to get the muskets.

"Let 'em be," Abe yells above the roar of the seals.

"Git the belaying pins. We're gunna use dem!"

A hesitant Blackwell passes out the pins.

The men stall, so Abe takes the lead. He passes the fur seals and walks into the horde of elephant seals and begins swinging the heavy, metal pin. The men stand there, astonished as they watch Abe swings left-to-right, right-to-left, smashing the heads of a different seal almost with each step he takes. He does it without missing a swing. As he does, he utters a shriek, a glee of delight. He seems possessed. He moves 20 feet into the cumbersome, defenseless seals before stopping and turning back to survey the path of destruction he has just wielded.

"My God," yells Blackwell. "Have you gone mad?"

A large grin spreads across Abe's mouth. His face, even his teeth, are smattered with blood. Blood still drips from his jacket as he reaches toward a seal closest to him that is still moving. The seal is still alive as he delivers another blow that separates the seal's proboscis-shaped nose from the rest of its head.

"Damn yuh," he yells back at his crew. "I told yuh ta git started. Wad's a matter? A bit squeamish are yuh? Git goin' or I'll use dis pin on yur backs."

"There was a strange look in his eyes," Blackwell tells Capt. Lester that evening after he gets back on the ship. "He was a crazed man. He was covered in blood. It didn't stop there. Abe turned back to the seals and continued his march and caused confusion among the helpless elephants. Then he turned to the smaller fur seals. The men began clubbing them but they were cautious and stayed away from him. Captain, he's nuts!"

"I did as I was told, an' so did da men wid me," Abe tells Andrew the next day after Hiram ordered him to go ashore and see if it is happening again.

"No one liked doin' dat work," Jolly said to Andrew.

"I stopped clubbing, dropped to my knees, drew my knife and began skinning the carcasses. Abe looked back and saw what I was doing."

"Maybe yah sissies should begin skinnin' out," he said to us. "I can kill enough tuh keep ya all busy fer a few days."

"We saw he was a mad man. I'd never seed anyone act so crazy, even when drunk. He's sick in the head," said Jolly.

To spread the workload with replacements off the ship, Hiram had Andrew rotate four men every four days, with the 8-man crew on shore. At times, when the number of dead elephant seals waiting to be rendered began to pile up, he would add two or three more men from the ship. No one escaped working ashore except for the carpenter and Michael Astor, the cooper who had their own chores.

After the first week, the biggest problem the men have is working their way in each direction from the trypot and dragging back their kill to camp. Finding more seals to harvest is never a problem. The daily trekking back and forth — even though the skinning took place where the fur seals were killed — is a miserable task for a man trying to walk on the rolling gravel beach while burdened with raw pelts. Carrying the blubber back to the trypots is even more wearing. Just getting back and forth takes a lot of time. And, it is getting colder each day they are there.

During the next three months the pelts of 925 fur seals are stowed in *Tranquility's* holds and the blubber from 608 elephant seals fills 498 barrels with oil.

Christmas comes and goes. Instead of chicken, which had all been consumed by then, the big meal is penguin. Everyone complains it tastes more like fish than fowl. New Year's sees an extra ration of rum, but the flagons bought in Barbados are nearing empty. Surprisingly missing is the discontent among the crew even though the work is difficult. The business of sealing consumes them physically. Only the idea that they are making money eases their disgruntlement.

Feb. 28, 1867, Day 450

"I believe it is time to move," Capt. Lester says to Jorge as he scans the beach from the bow of *Tranquility*. "It is consuming too much time and effort to haul the elephant carcasses to the try works. Tomorrow, we will begin dismantling the works and take down the tenting. We'll put two boats in the water to hasten the task. It can be done in two days."

"It may take less if the men think sealing is done," says the 2nd mate.

"Done?" says Hiram. "We may be just beginning."

Saturday, March 2, 1867, Day 425
37°23'0 S by 012°29'0 W

Two days later, *Tranquility* is drifting just north of the first island. When the bo'sun, manning the sounding lead, announces that the bottom had risen to 5 fathoms, Capt. Lester orders the anchor lowered.

During evening the winds grow with vengeance. They strongly rock the ship throughout the night. During the night the dense cloud cover opens and it rains heavily. Everyone is certain that no party would go ashore that day. And, none did. It blew for nearly a week, without let-up in either the wind or rain. On the last day, near day's end, the winds abruptly drop as if someone had closed a door.

March 10, 1867, Day 460

Tranquility is moved to the east side of the island where some respite can be found should the winds return…and they will. After setting the anchor, the sealing party goes ashore in two boats. They are greeted by hordes of fur and southern elephant seals and find the island infested with Rockhopper Penguins. Tufts of hair on their heads, modified feathers, make them look comical as they jump out of the path of the approaching men.

Two days after they start sealing, the weather turns squally, miserable, and is getting cold, real cold. The winds turn into squalls and a howling storm moves in behind them. Rain mixes from time-to-time with sleet and wet snow. The sleet feels like buckshot on the men's faces. It is difficult to look to windward. On the beach, the men find it impossible to keep fires going under the try pot and driftwood is scarce. The tried-out seal blubber provides a lot less fuel than the whales'. Life on the beach becomes impossible.

Chapter 28

The Horn Now or Never

March 14, 1867

"I fear we must retrieve our gear from this godforsaken island," Hiram says to Andrew as he watches the men ashore retreating to the caves at the bottom of the cliff.

"This isn't much of an island," Lester admits, "but it should have interrupted the wind's fetch and better protected us than it is doing."

Hiram and Andrew go below and take seats at the lounge table. Jorge and Diogo are already there drinking coffee. Abe is in the wheelhouse with the quartermaster.

There is a suddenly loud clap of thunder and the two Portuguese mates instinctively bless themselves.

"That one was close," says Ephraim as he enters the lounge and takes a seat.

"What I am saying," continues Hiram, "is that it is time we get out of here and head for The Horn. If not soon, the crossing will be that much more difficult."

"The Horn?" shouts Jorge as he jumps to his feet. "You never said we were to go to the Pacific."

"Are you afraid?" asks Ephraim.

"Of course not," answers Pilla, "I have been through it. You told me when I hired on that it was to be an Atlantic hunt. That's what I told Diogo and Nuno Dias. I led them to believe we would stay in the Atlantic."

"No one ever said that!" Lester returns to the conversation. "You must have assumed it on your own. Everyone was told that the voyage might take as much as three or four years. Those are not unusual lengths for a whaleship to be at sea.

"Would you have us go around in circles in the Atlantic? The first ride has not proven very successful. What do you think more turns on the wheel would produce?"

No one answers. A profound silence engulfs the cabin.

"We would not go into the Pacific," says Hiram, "if whaling had been better in the South Atlantic."

"We are being forced to go," adds Brown.

"Forced to? Who is forcing us to endanger our lives?" asks Pilla. "It is the greenbacks you seek."

"And what did you seek when you signed on?" Brown retorts. " Escudos? Yes, that's right. You, too, are chasing the greenback. Are you any different than we are?"

Silence again reigns in the cabin. After a few minutes, Pilla slaps his hand on the table as he and his uncle storm out of the cabin.

Word quickly moves forward, through the galley, steerage and finally the forecastle. The crew is enraged. It is especially heated among the Negroes.

"I never knew the captain could do sumpin' like dat," says Ben Johnson. "Maybe no one said it but we all got the feeling that this was going to be the last turn in the Atlantic and then head home."

"That's right. That's the way it was," pipes up Gerald LeRoy, a Bajan. I'd trade this for a sugar field in a moment."

"Me, too," seconds Obie Jones. "Someone ought to get Abe and see what he says.

"Who calls my name?" Abe says as he stands in the hatch opening into steerage.

"I heard ya bums bitchin' as I came across steerage," he says. "Ya ain't gots a chance. If Lester says Pacific, ya says yes sir an' suck it up.

"But, dere might be one chance."

"What's dat?" asks Jolly.

"I wuz listenin' to Cook the other day,'" says Abe. "He's complainin' dat we're running short o' food. Dat means Lester has ta put in at Sidney, in duh Falklands. Dat's the place ta jump ship. An' a big desertin' would end Lester's callin' as a skipper. Dat's one way o' gettin' even with duh bastard.

"Wad's even better is duh ship traffic dere. Dere's always boats comin' from New York and headin' fer the gol'fields of California. Yous gots a cherce. Pick a ship headin' home or pick one goin' tuh duh Promised Land.

"Whose wid me on dis?"

The number of ayes he gets surprises him.

Damned good, he says to himself.

March 15 dawns blustery and cold; winds blow consistently from the west. During the night, they had eased slightly. In the morning, as he comes on deck, Capt. Lester feels the difference. He glasses the shore and sees little activity among the men who slept in the caves. The weather had been so severe the day before that the men stayed over in the cave rather than risk returning to the ship. A small plume of smoke rises from one cave reveling that they made a fire and are preparing breakfast, or at least coffee.

Winds fall steadily throughout the morning. By noon, Lester believes that the waters are safe and orders away two boats. Their task is to begin the retrieval of the men, the try gear, any pelts they had skinned and 12 barrels of oil. The men on the beach are delighted when they see two boats coming. It can mean only one thing. By the end of the day all is secured aboard *Tranquility*."

March 16, 1867, Day 466

"This morning we departed the northern island under light winds," Capt. Lester enters in the logbook. "Weather is a far cry from what it has been for almost a week. This is an opportune time to make the move. Yesterday's weather was only a hint of the weather to come if we stay in these latitudes. I have been here before and don't pleasure to dally any longer that need be. I fear, I know, the winds will only get worse the farther to the south'ard we head.

"The Portygee were taken aback by the disclosure that I intend to reach the Pacific," Hiram says to his brother as they sit in his quarters. "I'm sure that word now has filtered through to the fo'c's'le. However, the attitude of the crew has been good despite the recent weather. Hard work is always beneficial to one's mind.

"Ephraim, however, believes that there is still time to harvest more seal pelts. He is encouraged by the unexpected return of mild weather after we left North Island. It defied my forecast."

Two days out (March 18th) they spot a pod of right whales and suddenly they are whalers again. Abe's and Jorge's boats are successful and they heave-to for three days as two whales are cut-in.

Chapter 29

Gough Island, Another Delay En Route

Thursday, March 21, 1867, Day 471

"We are underway again. I have heard no mention from officers or crew about heading to the Pacific," Lester writes in his log. "Maybe they've accepted the idea. I hope so."

"Gough Island is not out of our way," says Ephraim Brown. "I have heard you and the mates often talk of how great the herds of seals once were there. I think it behooves us to head for it, at least to see if it contains any great number. Besides, en route we can still look for whales. We have just added 35 barrels to our collection; maybe there are more barrels ahead."

Lester is now confronted with two choices, getting quickly into the Pacific or making money for the Company. He knows that his reputation as a whaling captain suffered from the last trip. True, he was hindered by an already faltering population of whales and the harassment by the Rebel raider. He knows this, but the Company members, dedicated merchants, are interested only in the bottom line. He remembers someone in the Company saying on his return from that voyage that he had lost his touch, that his was a less-than-greasy ship. Ever since, that phrase has been constantly battering about in his head. Lester is indecisive. Reluctantly, and against his better judgment, he decides to look and sets a course for Gough Island.

The island lies just over 200 miles to the south-southeast. They are delayed again when three right whales are spotted and the whaleboats are lowered and trying-out again further delays the reach for Gough Island. Delays, both good and bad, are badgering and confronting him. His wavering nature again does not reflect a captain truly in charge of a ship, even more import, of his will.

Monday, April 1, 1867, Day 481
Gough Island
40° 20'S by 10° 0'W

"We sit at anchor off Gough Island, almost astride the 40-line and yet the winds today are almost non-existent," Lester enters in the logbook that evening. "I fear the worst. Is it the quiet before a storm? It is like we are becalmed in the eye of a hurricane. I hope nature is not planning on playing an April Fool's Day prank on us. The days have been clear, sunny, yet the barometer continues to fall. Maybe I should throw that damned glass overboard. The island beaches are black with seals.

Despite Andrew's plea to make for The Horn, Hiram succumbs to Ephraim's constant badgering. He orders the establishment of a camp.

May 1, 1867, Day 511

A month after landing, Brown logged in his tally sheet that 1,200 sealskins, but only 317 barrels of oil, have been stowed. The lesser amount of oil rendered was not due to the number of elephant seals on the island but a reluctance of the men to work the blubber knives as opposed to skinning of fur seals. The try pots were moved three times before Lester, encouraged by his brother, finally made up his mind that it was leave now or winter on Gough Island and wait for spring to arrive in three or four months. Neither option was a good choice.

"Each day, almost imperceptibly, temperatures are falling," Andrew says to his brother as they share breakfast with the other officers. Hiram is more than aware of the deteriorating situation but is reluctant to make a decision. "The men are beginning to complain about working in the cold. Two have taken sick."

"But still," Hiram answers, "there is money to be made on these islands. Isn't that why we sailed to the south Atlantic?"

"That's not the point," says Andrew. "We are using up the time before real winter sets in here. Then, it will be impossible to cross into the Pacific. We really don't have an option. We may even be too late now."

"Captain," Diogo says to Lester, "you must make a decision soon. I, too, think that we are already too late to make a safe rounding of the Horn. But again, there never is an easy rounding of that godforsaken place."

"Diogo is right," Andrew adds. "The men sense that something is in the air. They are not stupid. You cannot continue to be indecisive in this matter."

"What? Think me indecisive?" asks Hiram.

Before Andrew can answer, Ephraim interrupts.

"There is no decision to be made," he says as he enters the discussion in opposition. "We came here to make money and while it has been slow during the past week or so, we are adding skins and oil to the holds. The men knew what kind of life lay ahead of them when they signed on. Besides, they, too, share in the profit."

"Profit? Profit? Wad profit?" asks his nephew Abe. "Duh lays each man gits is so small dat it ain't worth deir effort ta work so much. I gots no idea why anyone would sign on as a fo'c's'le man on a whaler. An' you ain't right. Most boat crews never been on a whaler before. Dey gots no idea of wad lay in store fer dem when dey signed on. If dey did, I knows day all tinks we should git da hell out o' here as soon as possible!"

Even so, Lester delays his decision until a vicious storm strikes on June 5th. The continued delays allow Lester to subject himself to a weakness in his personality, a dichotomy, a contradiction within himself of which he is aware but seemingly cannot control. He suffers in silence. His brother senses this but doesn't approach him. In a way Lester is using Brown's urging and insistence on making money as a foil, and bringing home a "greasy ship" as a reason not to confront the realities of the circumstances he is facing on this voyage.

"We have already overstayed our time," Lester finally tells his mates. "We must make every effort in the next day or two to retrieve the gear and pelts we have onshore."

The mates readily agree and bounce their coffee cups off the table in approval as if they were steins of beer. Brown is angered, rises from the table and stomps out the door leading to steerage.

The men make a heroic effort the next morning, pulling the oars over the 500 yards from the beach to the ship in 40-knot winds. Under duress they retrieve all their gear.

Chapter 30

The Falklands

June 8th, 1867, Day 549

Tranquility clears the east end of Gough Island and bears away in a west-southwest direction for the city of Stanley, the capital of the Falkland Islands. Heavy snow is now falling, almost vertically, in a near-windless sky. It obscures the horizon from the bow watch, forcing the helmsman to guide the ship by compass alone. He heads the boat into a future as uncertain as what immediately lies ahead.

Stanley is on the east coast of East Falkland Island and lies 3,300 miles away. It will not be an easy journey. They now buck not only the winds that shift from near nothing to 20 to 40 knots by evening, but also a circumpolar ocean current that flows in the opposite direction to where they want to go. They are also heading into the dead of winter, a winter such as only a few on board have ever experienced. Even those few crewmen who once rounded the Horn did it during Antarctic's summer months. With great trepidation, the men face a future among ice floes that increase both in numbers and size as they make way.

Tranquility is carrying a minimum of canvas, only as much as Andrew dared to set. Even though she is no longer in a cruising mode because of sea conditions, her forward speed is not much more than if she had been.

Lookouts are no longer posted on the fore- and mainmast yards because of the excessive swings of the ship. Nor are the captain and crew in a whaling mood. If successful it would be impossible to cut-in a whale with the strong winds. Even more tenuous would be launching whaleboats in 6- and 7-foot seas to plant an iron in an uncooperative whale.

Each day, as they move closer to Stanley, the air continues to cool. Precipitation vacillates between light snow and cold drizzle. It never seems to rain very hard, just enough to obscure the horizon and the sun. There are days on end when Capt. Lester cannot take a reading of their position because there is no sun; not even a bright spot in the southern skies.

One morning, a week after leaving Gough Island, the crew is surprised at daybreak to see the ship dressed entirely in white. During the night, the temperature dropped below freezing. The wet rigging is encrusted in frost and ice. Fortunately, it is a day when the sun unexpectedly rises. By noon it has melted everywhere except on the bow.

"Number 2," Capt. Lester says that evening, "tomorrow post two bow lookouts instead of one and have them carry belaying pins. The spray is now freezing on the bowsprit. We cannot let ice accumulate."

Into the third week, salt spray is everywhere forming into ice and many of the crew are put to work breaking it loose. An added safety line above the bulwarks is also rigged after one man slips on the frozen deck and is almost washed over the side. Now, waves regularly break over the bow. They do so with greater consistency as they near the 50th latitude. At one point in their southwesterly trek, they are less than 100 miles north of the permanent ice pack.

Monday, July 8, 1867, Day 579

After 30 days out of Gough Island, the weather abruptly changes. They are now precariously close to the Falkland Islands. Their location is not a problem as long as they have some degree of visibility. The winds abate to the point where Lester can again reset full sails. For a few moments, all looks good. But as they finish securing the braces, a fog bank lies ahead. Almost silently, *Tranquility* disappears into it. For three days, they are shrouded in fog that freezes on luffing sails and dangling sheets. Uncertain of where he is, Lester orders the bow watch to begin heaving the lead.

"I want a sounding taken every 100 yards," Lester says to his brother. Andrew passes on the word to the bo'sun.

No one likes heaving the lead in deep water so the men try to avoid the scanning eyes of the bo'sun as he enters the forecastle. They know what he wants. The shoal water lead is easy to toss because it weighs but 6 pounds. However, that weight would fall too slowly in deep water. Instead, in this case, a 25-pound lead is used, usually on 20 (120 feet) fathoms of line.

"Off sounding," comes the monotonous cry of the man on the lead when he finds no bottom. On the third day, the man sounding retrieves a long strand of kelp.

"This is not good," Hiram Lester says to his brother. "It means that the bottom is rising. The Falklands are a treacherous place to approach, even under blue skies. I have been here twice, and you, too. I know not what to suggest to you."

"We are in a pickle," says Capt. Lester to his mates assembled on the quarterdeck. "We are running blind in this fog and there is little, if anything, we can do, except lower the boats. We are not making way by sail. Only the current pulls us to the southeast. I have no idea where that will take us."

This is a statement Lester should never have uttered. His brother rolls back his eyes in disgust. He knows it is admitting defeat. Even if he does not know where to go he should never let the rest of the men on board know. Even Abe Brown knows this and a smile spreads across his face. Hiram Lester is looking for help, for suggestions. None are forthcoming.

The worry filters down to the crew and embroils the forecastle. Its messenger is none other than Abe Brown. Everyone onboard feels a sense of fear and helplessness. The fear intensifies as shoals of drift ice are now everywhere in sight.

"Fred," Abe says to Jolly as they pass in steerage. "I tink it's time tuh call dose tuhgether who plan ta jump ship. We're just a few days from Stanley. We can't meet in the fo'c's'le 'cause dere's spies among some of duh Greenies. I don't trust duh Indian. He seems too close ta duh captain's brudder. Make it tuh night, at 6 bells. Be sure tuh pick two men ta act as lookouts. Place one on each end of steerage."

That night, one of the mates knocks on Capt. Lester's door.

"Sir," he says. "I hesitate to wake you but the lookouts have reported that the winds have shifted."

"Are they strong?"

"No Sir, but they have cleared the sky. I see the Southern Cross."

Lester opens the cabin door while pulling up his trousers, then slips into his boots. He grabs a coat and follows the lookout up the ladder and onto the deck.

"Thank God!" Lester says as he glances across the star-studded sky, "Tomorrow there will be a sun."

July 11, 1967, Day 582
52° 23' 08" S, 057 ° 03' 11 W

At noon, Capt. Lester is topside taking a reading. His mates anxiously gather about him. All of the foremast crew not engaged are also on deck. Weeks have passed since they last saw the sun. Some even took to cheering as they climbed out the forecastle companionway and saw its light.

"Thank God the skies cleared," says Lester as Andrew jots the readings in his book. "We would surely be aground on this southerly course if they hadn't. We are at Latitude 52° and would soon run into the east side of East Falkland Island.

"Take a 190-degree heading," he instructs Andrew who passes it on to the helmsman. "That should bring us toward Cape Pembroke. From there we must pick our way to Jackson Harbor. Jackson is really a bay, not a harbor, as we know it.

"The waters approaching the point," he turns and addresses his mates, "are filled with rocky shoals. Stanley lies on its southern shore near the bay head.

"Number 1, keep the ship fully-rigged until sunset. The wind isn't fresh but should move us well against the current. We will heave-to at sunset and wait until daybreak. I dare not attempt to enter the harbor in the dark."

Jolly is on deck and headed for the bow when Abe stops him momentarily.

"Fergit 'bout meetin' in steerage tonight. Duh sun just screwed up our plans. Done worry, we'll git anudder chance fer sure."

Jolly doesn't respond but touches the edge of his watch cap.

Friday, July 12, 1867, Day 583

The ship averaged only 4 knots and took 35 days since departing Gough to arrive off East Falkland Island. Just after daybreak, the 3rd mate is again at the captain's door.

"Who's there?"

"Sir," he says after he stops knocking. "There's a ship approaching our transom. I'm not certain, but the lookout thinks she flies the Union Jack."

By the time Lester is topside, a British merchantman is within easy hailing distance as it slowly moves parallel to the starboard side of *Tranquility*.

"Ahoy there," yells a man on deck, "are you in distress?"

"No Sir," Andrew Lester yells back through his speaking trumpet. "We hove-to until we could see. We hope to enter Stanley today but our charts have little information of the surrounding bottom."

"A smart move, captain. I'm quite familiar with these waters. We, too, are headed there. You're welcome to sail in our wake."

"Gladly. Thank you," yells Lester. "I'll buy you a drink ashore."

"I'm already looking forward to it," he yells back.

The merchantman slowly pulls ahead as the crew on *Tranquility* begins to raise sails. As the ship passes she reveals her hail port. She is the *Orion*, out of Portsmouth.

Just about this time they sight Mt. Usborne, the highest peak on either East or West Falkland islands. As they move ahead in the wake of *Orion*, they discover that what at first appeared to be a relatively calm bay is covered by a thin layer of skim ice. Waters inside Jackson Harbor and at Stanley's docks, however, are ice-free. The amount of activity in the bay during the onset of winter surprises *Tranquility's* mates. More than a dozen ships are at anchor off the town wharves and an equal number are on several wharves that jut into the harbor.

Tranquility is turned into the wind and momentarily stops as she approaches the longest wharf. Lester and his mates spot a small, official-looking craft, flying an oversize Union Jack, approaching.

"Probably a customs boat," says Jorge to the men lined up against the larboard gunwale.

While waiting for his ship to be assigned a wharf, Hiram glasses the surrounding docks and yards and sees three vessels hauled out in the ways undergoing repairs.

Finally, a blue-uniformed man climbs the Jacob's Ladder on the gangway opening in the bulwark, and asks to see the captain.

"You're looking at him," Lester says as he waits along the bulwark.

"What's your business?" he asked Lester in clipped English. "Are you in need of repairs?"

"No repairs, Sir," he answers, "but we are low on some provisions."

"Do you possess a letter of credit?"

"Why would we need that?" Ephraim, who standing next to Lester, asks in amazement.

"Because you will find goods a bit more expensive here than in Sag Harbor. Everything here is brought in from the outside. The only local product is wool. Have you any need of wool?"

"Do your peddlers not respect the Greenback Dollar?"

"Aye, they do. You'll have no trouble here, that is, if you have enough of them."

"I'm not sure I like your attitude," Capt. Lester responds.

"Like it or not, that's the way things are here, especially in winter," the customs agent responds flippantly.

"How long do you plan to stay?"

"Three or four days should be enough," Lester answers.

"And where do you go from here?"

"That is none of your damned business," Lester says.

"We head for the Pacific," interrupts Ephraim.

"At this time of year? Are you mad?"

"Not mad, Sir," says Capt. Lester, "just your average American whaler."

"What is the daily fare at dockside?" asks Brown.

"For a bark of your dimensions, I think the wharfage is about 80 dollars. But, I'll have to measure her before I can give you an exact answer."

"That's outrageous!" exclaims Brown.

"Do you or don't you want wharfage?"

"Shut up, Ephraim," says Capt. Lester. "Yes."

"There is an opening on the north side of the main wharf."

The man points to the opening.

"Do you see it? Will you need help getting there?"

"And what will that cost? No!" Lester answers before the man is able to speak. We won't need further assistance.

"Number 1, make ready and launch bow and waist boats. We will come along the dock on our starboard side."

Tranquility is nudged into the open spot, immediately astern of the *Orion*, the merchantman she followed into the harbor.

"Number 1," says Capt. Lester as he watches his men secure *Tranquility* to the wharf's bollards, "please go aboard the *Orion* and ask her captain if he will join us for dinner at 8 bells this evening, or tomorrow evening if it is not convenient."

"Ephraim," says Capt. Lester, "find Cook. I think he has a list of what is needed. Then bring it to me for review when you have decided what we can do without."

"Yes, Hiram. I've already been developing a list of our needs. Shall I also include a flagon or two of rum?"

"I shudder to think what the price here might be. But," adds Lester, "you may investigate what it will cost."

An hour later, Andrew Lester returns to the ship.

"Tonight will be fine Capt. James Withers said," reports Andrew Lester. "I also invited his first mate. I hope that is alright with you?"

"Of course, Andrew," says his brother. "I would have thought less of you if you hadn't. I should have remembered to tell you that myself. I do have a great number of things on my mind. I fear that our cousin will soon confront me. At times his frugality is almost too great to bear.

"Oh! Andrew, please go by the galley and ask Batiste to meet me in my quarters."

"Captain," says Cook, "the 1st mate said you wanted to see me."

"Yes, John, I'm having a captain and his 1st mate joining us for supper tonight. Do you think you have enough time to make some of your plum duff? I also have asked Mr. Brown to see if he can secure for us a fresh lamb shank while he is in the town. It wouldn't hurt if you could give it one of your Cajun recipes."

"Of course, Captain. How many, in all, will there be?"

Lester hesitates for a second. "Four," he answers. "No, make it five. I guess I should invite the disburser. After all, I did ask him to secure the lamb. Also, be sure to tell the mates that tonight they will eat in their mess."

"Aye, Sir," Batiste says and leaves the captain's quarters.

"Capt. Lester, that was an excellent meal," says Capt. James Withers. "I didn't know that a whaler carried on board a gourmet chef."

"He really is," says Lester. "I must also admit that his plum duff is *par excellence*. In a way, I'm glad the rest of his cooking isn't as good or we all would have trouble sitting around this table."

"May I offer you some Barbados rum?"

"I hope you will forgive my impertinence," says Capt. Withers, "but I took the liberty of bringing along a bottle of Portugal's best, a bottle of aged port which I had hoped you and your mate would share with me."

"I'd be delighted," says Lester. "Pierre, glasses please."

Batiste, the captain's steward, anticipates the request and is at the table almost as soon as Lester asks.

"I genuinely appreciated being able to follow you in this morning," says Lester. "I have been here twice before and each time I scraped a bit of bottom coming in. I cannot understand why the admiralty, or the city council here, doesn't appropriate enough money to add buoys to mark the channel."

"Even I, too, wish it were so," says Withers. "However, there is a subversive power at work here that has stalled movement on such a corrective effort. Did you not see several battered wrecks on the rocks as we entered Jackson Harbor? And, did you see the three boats in the ways under repair? I'll bet half the vessels here at the wharves are manning pumps every hour of the day until they get their turn in the ways. And, the cost of work here is beyond reason.

"Fortunately, we carry the Royal Mail and are exempt from these prices. We also carry the yards' materials. The yards send their buyers to Portsmouth on every trip I make and fill the holds of *Orion* with almost everything needed to rebuild a ship.

"With traffic slowed at this time of the year, salvagers have even been known to take matters into their own hands and create wrecks. More than one ship has unexpectedly sunk at the dock. I suggest that it would be in your best interest to station an armed watch, one on both stern and bow, to protect your vessel.

"What are your sailing plans?"

"Pierre, my cigar box please," Lester says before addressing Withers' question.

"We had planned to spend a few days here, but not at these rates," answers Capt. Lester. "Then, we had hoped to make for the Pacific."

"I would caution you against it. Drake Passage is likely to be too violent during this and the next two months. And while it is usually open there is always enough shifting ice to make a crossing extremely dangerous. Half of its width is always covered in permanent sea ice. You might elect to run through the Straits of Magellan, but there, too, you will find little respite from the wind. The passage is very narrow in places but the wind seems even more forceful there than in the Passage. The land acts to funnel it and at times you will not make headway. If you do choose this route at this time, I suggest you allow four to six weeks to clear the straits."

"What would you do if you were in our position?" Lester asked Capt. Withers.

"First, I would get out of here. I'd look for a well-protected bay among these islands and remain there for two, maybe three months. I would wait for spring to arrive before I would venture a try."

"I have been here before," says Capt. Lester. "Twice before, but in December when it was summer here. I made a passage of the length of Falkland Sound. We overnighted one time in a small bay with a narrow inlet on the northern end of West Falkland Island."

"That sounds like it might be a good choice," agrees Capt. Withers. "I think that is called Port Howard. Some call it Adair's Harbor. I know not how it came by these names. It is a port only in name and there isn't anything there."

"I don't think anyone will bother you; West Falkland Island is still uninhabited," says Capt. Withers. "But, I don't think it will be for long. The government here is about to offer land on it at below bargain prices. They want to get British subjects homesteading on West Falkland Island to weaken any claims Argentina might have in regaining a foothold on these islands."

"I thank you for your advice and port wine," Lester says as he sees Capt. Withers rising from the table.

"It has been entirely my pleasure," Withers says. "But the night is drawing on, Captain, and I still have work to do before I can retire. We have but another day before we return to Portsmouth."

"How long does it take you to make the trip?"

"Depending upon weather and time of year, anywhere from 35 to 45 days. The ship's owners feel that an idle ship is lost money."

"Men after my own heart," says Ephraim Brown.

"Good night. And a fare thee well to you and your crew," says Withers as he and his mate walk down the gangway.

"Number 1," says Lester after the visitors leave, "break out the muskets and see that those on the night watch are armed. Place two men at each station and cut their watches to two hours. I want them fully alert. I don't think we will be here more than another night, maybe two."

"The prices are outrageous," Ephraim says the next morning as he storms into Lester's cabin. He and the cook had been in town and visited a commissary catering to transient ships. "I dared not make purchases until we both went over the ship's needs again to see what we might be able to do without."

Tranquility's food closets are no longer adequately stocked. But the prospect of lying at anchor for an extended period makes its conservation tenuous. The list is reduced by half. Still it is a hefty sum to be paid.

"Do your buying today," Lester says, "because we will sail tomorrow morning.

"I'm certain that our supply of coal for the galley stove is more than enough. However, I plan to heat the fo'c's'le while we wait-out the winter. If I don't we might get more than the usual amount of grumbling from up forward. While you're ashore, locate a potbellied stove for the fo'c's'le. Pay them what they might demand. We have no choice. Oh yes, be sure to pick up some stove piping. See if you can get a ton or so of coal. If they won't deliver it to the ship, come back and get some men to haul it. But, I don't think that will be necessary. You should also add some charcoal for our galley stove. That fuel will be our only source of heat when we make a home south of the 52nd."

"When we gonna do it?" Jolly quietly asks Abe as they pass each other on deck.

"T'night. Duh ship's pullin' out t'morrow."

"How many's goin?"

"Last time we figured about 10."

"I'll bet some's gonna back out."

"T'night, during duh First Watch. At 6 bells," says Abe.

"Who's got duh watch?"

"I do. It will be perfect."

"Git ta dos who said dey wuz goin' the las' time."

"Captain," says Jorge after he sees Ephraim leave the ship and clamber down the gangway, "I must speak to you at once."

"Well, talk."

"No, not here. There are ears everywhere. I do not know who can be trusted."

"I'm heading to my cabin. See me in a few minutes."

"What is it?" Hiram asks.

"I was just told of a plan to jump ship."

"That's always possible," says Hiram as he thumbs through his logbook. "There are always a few."

"It is not a few, Sir. It is supposed to be 10 or 12 men," says Jorge.

"That would cripple us," Lester says. "How did you find this out?"

"Egas," answers Jorge. "Egas Sanchez overheard them planning it a few nights ago. "It has to be tonight. Everyone knows we move out tomorrow."

"Jorge, find the bo'sun, and the other mates, but exclude Abe. Tell them to come to my cabin posthaste. But do it quietly, I don't want to raise any suspicion."

"Gentlemen," Hiram addresses his officers, "there is a plan afoot by a large number of men to jump ship tonight. We must not let this happen. I believe they will try to do it the hour before midnight. Who has the First Watch at that time?"

"Abe Brown," answers No. 1.

"I should have expected as much. I want you all armed. At 8 bells on the Dog Watch come to my cabin and I will issue you all pistols. Wear them unseen.

"Oh yes, I want the fore and aft watches replaced by the 2nd and 3rd mates. Andrew, go with them when they do this and gather the rifles and store them in my cabin.

"Bo'sun, get two hasps from the shipsmith now. At 7 bells, you and your mate must secure the two hatches leading into the fo'c's'le. Here are two padlocks. When the hasps are on, add the locks.

"Abe might see you locking the topside fo'c's'le hatch so we must get him off the gangway for you or your mate to secure that hatch."

"I have an idea that should work," says Bellingham.

"Good," says Hiram.

"All is well," says Jorge just as one bell is rung. Abe and his second, Harvey Bennett, exchange a few words with him as they relieve him of the watch at the head of the gangway. They watch as Pilla disappears at the ladder before the quarterdeck.

"I guess you're not comin' wid us," Abe says quietly to Bennett.

"I'd be nuts if I did. I've got a wife, family and farm back on Long Island. You've got nothing waiting for you there. Nothing anywhere. I can stick it out. Besides, when you're gone they'll need a 4th mate. Who knows?"

"Fuck you," Abe says.

"I'm goin' below fer coffee. Watch duh gangway!"

Bennett does not answer. He is still angry with Brown and has not forgotten that he accused him of screwing up the whale he stuck. It's good to get rid of the bastard, he says to himself as he scans the wharf.

As Abe stands at the galley counter pouring a cup of coffee, Jolly appears out of the hatch leading from steerage. He grabs a cup and then pours coffee from another pot.

"Yur not supposed tuh be here," Abe growls at Jolly. "This coffee's fer duh officers an' men on watch."

"Shut up and listen to me," Jolly whispers to Abe. "Somethin' strange is going on. I just saw the two Pillas and the captain's brother leave the skipper's quarters. Diogo was stuffing a pistol under his belt. I think the mates are armed. Someone must have spilled the beans."

"Dat's all okay. Done worry. Git back ta duh fo'c's'le an' keep duh men quiet," orders Abe. He walks to the gangway and tells Bennett to get coffee if he wants it.

Bennett doesn't say anything but simply turns away and heads for the galley hatch.

Jolly's no fool, Abe thinks. If he senses somethin's going on he might be right. He scans the wharf at intervals and sees the loading activity on the *Orion* still underway. He knows they sail at daybreak. Maybe I can get on her. I ain't been to England in years.

"Damn it!" he says aloud.

Whad a fool I am, he says to himself. If duh ship's secured by duh mates an' bo'sun no ones goin' anywhere. I've been left outa duh ring. I gots ta do sumpin' afore dey move. Damn dat bastard."

Abe sees Bennett emerge from the hatch, abandons the gangway and heads for it.

"Keep an eye open on dah Brits," he says as he passes Bennett. "Dere's a lot of leaving action goin' on derh."

Abe quickly passes through the galley, across the mess and approaches Capt. Lester's door. He can see light coming through the louvers and doesn't hesitate to knock.

"Who is it?" Lester asks.

"It's me. Abe. I gotta talk to you."

Lester opens the door and steps outside his cabin.

"What is it? Couldn't it wait until morning?"

"No, sir. Sumpin's goin' on, captain."

"What? What is it?"

"I tink dat some men are planning tuh jump ship."

"I don't think so. What makes you believe that?"

I done know sir. I just gots dis feelin' dat sometin' goin' tuh happen."

"I don't believe that. The men all understand that we must head for the Pacific."

"It's duh Greenies, Sir. I bin ahearin' some scuttlebutt over duh past few days an' it now seems tuh make sense tuh me."

"I think you're exaggerating what you've been hearing. What you've been feeling. Return to your watch. All will be okay. Believe me."

As Abe climbs the ladder to the main desk he says to himself, well I jus' saved my ass. No one can now accuse me of organizin' or even taken part in duh jump. I just outsmarted duh Lesters.

Just before midnight Abe sees bo'sun coming out of the galley hatch and approaches him.

"How are things going?" asks Bellingham.

"Fine, jus' fine, Bo'sun."

"It does seem to be getting colder, doesn't it?"

"Yes, sir," Bennett says.

"I just made a new pot of coffee," directing it to Abe. "I'll take your watch while you go below."

"Dat's not a bad idea," Abe responds. "I guess I will."

What's dat bastard up ta, Abe thinks. He's never been dis nice ta me. He must be part of Lester's plan.

"How about you?" bo'sun asks Bennett.

"That's not my problem. I really gotta hit the head."

"Be my guest," Bellingham says as the two men head for the galley hatch.

As soon as they disappear, bo'sun heads for the forecastle hatch and quickly screws the hasp on the door and snaps the padlock. He stops for a moment. He hears someone moving around on the other side. I don't hear snoring, that's for sure, he says to himself. He quickly returns to the top of the gangway.

Abe returns to the gangway before Bennett and thanks bo'sun. "Where's dat damn Bennett?" says Abe. "He mus' be shittin' his brains out."

A few minutes before midnight Abe hears pounding. He moves back from the gunwale opening. It is coming from the forecastle hatch. He walks up to it.

"Well, I'll be damned," Abe says as he sees the hasp and lock on the hatch. "So dats why Lester was so sure dat everythin' i'd be okay."

Just then 8 bells begins striking as Jorge and his mate assume the watch.

"It's a quite night," Abe says and smiles at them as they pass.

At 4 bells the following morning, the bo'sun and quartermaster are waking the mates and boat handlers.

"You're to get us underway. Tell the handlers. Be quick about it."

In minutes the men are topside hauling the slack out of the hawsers attaching *Tranquility* to the wharf. The men jump on the gangway as it is being raised aboard the ship. Andrew has two topsails raised, just enough to catch a brisk wind that pushes *Tranquility* away from the dock.

The quartermaster feels pressure on the wheel and watches as the bow slowly moves away from the dock. In minutes she overcomes the water's drag and slips past the seaward end of the wharf.

"Bo'sun," Capt. Lester says with one foot out of the wheelhouse. "Go unlock the fo'c's'le hatch and ask the men why they missed breakfast."

Chapter 31

A Forced Hibernation

Monday, July 15, 1867. Day 586

As *Tranquility* clears Jackson Harbor early in the morning, those still on deck are astounded by what they see when she rounds the headland. The lookout cries, "Ships ho!" and those still below decks rush topside. It is a magnificent sight. Ahead lay four vessels, all ships of the line, and all flying the stars and stripes from their main and mizzenmasts. Their poles are only lightly canvassed. From tall-unfaired stacks amidships, just after the main, they belch plumes of thick, black smoke. It looks almost like whalers' smoke.

The fleet is barely making way, as if waiting on station to intercept vessels departing the Falklands.

"The ships look like they are waiting for us to come out," says Bellingham.

The exception is one frigate in the lead. The helmsman slowly swings the bow of *Tranquility* northward and the other vessel picks up speed and approaches. It pulls along *Tranquility*'s starboard side. Running entirely on steam she slows as she comes abeam.

"What ship are you?" someone speaks *Tranquility*.

"The whaleship *Tranquility*, nigh onto 542 days out of Sag Harbor," answers 1st Mate Andrew Lester, who is in command of the watch.

"And what ship are thee?" Bellingham yells back.

"We are the *U.S.S. Pawnee*, part of the South Atlantic Squadron, Rear Admiral S. W. Codon, commanding. Behind me is his flagship, the *U.S.S. Brooklyn*. My captain is Commander T. H. Peterson," is the response.

"And who commands your vessel?"

"Where are you heading?"

"To the Horn," Lester answers.

"At this time of year?"

The response sounds familiar to Lester and his mates.

"Aye, at this time of year, but not directly. We plan to wait out the winter in a leeward bay on West Falkland before making the grand move."

"A wise decision," comes the reply from the *Pawnee*.

"To your first question, it is Capt. Hiram Lester," says Andrew.

"What is your business here?" asks Andrew.

"To ensure your safety. How did the British treat you?"

"They were thieves," Ephraim Brown yells back.

"Did they take all your money?"

"Never!" he yells back.

"Do you need any assistance?"

"We are well," Andrew Lester says after glancing toward his brother for approval. "Thank you."

"Safe voyage," he yells back as his ship retreats from the encounter.

All during the conversation with the *U.S.S. Pawnee*, Abe, Jolly and Bennett are along the bulkhead just aft of the forecastle.

"Dere's duh best reason I knows fer not takin' over dis ship," says Abe. "Da Navy would run us down in no time. Jumpin's duh best idea."

Tranquility is set on a northeasterly course as she leaves Berkeley Sound, a large bay on her larboard side. Expectedly, the winds pick up force as they round the northeast corner of West Falkland Island. They blow above 30 knots and create a snotty sea as the helmsman gradually begins turning the ship more southerly. Now on a west-by-northwest heading, the larboard side of the ship is being battered by the southerly winds. There is no sun so Lester cannot take a reading. However, he is not too concerned because the visibility is unlimited.

From a chart Number 1 procured in Stanley, Lester determines that they must cover 60 miles before they can turn at Cape Dolphin and head into the beginning of Falkland Island Sound. Nor will that be a pleasant ride because the ship will face headwinds. They will have to turn southwest to find a wind to push them. Lester estimates that it should be about noon the next day before they can turn directly downwind. Because the crossing the next day might be in shallow waters he orders the watch to begin taking soundings at daybreak.

Just before noon, *Tranquility* clears Cape Dolphin and enters Falkland Sound. The small pocket bay they are trying to locate is still another 30 miles farther. En route, they are lulled toward two false entrances as they hug the Sound's west side. Just before sunset, they stand off the mouth of what will someday become Port Howard.

"What was the last sounding?" Lester asks Jorge Pilla.

"Eleven fathoms, Sir."

"Number 2, prepare to lower the anchor. We will stay the night here. I dare not try to find an inside anchorage at this late hour."

Wednesday, July 17, 1867

"Mr. Pilla," Lester says to Jorge, "after you finish breakfast, have Number 3 lower his boat and take a lead with him. Number 1, accompany him. Find a suitable depth as close to the leeward shore as possible and then return. We dare not go in blind. Also, keep in mind that the anchorage you pick will be our home for the next 90 days, maybe more."

Two hours later, the whaleboat returns and comes alongside its mother ship.

"The depth in this small, well-protected bay is remarkable," says Andrew Lester. "In one place, we found 4 fathoms plus of water just 3 rods (49.5 feet) off the beach, and a sandy beach at that. The tide appears to be at dead low. It will only get deeper. The beach is about 7 rods wide and under a steep cliff that towers almost vertically for more than 200 feet."

"Have the watch weigh anchor," Lester orders.

After anchoring in Adair's Harbour, a part of Port Howard, life on *Tranquility* changes greatly, and to no one's benefit, other than they are still alive. Almost immediately, the ship is surrounded by forming ice. For the first week, no one can go ashore until the ice is thick enough to hold a man's weight.

Tranquility and her crew find themselves in a surreal world. A strange sense of immobility is cast upon them. Each man must now address this phenomenon in his own unique way. For some, boredom is almost immediate. The skies now are perpetually cloudy. Fog often moves in and lingers for days and weeks on end. It snows but it is never heavy, always light. Occasionally, it does get above freezing during mid-day.

In a very real sense, they are prisoners.

"Why are you rooting around the trunks?" a just awakened John Daily yells from his bunk in the shiphandler quarters.

"I'm lookin. Just looking," answers Henry Dibble, the ship's carpenter.

"Lookin' for what? Christ, it ain't even light yet. Chips, go back to bed!"

"I'm looking for some teeth, whale's teeth. I threw some back here a couple months ago; the last time we did a sperm. I can't find 'em."

"Damn it," Dibble says and stomps out of the shiphandler quarters.

I guess he's planning on more scrimshaw, Daily says to himself as he pulls the blanket over his head.

Not until October 23 will they haul anchor. They had imprisoned in limbo exactly 100 days.

The quickest way around South America, told by the mates who have sailed into the Pacific, would be Drake Passage that separates two continents. The passage lies closest to Cape Horn on South America. Then, they could swing to the south'ard once land is cleared. Some thought the skipper should play it safe and go through the Straits of Magellan. Bets are placed until the captain tells them the course is through Drake Passage because it is the quickest way into the Pacific.

CHAPTER 32

Ice Out

Wednesday, October 23rd, 1867, Day 686

Instead of running north, then west around the jagged coast of West Falkland, then sailing through a vast number of rocky shoals and threading through innumerable small islands, Lester decides to continue southwest down the length of Falkland Channel. *Tranquility* departs Port Howard near noon on October 23rd. In 24 hours, under half-sail, she covers the 120 miles to Cape Meredith, the southern tip of West Falkland Island. The ship continues in the same direction but now, as she clears the last land to the west, she feels the full brunt of the westerly winds.

This is a formidable undertaking for Lester, his crew and for the ship. Their destination, 25-mile wide La Maire Strait, lies 400 hundred miles away. It is likely to be 400 miles of the worst seas imaginable. Cape San Diego, the most easterly tip of the island of Tierra del Fuego, momentarily forms the strait's western shore. The other demarcation, on the east, is the western edge of Staten Island.

Gale force winds (39 to 54 mph) unmercifully batter the bark and her crew. Her forward speeds range between 3 and 5 knots. However, she isn't always moving forward. Not until the sixth day, Tuesday, October

29th, does the crew see Staten Island. They are spurred on because they know that the tip of South America is just over the horizon. However, there is a problem, there is no horizon. The winds blow furiously and for most of the time the sky is cluttered with hail or snow.

Rather than swing westward to enter the short strait, Lester decides to come up close to the north shore of Staten Island, looking for any bit of lee that he might find. He is hoping to wait out the raging storm and repair parts of the ship's rigging that have been shivered and ripped to shreds. Ironically, there is no good time to wait out the winds. On average, they are gale force for 200 days out of a year. During the remaining 164 days, the winds are "just blowing hard."

As they round a shallow point on the island, in a short bay, they are surprised to see another ship hove-to off the beach. "This looks like a good spot to spend a day or two," says Capt. Lester.

As they approach the ship from astern, her hail port reveals that she is the *Yankee Miss*, a whaler out of New Bedford.

She has just come through Drake Passage and has suffered damage to her rigging. The lee, behind Staten Island, is the first place her captain said he could reach to make repairs. The ship is laden with rendered whale oil. The Pacific has been good to them.

The crews exchange stories and the spirit of the men on *Tranquility* is heightened by descriptions of whales being everywhere in the Pacific.

"How long will you hold here?" Capt. Rufus Jones asks Lester as Jones enters Lester's cabin.

"Two or three days," he answers. "We have been holed up for a hundred days in West Falkland waiting for a chance to round the Horn. The crew is eager to get back to whaling, and maybe home before year's end. As soon as the weather breaks, we'll try."

"What course do you plan?" asks Jones.

"Why, though the Strait. Just as you did," Lester answers.

"You'd be mad to try that!" said Jones. "That is no storm you see blowing out there now. Captain, that is the way it always blows at this latitude. That is why they call these the Roaring Forties and the Furious Fifties.

"Have you ever run Drake Strait?"

"Yes, I have, twice," says Lester. "It was no Plum Pudding voyage but we managed. We passed with the ship fully rigged."

"What time of year was that?"

"The last time, it was just before Christmas, in '62."

"You don't know how lucky you were. I hear tell that occasionally the winds do go down to 10 knots when it's summer here. But these are rare occurrences.

"We made it through because we had the wind to our back," emphasizes Jones. "You will have it on your bow. I sincerely believe that most of the time your bow will be under water. Hell, Sir, we constantly rode on 30- and 40-foot seas, but the winds were on our backsides. The worst part was that we had little control going down the backs of the big ones and at the bottom we were often about to broach-to broadside to the wind. More than once I feared we would capsize.

"Yes, captain, we made it through but I will never make that trip again at this time of the year. Never!"

The next morning Lester asks his brother to assemble all the mates, shiphandlers and boat steerers in the officer's mess.

"As soon as we get a break in this wind, I want to strike for the Horn," Hiram tells to them. "But before we can, we must set the ship to rights, make her ready for the worst possible weather and seas we will ever encounter. I want you all to begin that work immediately. I know not when the winds might go down. I want the heavy-weather sails on the main and fore.

"If there are any sails that look weak, I want them replaced now and not in a gale. All the lines have stretched since we left Stanley. I want them all tuned, tightened. I want all the deck fittings checked and double-checked.

"Double both fore and back stays and temporary shroud supports added to the fore and main. It's unlikely we'll use the royals and topgallants until we again are on a northerly course. Store them below so we can reduce some of the weight aloft.

"I would like to bring both anchors inside but I can't. We may have to use them at some point if we lose control of the ship. However, make sure they are well lashed and secured. Make sure that the cables are clear on the windlass and not liable to jamming when we might need them the most.

"On deck, I want each boat crew to completely empty their craft and store everything in the blubber room. The 2nd mate will assign a space adequate to contain each boat's gear. Then, turn all the boats in their davits on their sides and secure them firmly against the hull. I want everything topside that can be moved, taken below decks for storage until we round the Horn. If it cannot be done then lash it well….very well.

"Take the two spare boats off the skids and lower them upside-down directly on the deck.

The shipsmith has access to a large number of deck rings. Have them double-bolted to the deck and secure the whaleboats to them.

"Chips, take a couple men with you and go into the hold and check every barrel. Make sure they will not move, even if we are turned upside down."

"Could that happen?" Ben who attended with Andrew asks.

"It could but I doubt it," Andrew answers.

"And, I ask each mate to make sure that all his men have heavy clothing and oil skins. If not, draw from the slop chest.

"Now gentlemen, let's make ready to round the Horn."

Three days after *Tranquility* anchors in the lee of Staten Island the winds began to fall. On the fourth day they are less than 10 knots. Ten-knot winds are unnatural for this time of year, or any time of year, in the 40s.

"The abating winds are luring us," say Capt Lester says to his brother. "I feel as if something tempting us the into a trap."

"Nonsense," says Andrew. "It is the long period of idleness that we all just experienced that has you thinking they way."

"If we are to go, now may be the time," Ephraim Brown says to Lester. "We cannot wait here indefinitely." His two superstitious Portuguese mates, however, are against it.

"It really doesn't seem to matter when we go," says Andrew. "We are sure to face rough seas at any time. We might just as well go now because waiting is likely to be a waste of time."

After a deliberation that must have consumed Capt. Lester from the moment he set the anchor behind Staten Island, he finally makes a choice.

"Make ready to weigh anchor," he says. "It is against my better judgment but we will go."

CHAPTER 33

Reaching for Horn Island

October 26, 1867, Day 689

Only 140 miles separate the Strait of Jacob le Maire from Cape Horn on Horn Island but it will be the most challenging 140 miles *Tranquility* will ever be called upon to cross. The winds are relatively light, 10 to 15 knots, as she rounds the west end of Staten Island on a southwest heading. This amiable condition lasts but 30 minutes before the seas rise in height and wind speeds climb. Two hours later, the winds again blow steadily at 40 knots. The ship bucks back and forth like a child's rocking horse.

Andrew Lester intently scans all the sails from the wheelhouse. He sees that there is too much canvas on the mainmast and orders men aloft to put reefs in the main and furl the three jibs. As the men attempt to go aloft, a large wave breaks over the larboard stern quarter and two men are swept against the safety rope that tops the gunwales.

This was a close call, Andrew says to himself, a warning, a hint of things to come.

The gray horizon ahead is dimpled with small icebergs and demands the helmsman to be on constant alert. The strain on the huge wheel is great but the quartermaster cannot clip the wheel because of the constant demand to change rudder direction. Seeing this, Lester orders Diogo to find another man to aid in holding the wheel. A few minutes later he returns with Egas Sanchez.

For a few moments, near noon, the sun appears as a bright spot in the gray overcast. Lester grabs the sextant, rushes outside, and attempts to take a reading. He is tossed back and forth against the gunwale outside the wheelhouse. Jorge grabs and holds him as steady as he can.

"Impossible," says Lester. "The glass is covered with spray. I can't find the sun."

Winds howl constantly throughout the night and tear furiously at the rigging. There isn't a line that isn't seen approaching its breaking point. At one time the wind's pitch rises so high that the sound pierces the ears of anyone who isn't below decks.

"It is like a troop of banshees screaming, shrieking and screeching," says Joshua Edwards.

Little sleep takes place that night in the fo'c's'le. The Greenies are so scared that a few tie themselves into their bunks. Nor is there a rush to visit the galley. A few who did brought back pockets of hardtack. About mid-morning, the solid overcast begins to reveal a layer of broken clouds. From time to time, the sun breaks through. By noon the sky over Antarctica is clear but the winds howl both day and night. They are a constant.

"We've made little progress," Andrew says. His brother had asked him to take the reading. "We've logged but 18 miles in the last 36 hours. It will take us forever to reach Cape Horn," he says with a bit of jest.

"That is," says Jorge, "if the ship holds together until then."

"This is a well-made, sturdy vessel," Lester defends her.

"That's true," says Pilla, "but only if we stay off the rocks. There are many shoals and rocks in close to Horn Island. A wide berth will put us away from land but into rougher weather."

"Which would you prefer?"

"Neither," says Jorge.

"I will settle for less of both and pray for help," says Andrew.

"Captain! Captain!" a man yells as he pounds on the captain's door during the next night. "There is a violent banging on deck. Mr. Lester says it is one of the spare whaleboats. It has broken free of its lashings."

"Has he ordered anyone to go forward to secure the boat?" Lester asks.

"He is in the process. He told me to relay the message to you."

"I'll be right there."

Wave after wave, sometimes with slush ice in it, sweeps over the bow of the ship each time she dips into the black-colored sea. The winds have risen above 40 knots.

"I sent two men forward to secure the loose boat," Andrew tells his brother as the captain enters the wheelhouse.

"Send four men into the main and bring below what's left of the top gallants and royals," says Hiram.

Andrew leaves the wheelhouse and disappears down the companionway, hurriedly passes through the mates' and shiphandler's quarters and arrives in the forecastle where few men are asleep. He orders the first four men he sees to go aloft.

In the Stygian darkness, the men labor for more than an hour in the rigging. They are slowed by bitter winds that cover them with freezing spray and snow. Their fingers are dulled, red, raw and swollen. As difficult as it is in the rigging, men trying to secure the loose whaleboat have an even more difficult task. Each time they rise on the wet, slippery, ice-covered deck to lift the boat back to the deck rings they are battered by powerful waves that persistently knock them down. The reduced sail has an immediate effect but causes the ship to slow only slightly. Sensing this, three men again attempt to secure the boat.

Again, as they are lifting the stern of the whaleboat, a horrendous wave plows under the stern of the ship. The men are smashed against the deck. This time, the stern of the boat comes down upon one man, violently landing on his legs. The others, struggle to survive, while half of the time they are under water. They haul themselves, hand over hand, back to the platform, using the boat's lines onto which they tenaciously hold. Once upright, they discover that the third man is missing.

Gerald LeRoy was knocked unconscious. The wave that flattened him pushed him to the gangway. Three lifeline ropes there were inadequate protection. In the darkness no one saw the event unfold. The escaping water swept LeRoy beneath the lowest line, washing him overboard.

Realizing what has happened, Andrew, who had been outside the wheelhouse near the base of the mainmast, orders the two remaining men below. He meets them in the forecastle and then tells four new men to secure the boat.

"Before you go topside," he instructs, "take enough line. Bend an oversized bowline on one end and double-loop it under your arms. Secure the bitter end to the mainmast before you head for the whaleboat."

"Gerald was a good man," says an exhausted John Coachman who had been trying to secure the whaleboat. LeRoy had come onboard in Barbados where they had been close friends. "He has a wife and four children. Now who will take care of them?"

There is no sunrise the next day as *Tranquility* continues to edge her way closer to Cape Horn Island. Her sails are reduced to a bare minimum, just enough to maintain forward movement and retain her ability to maneuver. There is no real reason to maneuver the ship because the wind never changes direction. The helmsman keeps the compass card at 225 degrees and the winds persist at speeds of 40 to 50 knots.

The ship labors for two more days before a slight break occurs in the winds. On the morning of the 10th of November, Ben and Edwards go topside to check the tie-downs on the whaleboats.

""Finally," says Edwards as they cross the main deck, "we got a break."

"It's my present from Michabo," says Ben.

"What the hell are you talking about? A present? Who's Michabo?"

"Today's my birthday. My other God is Michabo."

"They've dropped to 15 knots," says Edwards. "That was some present. Does he have any other presents up his sleeve?"

Immediately, Capt. Lester orders Andrew to unfurl all sails.

Andrew says to Ben as they both climb the rigging, that he doesn't think that this is a wise move. This is the first time he has ever heard Andrew criticize his brother.

The leftover seas are still mountainous and the bow occasionally plunges more deeply into a trough than is safe. After taking on a few waves, the captain sends word to quickly shorten several sails. By mid-morning, the sun breaks through a sky layered with fluffy, high cotton-like clouds. By noon Cap'n Lester is able to take a reading.

"We've come 75 miles from Staten Island," he says to the mates who regularly gather around him when they see the sextant in his hand. "If this weather holds, we can make Cape Horn in another full day of sailing."

Lester is fooled by a "sucker hole" in the weather that is short-lived. A half hour after the captain stows the sextant, the winds are again up. Within the hour, they are back to 40 knots as men race through the rigging, quickly shortening sails. The winds return with even greater vengeance, as if to make up for the lull.

The mate on watch at sunset notes the increasing number and size of the icebergs. Posting a watch in the bow is useless because that part of the ship again is constantly under water. Each time a wave smashes into the transom, *Tranquility's* bow crashes down with greater and greater vibrations as 20- and 30-foot waves pass under her hull. Near daybreak the following day, 11 November, during the change in helmsmen, the relief looks forward on the ship and realizes that one of the whaleboats is missing.

"Did you hear any noise?" Hiram questions the man who was relieved.

"Yes, Sir," he answers. "There were noises everywhere. The smashing of the ship into oncoming waves was so loud that it could have happened at any of those moments."

Scant pieces of debris lie scattered about the deck that had held the spare larboard whaleboat. The free ends of lines used to lash it down now lie haphazardly forward. Nothing else remains.

"Thank God she was a spare and empty of gear," Ephraim says that morning as he and the mates try to eat breakfast. "We still have to refit the other spare boat."

"Always thinking of money," Hiram says. "Always."

"Someone must," Brown answers.

"Don't you ever think of anything else? Food? Your wife? Home? God?"

He doesn't answer.

"Is money your real god?"

Still Ephraim doesn't answer.

Just before sunset on November 12, the bowsprit breaks loose under the weight of a massive wave. It is washed aft against the foremast. All the lines and stays that support it and hoist the jib sails are pulled out of the water. They now clutter the foredeck. Lester orders Diogo to get out a crew and clean up the mess. In the failing light, Miguel Dos Santos is washed overboard. Fortunately, his lifeline is short and saves him. He dangles off the edge of the ship with his feet touching water before the others finally pull him back on deck. It is a close call, too close a call. That bothers Hiram and he now believes that he made the wrong decision not to wait longer. Even one man is too much to lose, he thinks. What if Dos Santos hadn't tied a line on himself? *I will have to answer someday to God.*

Chapter 34

The Decision for Another Route

Wednesday, November 13, 1867, Day 707

"The seas are worsening," Andrew tells his brother as Hiram arrives in the wheelhouse. The small structure is also crowded with Jorge and Abe. "Winds now seldom drop below 50 and at times, I'm sure, reach 60 knots. I was in the bilge and found more water than usual. I have the inside pumps manned. It didn't take long to clear but there now is more seepage than in the past. I fear the planks cannot take much more of this pounding.

"Even if the ship can take this pounding, I fear the crew cannot and likely will not. The near loss of one man and the man over-the-side a few evenings ago has them arguing for a change of course. One cannot blame them."

"Dis is a hell of a time tuh be worryin' 'bout duh plankin'," Abe whispers to Jorge. Jorge does not answer but keeps his attention focused on the waves the bow of the ship is crashing into. Andrew, too, has heard Abe's comments but says nothing.

No one else ventures a response. The responsibility is that of the captain. It is evidently wearing heavily upon him. He realizes that his hesitancy is again getting him into trouble. He is losing face with his mates. Indecision is flashing back and forth across his mind. Without saying a word, he retreats to his cabin.

"Not much of a cap'in, eh?" asks Abe.

"What?" asks an astonished Andrew.

"If'n I wuz dah skipper I'd a turned her 'round a long time ago. Hell, can't ya hear her talkin'? She's amoanin' an' groanin'. She's bitchin' like a fat sow in heat. She's not gunna take much more of dis.

"I had enough of dis shit," he says and leaves the wheelhouse.

At noon on the next day the sun is no more than a hot-looking, bright, white spot in the southern sky. However, it is enough for Lester to shoot and get a rough fix on their position.

We've moved but 12 miles from where we were three days ago, he says to himself after calculating the new position. It's unusual that none of the mates are about me as they are when the position is read. He looks down from the quarterdeck and sees Diogo coming on deck.

"Diogo," he says, "will you get to the other mates and boat steerers and ask them to join me here immediately?"

In a few minutes, the quarterdeck is filled.

"Gentlemen," he says, "you all have been masterful in handling *Tranquility* in this dire situation. I believe that we could still round the Cape if we were to go on, but I feel it is too much of a price to ask of you and this fine ship. Therefore, when we break up, prepare to wear ship (turn the ship so the wind now blows on the ship's other side) because it is too dangerous to come about until we can find some wind to push astern. But fear not, the Pacific shall still feel the cut of *Tranquility's* keel.

"We are presently about 50 miles due south of the island of Tierra del Fuego and the entrance to Beagle Channel. I propose to cross into the Pacific through that waterway. Initially I hesitated to choose it because it is so narrow and long. My charts reveal that at times it narrows in width to less than 2 miles and will take some expert navigating and helm work. But, I know we can do it. It is about 90 miles long. If the wind direction holds, and I have no reason to believe otherwise, we will, most of the way, be on one long reach with the wind off the larboard stern.

"On our reach for the beginning of the channel, the winds are likely to be off our starboard stern. I caution you not to let the wind turn us about from the rear for that could capsize this ship. Otherwise, it should be a fairly fast run. We will not enter the Channel in the dark. Instead, we will come about and find some shoal water in which to anchor after the sun sets or, more appropriately the light goes out, and resume our direction at daybreak. If the winds be too strong, which I believe they probably will be, we shall wear ship rather than anchor."

Hiram Lester doesn't hear the cheer when news of his decision reaches the forecastle. It would have heartened him.

Rather than take a heading slightly east of north on returning to Tierra del Fuego, Lester chooses to shorten the distance somewhat to the actual point of entry to Beagle Channel by sailing west of two islands that guard the entrance to the passageway. The next morning, November 14, they reach Goree Roads, a passage between Navarino Island on the west, which forms the southern constriction of the channel for a third of its length, and much smaller Lennox Island on the east. Lester follows the east shore of Navarino as it slowly curves eastward and squeezes between it and Picton Island now on his starboard (north) side.

Just as the ship enters the passage the winds fall to just a breeze. It is the first time in days that *Tranquility* rides quietly in a westerly direction. Past Pitcon, the channel narrows sharply. Twenty-five miles into the channel Gable Island lies just ahead. It looks like a plug in a bottle with no way around. Lester quickly checks a chart he holds in his hands. He decides to skirt it on its north side. He is worried because the ship has had some difficulty making way in the light winds.

"We don't have a lot of maneuvering space," Adrian Moore, the quartermaster at the wheel says to Capt. Lester who is standing just outside the wheelhouse.

"We are being squeezed by that glacier," Lester says and automatically points to it. "It flows down from a northern valley on Tierra del Fuego and has sharply narrowed the passage."

"We may be lucky," Moore says to Lester. "The speed of the tide's current squeezed between the glacier and rocks has increased since we entered the passage. I can feel it buffeting the rudder."

The ship moves almost silently, swiftly, as it is about to clear the island. Suddenly the ship heaves forward then rights itself as a dull grinding sound is heard throughout the ship. It again stops, but just for a second as the grinding is heard again. In the blink of an eye, *Tranquility* is free and continues down a widening strait.

"That was close," says Lester.

"Bo'sun," Lester says to Bellingham who is also on the quarterdeck, "send someone below to see if there is any damage."

In a few minutes a crewman returns and says all is fine.

"Good," says Lester.

That evening, the ship is hoved-to and is anchored in a small cove off a nameless island. For the first time the crew has been able to see a glorious sun setting over snow-capped mountains with long glaciers filling the valleys.

The next morning, November 15, Lester faces an option. The chart reveals that the channel bifurcates just a few miles ahead of their anchorage. North Channel to starboard continues for another 50 miles while the south channel is only 25 miles long. South Channel abruptly turns south just before entering the open Pacific Ocean.

"We'll surely face gale winds if we take the southern course and are again on the open ocean," Lester says to his mates as they huddle over a chart on the table. He points to the place as he speaks. "It will be 20 or 25 miles before we can turn on a northwest heading. It will mean a beam sea for a few days. Once we near 50 degrees latitude, we should be sailing due north. It will save us two, maybe three days.

"I plan to take the shorter route!"

No one disagrees.

After the meeting breaks up Chips appears in the officer's mess.

"Sir, may I have a word with you?" asks Michael Astor.

"What is it, Chips?"

"I was below, shoring up some of barrels, when I noticed more than the usual amount of water in the bilge."

"Andrew," Lester yells to his brother who is on the ladder and heading topside. "Please come here a moment.

"Chips said there is more than the usual amount of water in the bilge. Will you go below and check it out?"

A few minutes he returns and enters Lester's cabin.

"It appears that the ship has sprung a leak," says Andrew. "It was either the rough pounding we took before entering the channel or the grounding that took place in the passage."

"Will you see to it?"

"Of course. Immediately."

CHAPTER 35

The Pacific, At Last A Real Reason to "....Splice the Main Brace."

November 17, 1867, Day 711

"At mid-morning, *Tranquility* cleared a delta of rocky islets that guard the western entrance to the southern approach of Beagle Channel," Lester writes that evening in the ship's log. "We are now in the Pacific. It is a grand occasion. I saw fit that the men should splice the main brace. I, too, even sipped a dram. So did the Indian. Everyone has earned it."

Though they are again being buffeted by strong westerlies, the winds seem to hang below 40 knots. Andrew is able to raise more canvas than they had flown when they first approached Horn Island. The ship's bilge pumps still need a watchful eye. Andrew has assigned Ben to check the bilge every morning.

November 21, 1867, Day 715

"Ben found 32 inches of water today," Andrew tells Hiram. "I went down to check it again with him and found a slightly-open seam. It was on the curve of the bow, in about 4 inches of water. I had Ben find Daily and he got some worn sail. I wrapped it around a board longer than the open seam and nailed it in place. Water now only slowly seeps in. It holds but bears continued watching."

"What a relief," Hiram says. "Now we can continue hunting as we head for Valparaiso. At first I feared we'd have to make a dash for land."

"We still might," answers Andrew.

November 22, 1867, Day 716

"Today we saw our first pod of whales," writes Lester in the logbook. "They were finback whales. They swim too fast for our whaleboat crews to ever hope to stick one. They, too, are heading north and disappeared ahead of us. Ben reported just 2 inches of bilge water this morning. It seems nothing to worry about."

Fifteen hundred miles separates *Tranquility* from Valparaiso, the seaport city that serves Santiago, the Chilean capitol at the base of the Andes Mountains. The ship's stores are low and were only scantily replaced in Stanley. Even Brown is in favor of restocking the larder. Andrew and Ben are still concerned with the leakage. It is like an albatross around their necks. Though it is still small Andrew knows it can open at any time. The pounding *Tranquility* took trying to round the Horn still haunts the ship. He knows that there is a naval base in Valparaiso and several big yards.

Two days later Andrew is startled by the water level in the bilge.

"I fear we must make for Valparaiso as soon as possible," Andrew says to his brother as he enters his cabin. "There was a foot of water this morning. I worry we might even spring a plank and it could not be filled before we could stuff the hole. I told Ben to check it at dinner and supper every day. It might even require a man on watch all the time."

"How much time have we?" asks Hiram.

"That I cannot predict. I do know that we are now approximately 1400 miles from Valparaiso. The distance can be covered quickly because winds now blow from the south along the Chilean coast and are in concert with the direction of the Peruvian-Chilean current."

Speed is not Hiram Lester's immediate goal, even though his ship's hull needs attention. After running north across the 50th latitude, Lester posts four men in the lookouts and cuts daytime watches to three hours. He plans to continue hunting whales and again has the ship hove-to each day between sunset and daybreak. All this activity spurs the boat crews into feeling that they are once again whalers. Nor did the sighting of the pod of finbacks hurt their rising spirits. His last order for the day is to relieve Ben of his bilge duty and turn over the responsibility to the watch on duty. They are to have the bilge pumped every four hours when a new watch takes over.

Chapter 36

Whales Galore

November 24th, 1867, Day 718

Early in the morning, just after the day watch and lookouts are set, as *Tranquility* begins moving through the water, the call "She blows, She blows! She Blows!" rings out from aloft electrifying the crew on deck.

"Where away?" asks Diogo Pilla, whose crew is on watch.

"To larboard! To larboard," the response comes from aloft.

By then, Hiram Lester is on deck.

"Two, three, maybe more," he says as he glasses the waters off the larboard bow of the ship.

"There she blows," comes the voice of a lookout. "They're sperms."

"I see. I see," says Lester. "Diogo, send men aloft to furl the t'gallants and royals. We don't want to override these fish. They aren't sperms, they're right whales. Sperms do not like an ocean as cold as we are now on."

Diogo calls down the boat crews that are aloft and finds a shiphandler to replace the lookout in the mainmast.

"We are about to go awhaling," he yells.

The whales eventually number four and three boats are fast after them. By noon, three right whales are along the starboard side of *Tranquility* and the try-stage is set and cutting-in has begun.

Andrew is in charge of the deck and cutting-in and tells Jorge to lower his boat. Those in Pilla's crew who are on the cutting stage are glad for the change in work. Before sunset, the fourth whale is towed to *Tranquility*, just as the last blanket from the second whale slides through the blubber hatch.

Not until November 28th, Thanksgiving Day, is *Tranquility* again able to continue her trek northward along the Chilean coast. Lester calls for the crew to meet before the mainmast.

"Many of you may have forgotten," he speaks from the elevated quarterdeck, "but today is a holiday for many Americans. We have no chicken, let alone turkeys to serve, but for this evening's supper Cook will prepare the last of the mutton we picked up in Stanley. He is also is preparing enough plum duff for the entire crew. There will also be a ration of grog. Sip it slowly because the flagons are near empty. Later, we will thank God for what he has seen us through, but now, get back to work."

The crew's cheers move Lester. He goes below before anyone can see his response. On the way to his cabin, he hears the lookout once again yell, "Whale Ho! There she blows! She blows. She blows!"

Ironically, in Washington, D.C., just a day earlier, President Andrew Johnson issued a proclamation designating the last Thursday in November as a national holiday. Just before noon, Chips and three men from the forecastle are seen rigging sawhorses just aft on the main deck behind the mainmast. Two long benches have already been constructed and are temporarily stacked against the starboard gunwale.

"Wad duh hell yuh doin' here?" Abe yells at Chips.

"Captain's orders," is all Chips says and ignores him.

Other crewmen are pushing long, flat boards through the blubber hole and onto the main deck. Close behind the boards is a long roll of sailcloth. John Daily is at the edge of the hole. With the aid of a crewman they haul the boards onto the main deck.

The crewmen begin laying the boards across the sawhorses. Chips and Müller are close behind with hammer and nails. A few minutes later Daily and a crewman load the sailcloth onto one edge of the boards and Daily rolls it across to the other end.

"My god," Abe exclaims, "it's a table."

Back at the blubber hatch, other crewmen are passing food tubs topside while out of the rear hatch Pierre Batista is burdened with a large pan covered by a heavy towel.

"Ben," he says as he approaches the table, "will you tell the mates that all is ready? Also, whoever is sent to get the foremast crew, remind them to bring their forks and plates."

"Abe," says Andrew, "that's your job."

Within minutes the mates and everyone not involved in handling the ship are on the main deck. Capt. Lester is the last to emerge from the aft hatch. He looks into the rigging and then tells Andrew to call down all the watches.

"That is the first time in my life that I have celebrated a Thanksgiving," Ben says to Jeremiah Kinder who is sitting on the bench next to him. "Even though most people on my reservation are now Christians, no one feels the need to give thanks for what has happened to our land and people. And, those who are now flooding onto our reservation may have been thankful that they escaped the South, and that Lincoln made them free men, but none seemed to be especially thankful for anything else."

There is not enough room at the table to seat all of the ships 35 crewmembers. Those without seats stand, forming a semicircle around the forward end of the table. Capt. Lester, at the opposite end, bows his head and leads those who would follow in a short prayer. Andrew glances across the table at Abe Brown as he sits with his uncle. His hands are not folded nor is his head bowed.

After eating the crew dispersed about the deck with only those on watch attending to running the ship. Ben made for the bow to catch the breeze where he saw Chips working away on something in his hands as he sat on one of two windlasses.

"Everyone seems to be lollygagging around," Ben says to the older man as he stands watching Chips scratch on a large whale tooth.

"It's kinda like a day off," Chips answers. "It's called Rope Yarn Sunday. I know it ain't Sunday but every once in a while the crew is given the time to repair their cloths or do anything they want. I like to whittle away on my scrimshaw."

"What are you making?"

"Nothing complicated," Chips answers.

"This tooth's big enough so I can scratch a drawing of *Tranquility*.

"How does it look?" Chips asks as he hands the ivory to Ben.

"It really looks good," says Ben.

"When we get the next sperm," says Chips, "be sure to ask the mate on the cutting stage to let you have one. You can borrow some of my tools."

Thanksgiving Day marked a visible change in the fortunes of the men onboard *Tranquility*. The promise of better whaling in the Pacific is beginning to ring true. They have already collected four whales and the captain said this is just the beginning. They have been underway, at just cruising speed, for just a few days when Mr. Lester, the 1st mate and captain of Ben's whaleboat, tells him that he is moving him permanently from waist to harpooner and boat steerer.

"Bring your gear whenever you want to the harponeers' quarters," Andrew tells Ben.

During the trying-out of the four whales they had just finished, Edwards had badly scalded his right arm and leg while scooping oil from the try pot to the cooling pot. His arm and leg are still swollen from the accident and he is in great pain. Andrew moves Jed Blackman, one Negro picked up in Barbados, to take Ben's 18-foot mid-ship oar.

Not long thereafter Ben is to be tested more severely as a harpooner when another pod of whales is found. On December 4, 1867, exactly two years, 728 days, since *Tranquility* left Sag Harbor. Just as the lookouts go aloft, early in the day, one spots a whale blowing, then two more. By the time Capt. Lester orders the boats away six different spouts have been seen. From their unique spouts Lester and others know they are sperm whales.

"Isn't it unusual to find sperms so far to the south, especially at this time of the year?" Andrew asks his brother.

"I would never had thought them to be sperms but their tell-tale spouting gives them away," say Hiram..

Ben feels strange being in the bow and looking back at all the straining backs and muscles. He, too, mans an oar, the 16-foot harpoon oar. Once they are going onto a whale he will put it aside for the harpoon. Ben catches Mr. Lester looking at him from time to time as he mans the tiller. Each time, a slight smile spreads across his face. Ben thinks Andrew is nervous about what he must do. Maybe I am too, Ben says to himself.

The ride is quick. The water is smooth but with large, long swells as they seem to glide up one side and down the other. The whale they are after stays on top. It disappears for only a moment between swells when all that the crew can see are the spoutings.

The whale is lollygagging on top and oblivious to the approaching boat.

"He is big, at least 50 barrels, maybe more," Andrew whispers to the crew.

One moment the whale is there then next it is gone. Nor is there a spouting to be seen. The whale sinks deep into the water as it dives for the bottom. Lester tells the men to stop rowing as he notes that the water's surface where it had been seems to boil for a moment. This is the result of a flip of its powerful flukes. When the water settles, there is only an oily patch.

"That oily patch is a glip," Lester says to the crew as they begin scanning the water around them for the emergence of the behemoth.

"He can be down anywhere from a half to a full hour before he again comes up. We'll move a few hundred yards to the east, the direction he was pointed before he disappeared. He is too big a fish to leave and seek another."

As they wait the ocean calms even more since they lowered.

Nearly an hour after it dove the whale unexpectedly explodes through the surface a hundred yards in front of the whaleboat. The crew is startled as its entire body clears the surface creating a tremendous splash as it lands on the water.

"Count the blows," Mr. Lester says to Ben.

"One, two, three," he yells aloud without turning towards Andrew.

"He dives," Ben yells. "He dives."

"Let's do it all over again," says Mr. Lester.

The crew rows another 300 yards when Lester tells the men to peak oars. They wait. This time the whale is down a half-hour before coming up again. The boat is 200 yards away. The men immediately begin rowing.

The whale blows once as they begin their approach. It blows a second time as the distance is halved. The third time it blows they are a dozen boat lengths away. But before they can get close enough for Ben to put in the iron the whale, it lobtails.

Its head is down in the water, almost vertically, and only its flukes are exposed. The whale slaps them hard then disappears into the depths.

"He must be feeding on a school of squid," Lester says.

"A little closer this time. He's still moving in the same direction. I don't think we've gallied him."

The crew rows 400 yards then stops on Lester's command.

Ben is already on the clumsy cleat with his knee in it and the harpoon in both hands. Out of nowhere, a flock of crying, wheeling gulls suddenly appears just ahead of the boat. They are circling, squawking.

"Get ready," Lester says, "the birds have seen him. He's coming up."

No more than 50 yards away, the whale breaks the surface in a slow arc rather than pushing its body into the air. The men stroke quietly, then stop. The boat slides silently to the whale as it blows the first time.

The crew is very careful, especially in the direction in which they approach. Sperm whales feed hard chasing their food. They are sight feeders. Because of this, their eyes can see well forward and abeam, but they're blind abaft of their fins. This knowledge has been pounded into all four crews.

"Be wary of the sperm's jaws and a right's tail."

"Stow oars," Lester says in a whisper, "and silence your paddles."

That is also the signal for Ben to man the iron.

"Ben, check to see that the wooden match is in the harpon's head."

"It is!"

"Good."

The whale blows a second time, not bothered by the boat's approach.

"Ready on the iron," Lester says as Ben rises in the bow and braces his knee against the clumsy cleat.

"Wood to blackskin," Ben yells as they move onto the whale.

"Now! Now!"

Ben hauls back on the harpoon and picks a spot between the fin and its eye. Just as he is about to thrust the iron, the whale's massive eye rolls back and looks directly at Ben. He looks into me, Ben thinks to himself. For a moment, the Shinnecock is stunned as the whale's eye moves back and forth trying to get a better look at what is suddenly upon its back. Its stare pierces Ben. It is as if he, too, is being shot. It is something he will never forget. Never.

Ben's arm is in continual motion, going up, going forward, going down. He feels the first resistance as the iron's point breaks the whale's skin, then as it slices through the blubber. The harpoon stops only when it sinks to the wooden handle.

"To the hitches. It's into the half-hitches," he yells.

"Back off!" Lester yells at the crew.

"Back off now! Damn it. Now!"

The crew has already reversed the direction of the oars. They push like hell because they know the whale is about to sound, to bolt and dive. The huge flukes come down almost upon them. They have now been through this routine enough times that no one really needs directions. Every man in the whaleboat knows what he must immediately do. They clear the flukes by four feet as it slaps on the water. The flukes create a huge depression in the water that returns upon the boat like a waterfall.

The sperm dives and line begins rattling in a blur as it races around the loggerhead. The noise it makes is like someone playing a tattoo on a drum. In minutes, the towline clears the main tub and begins taking line from the second tub. The ¾-inch line is capable of lifting 3 tons but the force of an escaping whale can multiply that force. The whaleboat is violently jolted ahead as Lester begins to snub the line around the loggerhead. Ben is knocked backwards and the hatchet flies out of his hand. Fortunately it drops at his feet and he scrambles to regain it. The bottom of the main tub is coming up fast as Lester manages to snub another turn on the wooden loggerhead without burning his hands on the line. The outgoing line gradually slows, then abruptly stops. The inside bottom of the tub is exposed but the end of the warp is connected to a second, somewhat smaller tub also filled with line.

Ben waits with hatchet in hand to see if the line rises toward the surface. If it heads downward again he must chop the line to save the boat and crew.

"Steady," Lester says as he stands at the stern and watches, waiting to see what Ben will do.

"I'll help you," he yells forward.

"Steady, Steady. How does it run?" he asks, even though he can see the line almost as well as Ben.

"No change, Sir. Not up or down."

"Good. Keep an eye on it. If you see a change, immediately call out."

Ben's eyes are frozen on the taut line as it slowly begins to cut ahead like a knife through the water.

"He moves," Ben yells. "He is again on the move."

Slowly, the boat begins to move forward. Minutes go by before the line's angle begins to change. Ben grabs a tighter hold on the axe handle and is ready to strike.

When he is certain, he yells, "He rises. He rises."

"The sperm breaks the surface almost the full length of line away from the boat. Between swells Lester sees the whale spout again and again as it regains air. The behemoth makes no effort to swim away or dive. It is exhausted, breathless.

"Bend the oars; bend them sprightly," Andrew encourages the rowers.

The whaleboat speeds quickly from swell to swell as line is hastily retrieved and coiled in the tubs.

As they come onto the whale, just a dozen yards away, Lester yells at Ben to come abaft. He slaps him on the shoulder as they pass saying, "Another good job, Ben."

After places are exchanged Ben mans the tiller. He must bring Andrew as close as possible to the whale in order for him to "…disturb the whale's lungs or heart." The boat must be brought within one or two feet of the body and the lance driven again and again into the whale's vitals. Only when there's blood in the spout can he be sure that his efforts have been rewarded.

No sooner does Lester grab the spade than they are at the whale. He shoves it deeply, again and again. The whale bolts, clears the water for a moment and then stops.

"There's fire in the chimney," Lester declares, as the whale's spout turns red with blood.

"A good hit," says Paul Hicks, on the tub oar just ahead of Ben. "He must have really scrambled the lungs. He'll die fast."

And he did.

After hauling the whale to the cutting stage, the crew rows their whaleboat around to their stern davit on the larboard side of *Tranquility*. As they rise in the davit they see Hiram is at the gunwale.

"I have bad news," he says to Andrew as the boat is locked into the davits and the crew begins stepping onto the ship.

"Bad news? What kind of bad news?"

"The Morning Watch reported that there was almost two feet of water in the bilge. The pumps have been manned for the last hour and the water is slow to recede. You must give it your immediate attention."

A half-hour later Andrew finds his brother in his cabin.

"It is bad news," he tells Hiram.

"I found the padded board that I nailed to one seam. However, the opening in the seam has lengthened. When the water level gets lower I think I might be able to jam a folded piece of sailcloth into it.

"Hiram, I think we should make for Valparaiso as soon as possible."

Hiram slowly walks around his desk, deep in thought and with his hands crossed behind. He stops for a moment and stares out the transom windows. He turns to Andrew.

"If we work the crew day and night we can finish the sperm in two days.

"We are about 1,300 miles from Valparaiso. Let's see, that will take about 8 days if we can, as you said, count on a fair southerly wind and ride the ocean current north. Let's do it. But, do not tell the crew until the last of the blubber is rendered and stored. I don't want anyone one worried about sinking and taking a short cut on oil so we could leave immediately."

However, two crewmen begin manning the topside deck bilge pump just forward of the foremast. A large stream of water pours onto the deck, escaping through scuppers under the gunwales. It is a steady stream because they can see that two more men are relieving the men on the pump every hour. The forecastle is aware of what is happening.

Two days later, the 6th of December, everyone is apprised of the situation. Knowledge of the growing leak became common knowledge because men on watch in the bilge as well as those on deck were rotated every hour until everyone had a hand in the effort. Abe has been in the forecastle stirring trouble by attacking Hiram Lester because he did not scuttle the whale and leave immediately.

"How's the bilge level?" Hiram asks Andrew while shooting the sun.

"The pumps are being manned day and night. They can't seem to get the level below a foot. This morning, it was 28 inches."

"Hiram, you must make a decision soon. Doesn't it seem damned ironic, just when we are finally into a horde of whales that we are confronted with a leaky ship and hungry men?"

"What would you do if you were in this situation?"

Andrew Lester ponders but a few moments before answering. These problems have also been on his mind because he, too, has been looking at them as the captain he was and not the 1st mate he is.

"I would wait no longer, there is too much to lose. I think we should try to make Concépcion. The distance is considerably shorter than Valparaiso, and given the rate we are flooding, we might not even make it there."

"Andrew, I believe you are right. It would be humiliating if we sank en route to Valparaiso when Concépcion is so much closer. Set the course immediately. Let's do it."

Chapter 37

The Run For Land

December 3rd, 1867 Day 730

After more than a week under full sails, both day and night, *Tranquility* is a hundred miles out off Concépcion. En route only one whale is spotted. The crew knows for sure that the ship is in trouble when Capt. Lester doesn't hove-to *Tranquility*. Even Ephraim doesn't feel bad because the whale never resurfaces.

"This is the first time on this voyage," Hiram Lester says to his brother as they share a corner of the quarterdeck, "that I don't mind not seeing whales resurface."

Hiram leaves but Andrew enters the wheelhouse.

"Have you checked the log lately?" he asks Quartermaster Moore.

"I have, Sir. We are making only 4 knots. I would have thought, with the current and a fair wind and all the sail we have aloft, that we would have been making 7, maybe more."

"How does she run?" he asks

"She seems to be lumbering, sluggish and slow to respond to the wheel," he answers.

"I, too, notice that," says Andrew, "the bow dips deeper into the back of a wave than she should. I think I know what is causing it."

"What is that, Sir?"

"We are riding lower in the water and that is slowing us. We are carrying too much water in the bilge. I'm going below to check."

Andrew is taken aback by what he hears as he drops down the ladder in the darkness to the bilge. Water sloshes back and forth as the boat lunges forward then aft as the bow rises and falls.

Where's the watch? He asks himself. Someone is supposed to be here all the time.

He lights a lantern hanging just above his head.

"My God!" he exclaims as he sees the amount of water flooding the bilge. He abruptly turns and climbs the ladder and races toward the galley. He sees Bellingham filling a coffee cup.

"Bo'sun, who has the watch?"

Bellingham pauses for a moment. "It is Abe Brown's watch, Sir."

"Where is he?"

"I saw him in his bunk a half hour ago."

Andrew rushes to the mate's quarters and sees Abe thumbing through a well-worn magazine. He drops it when he hears Andrew yell.

"Where's your man on watch in the bilge?"

"In dah bilge, I guess."

"He's not! Find all the men on your watch and lay below with them and man the pumps before we sink."

A half-hour later Andrew returns to the bilge and sees Abe and four of his men. The crew mans both bilge and deck pumps and is working furiously.

"Not much progress," Abe says to Andrew as he checks the water level. "I don't know what more to do."

"I do," says Andrew and rushes back up the ladder.

"Any progress?" asks Bellingham.

"No! Get help and find every bucket on this ship. Get a man for each bucket and send them down to the bilge. Oh yes, be sure to uncap the scuppers on steerage."

Within minutes 14 men and their buckets are in the bilge.

Andrew lines them up, an arm's length apart. They extend from the bilge to the second deck where steerage has scuppers leading to the outside.

The men need no further instructions and begin passing buckets of water from the bilge to the steerage deck.

Andrew again finds Bellingham and tells him to have the men from next watch relieve them after an hour.

"Give them an hour on and an hour off," says Andrew.

It is noon and Andrew knows where his brother is likely to be.

"What's all that commotion below decks I hear?" he asks Andrew.

"The ship was on the verge of sinking," Andrew says.

"Moore and I noticed that the ship was not moving well and I thought it might be the leak in the bilge. I was right. It seems like the barrels of oil might begin floating at any moment.

"There was no one on watch on the pumps."

"Who has the watch?"

"Abe!"

"I should have figured as much. What did you do?"

"I had bo'sun set up a bucket brigade."

"After two hours I found where the garboard plank next to the bow stem had opened. I stuffed a shirt in it and backed it up with a board, then nailed in place.

"How runs she now?"

"She holds but I know not for how long."

"Did you get our position?"

"Here it is. Plot it on the chart."

Andrew disappears into the wheelhouse and spreads a chart on the table.

"We are 92 miles from Concépcion. We should be there late tomorrow if the patches hold."

"God willing," says Hiram.

"Why not tell the crew that we are headed for Concépcion instead of Valparaiso?" asks Andrew. "I know we spoke of this earlier, but have not circumstances changed enough to inform the men?"

"Yes, I guess so. You tell the mates and let them pass the word on to their crews and the shiphandlers."

CHAPTER 38

Shore Leave in Concépcion

December 5, 1867
Concépcion, Chile, Day 735
36°49'60" S, 073°2'60" W

Tranquility is within sight of the narrow, steep peninsula that comes off the continent and turns sharply north for a few miles. In doing so, it creates one of the safest harbors in the world. As she enters the harbor, Lester asks his brother the state of the bilge.

"The leak is still worrisome even though the patch is holding," says Andrew. Water rises about a foot every four hours. The men on the pumps can again handle it without putting the bucket brigade back to work.

"There is some good news. I had feared it might have been along the garboard planks but yesterday I traced the main seepage to several planks about two feet below the waterline, just abaft of the stem, on the starboard side. They had opened enough to show some inward flowing water. I believe it is the caulking that has let go. I tried caulking it from the inside but that did not work."

"I looked for a site as we approached the inner harbor but I found that there is nowhere to careen the ship," says Hiram. "I guess we will have to find a yard that can pull us partially out of the water. Andrew, as soon as we dock, go along the ways. Find where it can be done as soon as possible."

The city's harbor is well developed. Its long wharves can easily handle more than a dozen large sailing vessels. Like Stanley in the Falkland Islands, and Valparaiso to the north, all three ports benefited from the 1849 discovery of gold in California.

For a change, all progresses exceptionally well for *Tranquility* and her crew. Andrew finds a yard with empty ways. An exceptionally high tide is predicted for the next day. At mid morning, *Tranquility* is there a few hours before the top of the tide and is warped tightly against the cradle on the incline's sliding ways. Inch by inch, as the tide rises, she is warped ahead. At 10:30, the yardmaster sees that the tide has topped and all the ship's forward progress has stopped. Before the tide begins its retreat, he calls to his men to secure the ship. She is warped around two bollards and cannot slip back.

After two hours of ebbing water the cutwater and bow are completely out of the water. The seams that had lost their caulking just astern of the ship's stem are exposed. The yard's caulkers quickly move in. In an hour their work is completed.

"Captain," says the yardmaster. "We can get you back into the water in two ways: either by letting her slide down the incline or waiting for the tide to again rise to its top. That would be close to noon, tomorrow."

Lester has already made up his mind but asks the yardmaster which he prefers.

"The latter would be the surest," he says, "but all we need do now is loosen the lines and give her a push. The ways are well greased. With a little shoving, she should float off on her own."

"The wind might even help," Andrew says.

"What do you mean?" asks the yardmaster.

"The wind is from the bow and I could have the main and topsail raised in a minute or two. They would do the pushing for us."

"Sounds great," says Hiram. "Let's launch her."

"Never has a ship sailed out of my ways, but it sounds possible," says the yardmaster as he looks on.

Almost as soon as the lines are loosened, *Tranquility*, on her own, slowly begins to move down the incline. The pace is steady, continuous, without stops or even slowdowns, though still under control by heavy lines that are steadily payed around the bollards. In a few minutes, the stern rises and is afloat. Finally she rocks. She is fully afloat. The ship is towed back to the wharf by two of her whaleboats.

"I hope you find prices here more to your liking," Capt. Lester says to Ephraim Brown as they watch *Tranquility* being secured to bollards along the wharf. "I think it only fair that you should secure enough food and other needed supplies to extend our stay at sea…. for another two years. Be sure that Cook accompanies you."

Much to Ephraim Brown's chagrin, Cook brings onboard several crates of oranges and grapefruit as well as the needed staples. The grocer wants to be paid before his goods can be offloaded from his wagon. After hearing his vocal demands from the wharf, Lester looks at Brown. He doesn't need to say a word. Brown disappears down the after companionway to his locker.

The captain's lounge is separated from the mates' quarters by their mess room/lounge, through which Brown passes to get to his locker. His nephew and Jorge Pilla are sitting at the table drinking coffee and discussing the pending watches. The door between the two areas is always hooked open.

The mates' sleeping quarters are comprised of four double bunks, one atop the other, two on the larboard bulkhead and two on the starboard side of the ship. Bunks against the starboard bulkhead are used by the bo'sun and quartermaster, and privileged guests, in this case, Ephraim Brown, the disburser.

Brown scurries to his chest, gets down on his knees as he fishes a ring of keys from his vest pocket, finds the right one, and undoes the padlock. He is rummaging through a cloth sack in the oversized chest when the clinking of coins catches his nephew's attention. Abe turns his head away from Jorge and watches through the doorway as his uncle places a handful of dollar coins in one pocket then a pile of newly-printed greenbacks in the other. On second thought, he retrieves each and counts the money just to be sure. When he believes he has enough to pay the waiting merchant, he slams down the lid and quickly snaps shut the padlock. He rises and hurries topside.

The merchant is onboard waiting at the top of the gangway. He is satisfied with what Brown pays him. He drops down to the wharf and directs his and the cook's helper to unload the food and stores. Andrew has called two Greenies to fill out the work party. As Hiram Lester and Brown watch them unload the wagon, Brown again complains about the cost of the provisions, then adds the yard costs to the conversation. His bewailing falls upon deaf ears. The yard costs amount to $225. That is not outrageous and comparable to what any yard in Sag Harbor or New Bedford would have charged.

"Will there be liberty for the men in Concépcion?" Andrew asks his brother. "It is not too soon that they should get some time ashore. It has been 735 days since they were free to wander the streets of Angra."

"I don't see why not. It should change their mood for a while. Especially when they can now get a full meal onboard."

To the disappointment of the crew, there is no liberty that night Friday Dec. 6th, because it isn't until well after dark that the ship is finally secured and all provisions stored. The following evening, Andrew and Diogo Pilla's watch have liberty.

Jorge has the gangway, while Abe, from the bow, watches as the last three men of the liberty watch walk down the gangway and head to the end of the wharf. Within minutes, they are consumed by the bustling crowd, food stands, and hawkers in the town's commercial square. Brown turns and walks toward the gangway. He tells Pilla he will take the first part of their watch.

"It's yours," Jorge says. "I'm going below to see if there's any coffee."

While the captain's revelation of their run to Concépcion immediately took the steam out of Abe Brown's forecastle rhetoric, it may also have again given rise to thoughts of desertion.

As Abe glances into the glitter of lights in the market place Fred Jolly emerges from the forward companionway and heads for the gangway. He is about to start down to the wharf when Abe stops him.

"Hey, yuh ain't goin' anywheres," Abe says roughly.

"I know it. I was just looking to see what the town looks like from the end of the wharf."

"You'll have tuh wait 'til tomorrow night fer a real look.

"Dat remin's me," Abe says as Jolly steps back on deck, "ain't it yuh, who back at Trindade Island, said he's gunna jump ship duh first chance yuh git?

"Concépcion is duh right place tuh do it. It's a big city an' dere's always ships goin' up duh coast tuh California. I done tink Chilies care who yah are as long as yah gots a few bucks."

"That's the problem," answers Jolly. "I have only a few bucks. I'll bet that even if I saw this trip to the end, that's all I'd get, a few bucks. I don't know why the hell I signed on again."

" 'Cause you're stupid an' can't do anythin' else but cook whale blubber."

"Maybe so, but I bet I could knock you on your ass for starters."

"Yuh an' who else?" Brown says laughingly.

Jolly doesn't say any more because he thinks that maybe Brown is right. I've never seen him without that knife on his belt, he thinks as he heads for his bunk. Then again, he ponders, almost everyone in a boat crew carries a knife. Jolly takes the steps, two at a time, down the forward companionway into the forecastle quarters.

"Where's everyone?" Jolly asks James Blackwell who is lying awake on his back in his bunk.

"Most went back to the galley. Cook made plum duff for those who have the watch."

"Why didn't you go with them?" asks Jolly.

"I don't like plum duff."

Jolly jumps into his bunk and silently lies there for several minutes.

"What are you thinking?" he queries Blackwell.

Blackwell doesn't answer immediately.

"I'm tired of this shit," he finally says. "It's like being a fuckin' slave."

"Then do something about it."

"Do what?"

"Jump off this ship."

"You first," Blackwell says jokingly.

"I might just do that."

"When?"

"We got liberty tomorrow, ain't we? And the ship's supposed to pull out early Monday morning to catch the tide."

Purposely Abe quietly treads down the ladder so the two men do not hear him approach. He has heard their entire conversation.

"Wad are yuh guys plannin'?" they hear Abe Brown ask. Jorge had returned to the gangway with coffee and Abe told him he'd be back soon.

"I should haul ya both up tuh duh cap'in. Right now!"

Blackwell swings his feet off his bottom bunk and sits up on his bunk.

"He won't believe you," Blackwell says. "He won't believe a thing you say. You're lucky you are still an acting mate. Besides, I think you're about to join us. I'm not as stupid as you think."

"Yur not as dumb as yah act," Brown says. "Lester's too stupid ta believe anyone'd jump his ship. His brother might. He's dah one yuh gots ta watch."

Sunday morning, after breakfast, a dozen or so Catholics in *Tranquility's* crew are mustered near the gangway. Jorge, the ship's 2nd mate, is making a list of the names of the men assembled. Nuno Dias comes out of the forward companionway.

"No one else is going to attend services at the church," he tells Jorge.

"What about Sanchez? Why isn't he going?"

"He is a Protestant. Didn't you know that?"

"A Protestant Portygee. What is this world coming to?"

The rest of the ship turns to readying *Tranquility* for her departure the next day.

"It's damned busy work," Fred Jolly complains to others in the crew's quarters. "Can't he leave us alone? It's Sunday. Do we gotta to go to church to get out of work?"

"Quit yur bitching," Abe says as he comes down the ladder. "I needs two volunteers tuh work on a detail in the bow. "You two," he says to Jolly and points to Blackwell, "will do."

Begrudgingly, the pair follows Brown up the ladder and forward of the capstan.

"What do we gotta do?" Jolly asks.

"Keep yur mouth shut an' listen. Can yous do dat?" Brown asks.

"I'm going to jump ship. I've had enough of this crap. Duz yah two wants ta come along wid me?" asks Abe.

"I thought we was goin' to take over the ship. What happened to that plan?"

"Der ain't enough bums who wants to go. Not enough hands. Jumpin' ship's all we can do. How much money yous gots?"

"I ain't got money," Jolly answers.

"I don't have much. A few bucks, that's all," adds Blackwell.

"Done worry 'bout duh money. I'll take care of dat. Yous can pay me back when we gits ta Frisco. I knows we can git a ship an' work our way dere. An', we might even git a buck or two extra.

"Are yous in?"

Both answer affirmatively.

"Is dere anyone else who wants to go?" asks Brown.

"Maybe Bennett."

"No! I done trust him," says Abe.

"There's only Kinder and Whetstone," says Jolly.

"I done trust dem either," says Abe.

"Neither do I," says Jolly.

"There's only Niggers left," says Blackwell.

"Dat's it. Just us. Dat's easier dan a bunch of guys.

"Here's wat we're gonna do. Liberty starts at 6 bells. It'll be dark by den. Yuh two goes ashore a half hour later. Hang aroun' duh market square where I can find yous. Understand?

"If word of dis leaks out ta anyone, you guys are dead men. Both of yous. Understand?" Brown says as his right hand goes to the sheath hold the knife on his belt.

Just before supper, Abe is in the mate's quarters. His bunk is immediately next to his uncle's.

"Are yuh goin' ta town ta night?" Abe asks.

"Of course," Ephraim answers. "I hear there are some fine restaurants here. Will you be going in with me?"

"No, I've been here once, a few years ago. A couple of my crew wants me tuh have a few drinks wid dem. I tink I will."

Ephraim is not subject to the watch restrictions. He and Andrew decide to skip supper on the ship and dine ashore. By 5:30 they leave.

Abe planned that this would happen. The day before, he had glanced at his uncle's sea chest shortly after he saw him take out the money to pay for the new provisions. He noted that in his haste, his uncle had not fully snapped shut the padlock. No one would know for a while that he had been there because he would fully snap it shut when he was finished.

Abe watches the mate's mess through the open door as he lies on his bunk. Diogo is alone in the mess. When he finishes Diogo goes topside using the after companionway. Brown knows it will be another 15 minutes before the harpooners and men from steerage will be served. Just to make sure no one sees him, he closes the door into steerage and slides the bolt locking the door.

With all speed, he dashes back to Ephraim Brown's sea chest, conveniently next to his, and opens the lock. He doesn't bother with coins but grabs a handful of paper money. He quickly counts it. There's almost 300 dollars, he thinks to himself. That is about what my lay would be if the ship returned with a full hold. I'll take my pay now, he says to himself, and smiles.

Quickly he closes the lid, snaps the lock firmly to make sure it has closed and runs back to the steerage door. He unbolts it, and locks it open by the hook on a nearby bulkhead. Only Dibble and Astor are in the room, and in their bunks. Probably asleep, Brown thinks.

Back near his bunk, he moves some of the bills to the left pocket of his pants so no one could see them bulging.

On the quarterdeck, Hiram has joined Bellingham as they watch the men go on liberty.

"I wonder how many will come back," he says to him, as they watch the men scamper down the gangway. There isn't a single man on the Larboard Watch who doesn't go into Concépcion.

"I know of a few I would like not to," answers the bo'sun.

They both go below and miss Abe's departure.

After a half hour, Abe is off the ship and heads for the market square. At the end of the wharf, he stops and looks back at the ship. A smile spreads across his face and he spits in her direction. It takes him only a few minutes to find Jolly and Blackwell. They are sitting at an outside table in front of a tavern. Each has already downed a pint of beer.

"Let's go," Abe says and takes the lead as they rise from their chairs.

They leave the market square and walk hurriedly up the main street that leads away from it. The street rises on a steady grade. After 20 minutes Jolly begins complaining that he's out of air and needs a drink.

"Not now," says Brown. "I wants tuh git away from places where some of deh crew might be. The fewer who sees us duh better."

As they continue uphill, following the street, the streetlights abruptly end. And, so do the shops. The character of the street changes from commercial to residential. From here on, the once wide, tree-lined boulevard grows narrower and narrower. Eventually, the cobblestones give way to hard-packed dirt.

Now, about a mile from the docks and well above the city, Brown spots a side alleyway. Halfway down its length is a lighted sign that announces there's a tavern beneath. Small lanterns on each side illuminate the sign. This is the only source of light on the entire block. They turn into the alley and approach the tavern. Brown hesitates for a moment then pushes through a pair of swinging doors. His companions follow.

Lighting inside isn't much better than outside. The bar is a local establishment and only Chileans inhabit the place. A waiter in black, wearing a white, ankle-length apron, approaches them and points to an empty table. The trio takes it. Brown orders a bottle of rum as they sit.

In less than an hour they empty the liter bottle. Jolly is about to ask the waiter for another when Brown stops him.

"Dat's enough fer now," Brown says. "We gots ta fin' a place tuh sleep tonight." He asks the waiter. The man points to the entrance door, then to the ceiling.

"*Exterior. Externo,*" he says. "*En al peso de arriba,*" he says and again points to the ceiling.

"Senoritas?" Brown asks.

"*Mucho,*" he answers and again points to the ceiling.

Outside, there is another door next to the swinging doors that open into the tavern. Brown leads the way and climbs the stairs. At the top a lone woman is sitting on a wooden chair, partially blocking the hallway. Next to her is a small table. On it is an empty glass and a stain from what was in it at one time. The glow from a single lantern, a dozen feet deeper into the hallway, renders her as a silhouette. She slowly strums a guitar and stares at the floor, never lifting her head to see who is coming. She crowds the narrow hallway. Brown stops in front of her waiting for a response. She doesn't move. She ignores him and keeps on playing without ever looking up.

"*Senoritas?*" Brown asks. She doesn't answer. He kicks her foot and she explodes, jumping to her feet.

"*Senoritas?*" he again says.

"*Animal,*" she responds in Spanish and points to one of three doors that open into the hallway.

Brown opens it. For a moment the unexpected brightness blinds and hurts his eyes. There are lanterns and candles everywhere. A light blue haze surrounds the candles. A sweet, sickening aroma fills the air. That smell's familiar, Brown says to himself. It's been a while since I smelled dat stuff.

A matronly woman, sitting on the far end of an ornate sofa is talking to two young girls. When she sees Brown enter she stops. Quickly she rises to her feet, pulls down the hem on her wrinkled dress, and approaches him.

She is Asian. Chinese, Brown thinks to himself.

She is over 50 years old. Her hair is still pure black and pulled back in a ponytail. She is slim, petite. Her initial appearance is deceiving but her life can be read in the many lines in her slightly-gaunt face and thin crimson-painted lips. Her high cheekbones are accentuated with blotches of rouge that make her look almost comical. There is no doubt that she is in charge. To Brown it seems incongruous to hear her give instructions in Spanish to two girls she left sitting.

Suddenly, Brown recognizes the aroma in the room. It instantly brings back memories of other brothels he has known. It is the smell of cheap perfume clashing with that of hashish. Dat's wat's wrong with da bitch outside, he says to himself.

"You wants young girl, womans, or old womans?" she asks.

Brown hesitates to answer. The climb up the stairs and the surfeit of rum is beginning to take hold of his mind.

Impatient for an answer, she continues. "Maybe you like a young boy? You sailor man, yes?" Then she feigns a laugh and momentarily exposes two rows of exceptionally white teeth.

"Bitch," Jolly blurts out. "Young senoritas. *Mucho.*"

The woman disappears into an adjoining room. A few minutes later she returns.

"You take pick," she says. "Maybe you first want drink?"

In about 10 minutes, one by one, the first of a dozen or so females parade in from the other room. They range the gamut of age, from 15 to

50, and in height from 5 to 6 feet, and in width from under a hundred to over 200 pounds.

When the heavyweight shows up, the matron apologizes for her obesity. "Maybe you likes fat womans. Some men like soft ride. She is one."

And they range in color, from Negroes to Asians, to pure-white Spaniards to tan-skinned mulattos.

"Yankee, you got dollahs?" the matron abruptly asks, showing her displeasure because of the time it is taking the now inebriated men to make a decision.

"We gots dollars as long as you gots *puta!*" Brown says.

"How long?" she asks. "One time or all night?" She then steps back from Brown, scanning him as if she is looking over a horse before buying it. "Maybe just one time, I think," she says, then giggles.

"How much?" asks Blackwell.

"Two dollah, one time; five dollah all night."

"How much for two women, all night? I've been at sea for a long, long time."

"Two womans, one time, three dollah. Two womans, all night, ten dollah."

"Does that include breakfast?" Jolly asks laughingly.

"What you want eat?" she surprises them.

"Half-dollah if you tell me now. One dollah breakfast if you ask tomorrow.

"You pick womans now? Yes?"

The women are still arrayed against the far wall and chat endlessly among themselves as the *gringos* try to decide which one they prefer. Finally, each man picks two women. Brown is in the lead and about to follow his two women into the back room when the madam quickly comes between him and the doorway.

"You pay now! " she demands. "You pay me now, here, not girls. No pay now no fuckie, fuckie!"

"How much?" Brown slurs his speech as he speaks.

She hesitates for a moment as her mental calculator works at top speed.

"Thirty-five dollah," she said.

Brown hesitates, then says: "You're duh first Chinee I've ever met who don't know how ta count. Dat's 34 dollars. Do you tink I am so drunk I cannot count?"

She thinks for a moment. She has been caught.

"That cheap," she says. "I give you good price. That include breakfast and I no charge you, just your boys. Gimme 35 dollah."

Both Jolly and Blackwell feign searching for money in their pockets. Brown sees through their charade. Dis one's on me boys," he says and sticks his hand into his right pants pocket.

The madam gasps when she sees him pull out a roll of green bills. He peels seven $5 bills off the outside then stuffs the remainder, with some degree of trouble, back into his pocket.

Brown grabs the wrist of one of his girls then turns to the madam. "Tell the other one to come back in about an hour. One at a time."

The room is little more than a cell. There is one single bed against the far wall, next to a window that looks onto the alley. On the other side of the window is a chair and small table. A single rose, now long dead, had been stuffed into an empty beer bottle. On the far side of the table is a large ceramic pitcher of water sitting inside a large washbasin. Over the back of the chair are several small towels. To one side of the bed is a small bench, with a larger towel on it. Several candles, placed on one corner of the table, light the room. Wax from those that burned their wicks to the end covers the end and some has collected on the floor where it had dripped. On the other side of the wall is a large picture calendar of a toreador dodging a bull. The room smells musty, like dried grass, as if its window has never been opened.

Brown follows his choice into the room. She takes off her clothes then disrobes him. As she does, she again notices the bulging pocket in his pants. She lies on the bed, looking at him, then lifts her arms, inviting him in. Brown is still in command of himself as long as he is standing. But when he begins to mount the naked woman before him, his head begins to spin. He abruptly rises to his knees in an attempt to stop the spinning and hears the door open into the room. He turns and sees the madam.

"Ah," she says, "I see you slow to start. Maybe you shy."

"What the hell do you want?" he blurts.

"You good customer," she says, then reveals a nearly empty bottle of rum she is holding behind her back. "I give you drink, no charge. Now you get busy. Yes?" She again giggles, then places the bottle on the small table before closing the door.

Brown again lies atop the motionless girl. He looks into her black eyes as his face moves unsteadily closer and closer to her. I've almost forgotten what it is like to be with a woman, he thinks. He closes his eyes and lies on her, motionless. His head is wildly spinning. He passes out.

Thank God he isn't heavy, she thinks, as they lie motionless together. The slight girl, in her late teens, has seen this skit played out before and, willing or not, she is a participant. She knew the bottle of rum was brought in to get this man drunk and to have him pass out. She didn't have to induce him to have another drink. He already had enough rum in him to do the trick.

She, too, has seen the roll of bills Brown pulled from his pocket to pay the madam. From where it is kept, she knew it could be nothing else. Soon the madam would be in here to pick clean his pocket, she thinks to herself. She will keep it all for herself. Maybe I can get some before she comes in.

Cautiously, she begins slipping out from under Brown.

He is heavier than I thought, she thinks. Slowly, she manages to free one leg, then the other and then her torso. Just as she breaks free, Brown moans, then moves his arm around her waist and pulls her close. She freezes for a while and listens to his breathing. When it returns to normal, she again moves. She uncouples his arm and lays it between them. She stops. He doesn't move. She eases off the edge of the bed, feet first, then pushes away from him. Brown belches. She freezes, waits, then all is again silent.

She quickly moves to the low bench where she laid his clothes as she undressed him. She finds the bulging right pocket. Without counting, she strips several bills off the roll then tries to put the remainder back in the pocket.

"Bitch!" yells Brown, "fuckin' whore!" He startles her.

Engrossed in taking the money, she hadn't heard him get off the bed. He grabs her hair with his left hand and pulls her off her knees. He lifts her almost off her feet. He holds her there while with his right hand he punches her squarely in the face. Blood immediately gushes from her nose and mouth. He lays a second blow on her that is so hard it tears her head from his hands. She falls backwards, over the bench.

As she does, the madam throws open the door. She must have been waiting outside the door for Brown to pass out. When she sees what he has done, she begins screaming. She lunges toward him but even in his alcoholic stupor he is ready for her. He lands a fist on her face and she goes down in a heap.

Brown grabs his pants and is stumbling as he puts on his shirt and bursts through the door and into the hall. Jolly and Blackwell erupt into the hallway, responding to the madam's screams.

"We gotta git outa here fast," he yells to them. "I caught da fuckin' whore picking my pants. The Chinee was in on it."

Fortunately for the guitarist she had left the hallway. As they run down the stairs, half stumbling and half jumping, the madam regains consciousness and is at the top of the stairs, screaming as loud as she can.

The noise alerts several men still in the tavern. They come out just as Brown and his crew open the door. They run over and knock down the first man and the others pile atop him. Brown, followed on his heels by Jolly and Blackwell run up the alley to the boulevard, then turns right, running uphill. Looking back occasionally. Brown no longer sees the tavern men in pursuit. They continue to run until they can run no more. Out of breath, exhausted, they collapse onto the dirt street that is now no more than a path.

Gasping for air, "What do we do now?" asks Jolly.

"Let's try to get back to the ship," Blackwell suggests.

"We can't," answers Brown. "At least I can't."

"Why?" asks Jolly.

Suddenly, Brown senses that there is someone behind him. He turns around as well as do Jolly and Blackwell. Emerging from the darkness are half a dozen men. In what little light that comes from the city below, they see the flash of knife blades. Brown automatically reaches for his. The sheath is empty.

Chapter 39

Troubles Comes in Threes

The sun has yet to rise as Andrew Lester rises from his bunk and begins dressing. For the last hour, he lay awake planning the routine for departure of the ship, which is always his responsibility. A lone lantern hangs in the mess room and casts a weak light into the mate's quarters. He glances around and sees that Abe's bunk is empty. At first, he thinks nothing of it. He surmises that maybe Abe is already up and readying his watch for their part in the ship's departure from the wharf. He glances over to Abe's uncle. He is snoring away in a blissful sleep. He remembers how they had enjoyed dinner the night before at a restaurant.

Lester slips into the galley and pours a cup of coffee from the ever-active pot. It tastes burned. It has been on the stove too long, he thinks. Still, it's coffee. He walks forward looking to see if anyone in steerage is stirring. He notices that the bunk of Harvey Bennett, Abe's harpooner, is empty. It is disheveled and looks as though he has just crawled from it. He walks farther forward on the second deck and encounters Bennett.

"Good morning," Lester says first. "Is Mr. Brown forward?"

"I haven't seen him, Sir. In fact, I was looking for him."

"Go to the fo'c's'le and see if anyone is missing," Lester orders. "His uncle, last night, said Abe was to meet a few men ashore for a drink."

Who had the Mid Watch? Lester asks himself. As he scurries back to the mate's quarters he remembers it was Diogo Pilla.

Pilla had gone off watch at 4 a.m. and is sound asleep when Lester shakes him by the shoulder.

"Diogo! Diogo! Did you see Abe Brown come back from liberty while you had the watch?"

"No," said the startled 3rd mate. "Is there something wrong?"

"Were you alone on watch?"

"No, I had one of my crew with me. At least one of us was at the gangway all the time."

"Who was that?"

"Kinder, Jeremiah Kinder, the farmer from Sag Harbor. Kinder would have told me if he saw Brown come onboard."

"I fear we may have a problem," Lester says as he turns and makes his way toward the forecastle. The traffic between the mate's quarters and steerage arouses several men. As Lester is about to enter the forecastle Bennett appears in the doorway.

"Two men," says Bennett. "Two men, Jolly and Blackwell. Their bunks were never slept in."

Lester turns and races aft. Diogo is already up and finishes getting dressed when Lester passes him.

"Take someone with you and go immediately to the police station," he tells Diogo. "See if they are holding Brown, Jolly and Blackwell. We may still be able to shove off at sunrise if we can get them back. On second thought, wake Mr. Brown and let him help you find his nephew."

Lester turns and heads for the captain's cabin. He knocks on the door. There is no answer so he opens it. His bed is still unmade. Lester rushes up the aft companionway and out on to the main deck. He sees his brother in the wheelhouse talking to Quartermaster Adrian Moore. They are going over the route to be taken out of the harbor when Lester enters.

"Good morning Andrew," Capt. Lester says. "What's causing all the noise I heard from below decks? Is something wrong?"

"I fear so," says Andrew.

"Abe Brown and two men never returned from liberty."

"Have you checked with the watch?"

"Aye, Sir, I have.

"I was on deck from 10 to 2 and saw only the rest of the liberty watch returning. Diogo Pilla was on the Mid Watch and said he saw no one else come aboard."

"Damn it," Lester says. "Have someone go to the police station and see if they are there."

"I already did that."

"How does this affect us in departing?" Hiram Lester asked his brother.

"It hurts. We can compensate for the loss of men in getting off the wharf and underway," says Andrew. "But we will be handicapped without them if we run across a pod of whales. We will be able to put only three boats in the water. Bennett is the harpooner on Brown's boat. He can also act as boat steerer. Jolly and Blackwell are mid and tub oar. We'll need two men to replace them."

A half-hour later, Diogo Pilla is seen running down the length of the wharf toward the ship. Ephraim Brown, who had accompanied him, is still somewhere in the marketplace but on his way back. Diogo rushes up the gangway just as the sun breaks over the saw tooth profile of the Andes Mountains. He sees Andrew and the captain outside the wheelhouse.

"Are they locked up?" Capt. Lester asks before Diogo can catch his breath.

"I wish they were, Sir.

"No, Sir. They are not there."

"Damn! Damn! Damn!" Lester says as he pounds his fist on the top of the gunwale. "We dare not leave without full boat crews, let alone a spare man or two. We have another year or so to sail and there are no ports with men available where we are going.

"What's the Spanish word for crimper?" he asks Diogo.

"I do not know, Sir, I am Portygee. I think it may be *encrespar*, but I do not think it means quite the same as it does in English."

"Andrew, take Diogo with you. Go first to the American Consulate and see if they know of any Americans, or Brits, for that matter, who are looking for work. They might even know of a few stranded New Bedford men who might join us. If they cannot come up with anyone, ask them if they know of any Chilean agency that outfits ships with men. There must be such a group here, after all, this is a seaport. Tell him square-rigger men are preferred, but at this point anyone will do.

"If we don't we may have to postpone sailing until tomorrow morning's tide."

By mid-morning, Jorge, has the gangway watch and is knocking on Capt. Lester's cabin door. The door quickly swings open because it had been left ajar. Lester, sitting behind his desk with a chart, is momentarily surprised by Jorge.

"There's a policeman on the wharf, Sir. He's tying his horse to the gangway and wants to speak with you."

Lester drops what he has been doing, grabs his semi-formal frock coat from the closet and captain's hat, and rushes topside. The policeman is at the top of the gangway.

"Captain," the policeman says in near-perfect English, "may I come aboard?"

"Of course," answers Lester as he returns the policeman's salute.

"I am detective Miguel Valdez. I am with the city's homicide department. I have just left a brothel on the east side of the city. A young woman, a prostitute, was killed there. The madam said that it was done by one of three whalers who were there last night. I would like to interrogate them, if I may."

Valdez is taller than most Chileans Lester has met. He is a bit over six feet. His trim physical condition belies the fact that he is in his early fifties. He wears civilian clothing but the saddle and blanket on his horse reveal that he is a member of the city's police department.

"I can see from the way you carry yourself," Lester says, that you are a military man."

"Naval," Valdez corrects. "Up until a few months ago, I commanded a coastal frigate. A barque about the size of your ship."

"We are short three men who didn't return from liberty last night," Lester says. "I think they are the ones whom you might want to question. My 1st mate just returned from your station in the square, hoping to find them locked in jail. But he reported that the police have not arrested any Yankee whalers."

"How was the woman killed?"

"I'm not certain at this point because I am not a medical person, but it was obvious from the blood that she was punched in the face. She fell backwards over a bench and may have broken her back. She was in that position, over the bench, when I saw her."

"Then it wasn't murder, was it?"

"Technically, it is manslaughter.

"If I find anything else, or your men, I will immediately send you word."

"We had plans to sail today but I will hold off until tomorrow's tide."

"Sir, thank you for you time," Valdez says. He salutes Lester, turns and leaves.

Andrew Lester and Diogo Pilla return early in the afternoon. Lester immediately goes to the captain's cabin.

"We're in luck," he says to his brother.

"The Consulate said there is a young American, a man from Pennsylvania, a coal miner. He claimed he was shanghaied while he was dockside in Philadelphia. His name is Rusnak, John Rusnak. He jumped ship a week ago and is waiting for a ship headed for California. Diogo and I found him and he said he is willing to sign on. We said we'd give him a full lay as an oarsman, just as if he had signed on in Sag Harbor."

"That's fine," Lester says. "Did you find any more?"

"The best Diogo could do was two, maybe three Chilean farmers.

He stopped by a church and spoke to the priest. The priest told him of two young men out of work and sent a runner for them. They both were eager to sign on. In fact, there were three, if you need another man. They are all in their mid-20s, short but powerfully built. I don't think any of them would have a problem bending an oar."

"Have them all here before supper," Lester says. "Let me look at them and let them look at the ship and see if they still want to sign on. I don't want them jumping the first time they see land."

Later that afternoon, Capt. Lester is at the bow of *Tranquility*, checking over the anchor cable for signs of wear and waiting for Diogo to show up with the men. Ephraim is also topside, working his way forward, when he sees Lester in the bow. He had heard that Lester was about to hire several new men. Of course, he wants to know why, how much and how many.

Just as Brown approaches him, Lester hears horse hooves clattering on the wharf. He looks toward the city and sees Valdez approaching the ship. As he pulls up to the gangway, Lester is there to see if the detective has found anything.

"Have you news?" he asks as Valdez steps onto the ship.

"The worst kind," answers the detective.

"We have found two of your men. They were on the outskirts of town, near where the squatters live."

"What were they doing there?" Lester asks.

"I don't know captain."

"Where are they now?"

"They are being taken to the morgue."

"The morgue. Are they dead?"

"Both men had their throats cut. All their clothing and shoes were gone. It must have been robbery. The men should not have strayed to that part of the city. Even I won't go there at night unless I have a few armed men with me."

"What do I do next?" Lester asks.

"Nothing. They are under my jurisdiction."

"But we cannot hold the ship until your investigation is over."

"I know, captain," said Valdez. "The American Consulate will see to their remains."

"I want to see them before we pull out," Ephraim Brown says.

"Why?" asks Valdez.

"Because one of the men might be my nephew!"

"Certainly," answers Valdez. "I will leave word at the morgue that you may view them. Incidentally, the morgue is in the basement of the hospital. It is but two blocks, on the main boulevard, from the square.

"*Via con Dios,*" Valdez says as he turns to leave and salutes the captain. "I hope the rest of your voyage is more successful."

"Well?" asks Hiram Lester as Brown bursts into his cabin late in the afternoon. "Are we free of your nephew?"

"He was not among them. No one knows where he is, either dead or alive. We cannot sail until we find him."

"Are you again commanding this ship?" Hiram asks his cousin.

"Well, well, no. But we cannot leave until we know his fate."

"Yes, we can," answers Lester.

Tuesday, the next morning, before they begin the process of warping ship, at the captain's behest Andrew Lester calls the entire crew to muster forward of the wheelhouse. He tells them of what happened even though they knew it the day before, almost before Valdez had mounted his horse to leave. He asks that they all say a silent prayer for their dead shipmates. After a few minutes, Bo'sun Bellingham moves the shiphandlers into action.

"Mr. Brown," Capt. Lester addresses Ephraim who is about to leave the service. "How did you fare in the search for your nephew?"

"I didn't go ashore."

Brown seemingly embarrassed, silently walks away

By late morning, *Tranquility* has cleared the peninsula created by Concépcion's unique harbor and is now standing out to sea. Captain Lester is on the transom, studying his ship's wake. She runs true and clear with a minimum of white water. He hears someone approaching.

He turns and sees Roger Whetstone. He knows Whetstone had been injured during the battle of Gettysburg but never knew how. He watches the slight limp in his gate as he nears.

"Sir. May I speak with you?"

"Of course."

"In strictest confidence, Sir?"

"Certainly, why ask?"

"Because you won't want the rest of the crew to know what I am about to tell you."

Before speaking further, he hands Lester a piece of paper with some awkwardly written words.

"To who it concerns," Lester reads quietly so only he and Whetstone can hear. "I give all my lay this day, Dec. 5, 1867, from the whaling voyage of *Tranquility* to my friend and shipmate Roger Whetstone. I do this because he has loaned me 21 new dollar bills. I also give him my ditty bag and any of my personals. Fredrick Joseph Jolly."

"Why did he do this?" Lester asks. "Why did he need the money?"

"He told me to show you this after we sailed. He was planning to jump ship."

"Jump ship!" Lester repeats. "I felt this might happen again. Was this what Mr. Brown and Blackwell were also doing?"

"Yes. He said he needed it for passage to San Francisco."

"But that wouldn't have gotten him very far."

"He knew that, but later, after I gave him all the money I had, he said that he found out, later that day, that Mr. Brown had come into a lot of money."

"What did he mean by that?"

"I didn't understand what he meant. But he said that Mr. Brown's uncle would be helping them out."

"Is there any more?"

"No, Sir. I have told you all I know."

"That is good. It is good that you didn't tell anyone in the crew."

"Will I be getting back my loan?"

"I don't think you will get money but you can have the other things he assigned you. I will look into that."

Lester leaves the transom. As he goes below he encounters Jorge coming up the companionway ladder. Before Pilla can say anything, Lester tells him that he wants to see all three mates in his cabin, including Mr. Brown. Pilla returns below and goes forward passing the word. Pilla thinks to himself that it is highly unusual that the captain would hold a meeting in his cabin and not the lounge. It must be something important.

A few minutes later everyone is there except Ephraim Brown. Andrew is about to close the door when he hears Brown coming down the companionway. He passes through the captain's lounge, and enters the cabin.

"Gentlemen," Lester says as he continues to look out one of three, large transom windows against the stern bulkhead of his inner sanctum. Then he turns and addresses them directly. "What I am about to tell you should remain in this cabin until I can decide on what further I must do.

"Abraham Brown, Fred Jolly and James Blackwell are deserters. They were in the process of jumping ship. I don't know what happened in the whorehouse but someone must have discovered that Brown was carrying a sizable amount of money. It is not uncommon for seamen, especially drunken seamen, to be rolled once ashore. That is what I conclude must have happened."

"How dare you say that of your own kin?" Ephraim yells out.

"What evidence do you have of this?"

Lester hands the note to Brown who in turn passes it among the three mates.

"Roger Whetstone told me that Jolly had told him this in secret and that this paper would get him back the money he had loaned Jolly."

"But Abe didn't have any large amount of money," claims Brown.

"If he did, where did get it?"

"From you," Lester answers.

"That's absurd. That's impossible. I never gave him any money. I never would. I don't even have much of my own."

"You do have Company money, don't you?"

"Yes, I do, but it's locked. It is well secured."

"Mr. Brown, I have a witness who claims that Abe said '…that Mr. Brown's uncle would be helping them out with the money they needed.' Has Abe any uncles here other than you?"

"I never said that. Why you….you know you cannot believe everything Abe says. You have caught him in lies, have you not?"

"There's one way to prove it."

"How's that?"

"Go check your chest. Isn't that where you have squirreled away the Company's funds? "

"Take the time to go to your hoard and count it."

"There's no need. Abe would not steal from the Company, nor from me."

"Damn it, Brown. I am not going to argue with you. Go check your chest. If you won't I'll have the bo'sun go there and use a crowbar on it."

Brown turns and leaves. In defiance, he leaves the cabin door open.

In a few minutes, the mates and Lester hear a loud shriek. Seconds later, Brown is rushing into the captain's cabin with a cloth bag in his hand and his mouth agape. The bag still contains some money.

Brown stands before Lester who was now seated behind his desk. A thin smile, a rarity, spreads across Lester's lips. Has Lester at last obtained retribution against the Browns?

"That bastard robbed me. He robbed me!"

"He didn't rob you," Lester says. "He robbed the Company."

Chapter 40

Riding the Humboldt Current North

December 8, 1867, Day 766
38°47'00" S, 073°0' 6" W

Tranquility departs Concépcion shortly after sunrise on December 8th on a northerly heading, paralleling the coast of Chile, just two or three miles off the beach. The winds have a northern cast. Capt. Lester fears that it bodes bad weather. He has little faith in the ship's barometer. He believes it was damaged when they rounded The Horn. To replace it he had Andrew picked up a new one while they were in Concépcion.

"I am deeply grieved by the entry I must now make," he writes in the ship's logbook at the end of the day. "'Three of my men--Abraham Brown, acting 4th mate; Fred Jolly, oarsman; and James Blackwell, oarsman--were murdered two days ago, December 5th,' while we were in Concépcion. I add Brown to the list though his body was never located by the police. Because of the brutal way the other men were slain I must assume that he, too, experienced the same fate. The cause was robbery.

"In addition, we have discovered that Abe Brown robbed the disburser, Ephraim Brown, of Company funds amounting to nearly $500, according to Ephraim. They were in the scheme of jumping ship. I have in evidence a promissory note Jolly wrote as a receipt for money

Roger Whetstone had given him to be repaid as part of Jolly's lay. May God have mercy on their souls.

"The murderers are believed to be, according to Concépcion's investigative detective Miguel Valdez, local people. The American Consulate will be responsible for the proper care of their remains."

Lester lays the pen aside and slowly closes the logbook. He places it in a desk drawer and rises. He empties the last bit of port wine into a tumbler and returns to the stuffed chair that overlooks the wake of his ship. There, he eventually falls asleep.

Early the following morning Hiram Lester is inside the wheelhouse to confirm that the ship is still on a northerly course. He gives the quartermaster a new heading, north-by-northwest. Slowly, *Tranquility* begins to turn away from the continent. Lester remains on the quarterdeck checking the rigging. He turns to the east and watches the white, snow-covered peaks of the Andes, turned red by a setting sun, grow smaller and smaller. He hears a noise and turns forward. He sees Ephraim Brown rush out the companionway and take the port ladder onto the bridge.

Idiot, Lester says to himself, will he ever learn to use the starboard ladder when coming up?

"Where are we now headed?" Brown asks Lester as he stands next to him, also viewing the Andes.

"To an island group about 600 miles off the coast of Chile."

"What island?"

"San Ambrosio."

"How far away is it?"

"About 550 miles!"

"Why there?"

"Damn it, Ephraim. Don't you have anything else to do but stand here and interrogate me?

"Why not go below and count the number of casks we have filled. When was the last time you did that?"

Brown doesn't answer. He has not been on top of his duties. He turns away from Lester and retraces his steps, disappearing down the companionway. He stops at Andrew Lester's desk, takes paper and pencil from it, then removes a lantern from the mess table and lights it. He is about to drop down another ladder into the bilge.

"Where are you going Mr. Brown?" asks Michael Astor, the ship's cooper.

"Ben and I were just about to count the casks,"

"I, too, am going to make a barrel count," says Brown. "You can carry the lantern for me."

Astor leads the way down, followed by Ben and then Brown.

They begin counting the first row of filled casks when Ben hears something.

"What's that?" he asks.

"What's what?" asks Chips.

"Hear that sound?"

"No."

"It's coming from over there."

Chips moves to the next row of casks and swings the lantern around the first one.

"My God! My God!" he exclaims.

"What is it? What do you see?" says Brown as he quickly follows Astor.

"Abe! Abe!" Brown yells and rushes to his nephew who lies on his back on the bilge deck. His jacket supports his head.

"As the trio approaches," Abe lets out another moan.

"Water. Water," he mumbles almost inaudibly.

Astor brings the lantern closer. They see Abe's face is smattered with dried blood. His shirt is bloody and torn. Dried blood mats his hair. Ephraim slips one arm under Abe's head and lifts it slightly.

"Are you all right?" he asks.

Abe doesn't answer.

"Ben, get some water and help," Chips tells Ben.

Capt. Lester has returned to his cabin desk and pulls the logbook toward him. He is about to make the day's entry. He stops for a moment because his thoughts are interrupted by a commotion outside his door. He hears men talking and is about to rise. Suddenly, the cabin door is thrown open and bangs violently against the bulkhead. Lester jumps up and sees Ben in the doorway.

"What is it?" Lester yells.

"We found him! We found him!"

"Who did you find?"

"Abe. We found Abe."

"Where?"

"In the bilge. Chips and I went below with Mr. Brown to count casks and he was there, lying among them. At first, we thought he was dead. Then he moved. I just told Mr. Lester and he sent men down to help."

"I pulled him from between casks," Andrew tells his brother. "We carried him to steerage. Cook and others are now there with him."

Lester rushes out the door passing Andrew who is carrying the medicine box. Other mates are around Abe as Cook attends to him. He is laid out on his bunk.

"Is he alive?" Lester asks.

"Yes, but barely," answers Cook.

"He must have been in some fight by the number of cuts," says Diogo.

"He is pale," says Andrew. "He has lost a lot of blood."

"Abe, can you hear me?" asks Hiram.

Brown momentarily opens his eyes, then closes them. He babbles a few incoherent words.

"He is delirious," says Andrew.

"We must keep him warm," Cook adds, as he finishes binding the open cuts.

"Get another blanket off one of the empty bunks," says Hiram.

For the next several minutes the men wait around Abe. His uncle has composed himself and now sits on his bunk, looking at his comatose nephew next to him.

"Oh God," he says in a weak voice that is just barely audible, "what has brought you to this state?"

"There's nothing more we can do," says Cook. He gathers up his torn linens and disappears in the galley. The others break away and leave.

"What do you think?" Andrew asks his brother as they move astern.

"I think I must make a revision to the logbook. If he does come awake, he will have a lot of questions to answer.

"Andrew, we must talk with Abe as soon as he is lucid, before anyone, especially his uncle, who can give him information about what has transpired. We do not want Ephraim to prejudice him."

"I know," says Andrew. "I will post Ben for now to watch on him. In the meantime, might it not be a good idea to also speak to Ephraim and forbid him to talk to Abe without us, or anyone else present?"

"Yes, that's a good idea. I will do that. You tend to the watch."

"I know the perfect man to do that," says Andrew.

A few minutes later Andrew is in the forecastle. The men there already know that Abe was discovered in the bilge. He looks around and sees Obie Jones.

"Jones," he says, "follow me and bring your donkey breakfast (straw mattress) with you."

Andrew leads him into the mates' quarters.

"Wait here a moment," he says as he goes aft to the captain's lounge. He lifts the seat from the table where Abe sits for his meals. He sets it down across the room from Abe's bunk.

"Sit here and keep an eye on Brown. Never leave him out of sight or earshot. I will make sure the cook's helper gets you your meals. If you feel you must relieve yourself, have someone contact me and I will get someone to stand guard. Do you understand?"

"Aye, Sir, I do."

"Do not ever leave this position unless the captain or I tell you to. Do not listen to what Ephraim Brown might tell you to do. You must be vigilant. The moment you think Abe is awake, call out for me. In the meantime, I will find someone to replace you in the morning. I will bring him to you."

The next day (December 9th), as Lester is taking another sighting, Ephraim Brown comes on deck and stands silently beside him.

"We had planned to pull into Valparaiso," he finally says. "Is that still your plan?"

"No!" Lester says to Ephraim.

"How is your nephew?"

"There's been no change. He either sleeps or is unconscious. Neither I, nor anyone who has looked at him, can discern the difference. There is one change. He seems to be running a fever."

Lester does not respond immediately.

"I think we shall pass it by…even if whaling is slow," he eventually answers.

"On the day we arrived in Concépcion, while you were shopping, I had a visit from Andrew Benoit, the American Consulate. He said Valparaiso is not a pretty city since the end of their war with Spain. The Spaniards and their sympathizers are still strong in Peru and would like to regain control of Chile. They continue to occasionally bombard the city. It is in shambles."

"But that war ended more than a year ago." Brown says.

"Still, he cautioned me about going there. Spanish *"amigos,"* the Peruvian insurgents, are still making trouble.

"Besides, we took on sufficient food stores in Concépcion. Didn't we?"

Brown doesn't answer.

"We are again whaling, our primary business. Tomorrow I will return the ship to cruising. We have no schedule to maintain.

"Is there anything else that concerns you?"

"No. Not at the moment," Brown answers.

Strange, Lester thinks to himself as his cousin goes forward and disappears down the starboard hatchway. He seems in a somewhat contradictory mood. I would have thought he would have been a bit more morose after his nephew's supposed death, but he wasn't. Now, that he knows he's alive, he seems more concerned than before. I realize they are not close but still, why the change? He said that there was $500 missing from his locker. I dislike thinking this, but it would have been an easy opportunity for him to add dollars to his own pocket. I think he is capable of it. But who can challenge him if he did? Oh well, I must stop thinking in this vein."

That evening at dinner, Capt. Lester tells the mates that they will have to shuffle around the boat crews, to think of who could be placed elsewhere to make four efficient whaleboat crews.

"There are three Chileans and the Pennsylvania man from which you can choose. Make your decisions tonight because we could be into whales tomorrow! Place Bennett in command of Abe's boat and someone as the harponeer."

"Is he the 4th mate?" asks Ephraim.

"No, answers Hiram, "he is just filling the position for now."

Once *Tranquility* leaves Concépcion the attitude of the crew changes, not for the better nor the worse. The murder of their two shipmates has an affect on them and is still the topic of discussion, but there is something else that affects them.

Several crewmen are again working holy stones over the deck.

"I'll be glad when we spot some whales," says Kinder. "I don't mind cutting-in, or even going down on a whale, it's the make-busy work that bothers me. This is the third time we were told to do the deck since that last whale was cut-in."

"I think you're right," says Harvey Bennett who is overseeing the work. "For sure, it makes the time go faster. You don't get too much time to think when you working your ass off."

Captain Lester let his brother shuffle around the boat crews because of the loss of two men in his boat. Some men liked the changes, others grumbled about it. To most it makes no difference. You have an oar to pull, a job to do. It doesn't matter which boat you are in.

The weather is unusually pleasant for the first week but that begins to change. Until then, *Tranquility* had been on a tack that gradually took her away from the coast, toward a group of islands now some 550 miles off Valparaiso. The shoals around the islands, according to Mr. Lester, had been known for concentrating right whales. The ship is within two days from reaching them when violent weather hits just before sunset. Within an hour, it goes from flat seas to a howling southwest gale.

The watch is just able to lighten sails ahead of the growing darkness as the ship heads into heavy weather. For three days the gale blows and the ship runs under bare poles, except for the jibs. *Tranquility* gains 60 miles downwind before the winds start to die. By noon on the third day the winds begin veering to the south. Lester is able to take a reading and tells the onlookers that they are but a day away from the islands.

In late afternoon, the lookouts see spouting in the far distance. Andrew quickly has bo'sun raise the course and topsail on the foremast as they bear down to the location. There are four whales but Hiram hesitates lowering the boats because of the lateness. Brown convinces him otherwise. Andrew does not lower because he sent two men of his crew to fill out the other boats. In no time the others upon the whales. Two boats are fast to whales as the sun is setting.

"Why didn't you lower your boat," Hiram asks Andrew.

"Because we are two oarsmen short. Rusnak and one of the Chile men have not yet bent an oar. I thought it is not wise to send them after a whale without any experience. Besides, there is the stage to get ready. Instead, we began setting up the try works and lighting lanterns for the boats to see.

Josh Edwards, Andrew's harpooner, is temporarily added to Jorge's boat. It is near midnight when Pilla's, then Abe Brown's boat, now run by Harvey Bennett, come into view. The whales are secured alongside and the crew immediately begins cutting-in.

Chapter 41

A Stoved boat!

December 17, 1867, Day 777
33° 13' S, 078° 50' S

Tranquility is somewhere off Valparaiso when Lester decides to change course. Earlier, he had decided to pass up another group of islands, Juan de Fernandez Islands, because, on his last voyage in the Pacific, he had not seen any worthwhile number of whales there. But, because they are so close, a hundred miles away, he decides to take a chance, and gives the quartermaster a due west heading.

The next day at daybreak the lookouts, as they go aloft, spot a pod of finback whales. Their presence is short-lived as the fast-swimming whales quickly bear away and disappear. That does stir the men in hopes more whales might now be in the offing. Near mid-morning, a lone right whale is spotted but does not rise again.

Early in the afternoon the lookouts spot a pair of sperm whales, one large and the other very small.

All four boats are lowered and make a chase. Rusnak and a Chilean have been added to Andrew's boat. The two whales, oblivious of what is approaching them, swim on the surface and close together.

"The smaller one's a pup," Andrew says to his crew.

He turns the whaleboat away, toward the mother. "It is one of the biggest sperms I have ever seen," he tells them. At first, he believed it to be a big bull. A schoolmaster. "Pups as small as this one still follow their mothers for milk. It is a cow, he says to his crew."

Ben is spurred on by Andrew's words and grabs the harpoon as the boat comes to the whale's side. He is about to lift the iron when he momentarily pauses. A fleeting series of thoughts rush through his mind at lightning speeds. He remembers the look in the eye of the first whale he killed. The pup will not live if I kill its mother, he thinks. I would rather not. The choice is not mine. This is a terrible business. But, all her oil may hasten our return home.

The hit is good as the harpoon sinks to the wooden handle. The whale immediately bolts. The crew backs off quickly. But instead of diving, as it should, it turns sharply and looks at the boat. Then it turns completely. In seconds it is pushing a wall of water toward the whaleboat. The men are stunned.

"Pull! Pull," Lester yells as he tries to steer the boat away from the oncoming whale.

But the move is too late. As the whale approaches the boat, it lifts the top of its huge head out of the water and drops its lower jaw. Ben, still standing, looks down the throat and sees a jaw lined with rows of big, white teeth. For a moment, he imagines what Jonah must have gone through. In seconds, the whale grabs the boat amidships as the head comes crushing down. The boat splinters into pieces as lines, irons and men are flung into the air. Ezekiel Jones is in the whale's mouth, cut almost in half, as the whale rises and shakes its head like a bulldog. Paul Hicks is somewhere beneath the whale.

Ben lands on the water almost atop John Rusnak who sat behind him. In the tumult of waves and confusion created by the whale, Ben does not see Andrew who was in the stern of the boat.

The whale swims off with its mouth full of debris and drags lines and pieces of the boat with it. It sounds, taking all beneath the sea.

"Ben, are you all right?" Andrew yells from behind.

Ben sees him holding onto a piece of flotsam that helps him stay afloat.

As Ben looks around for help, he sees Bennett, now in command of Abe's boat, fast on the pup whale. Maybe it is better this way, Ben thinks. It won't live without a mother. Then he sees Diogo's boat heading for him. As they float about on the site where the whale sounded, bits of rubble and ruin from the boat continue to pop onto the surface. Then they see Hicks' body come to the top. Pilla's boat first retrieves the body. Everyone is pulled into the boat and wait, gathering what is salvageable and looking for Zeke. He is never seen.

Ben stares at Hicks' lifeless body and is moved. It could as well been me, he thinks.

"Tranquility raises the flag ordering everyone back to the boat. Abe's boat is already at the cutting stage when Diogo's laden boat arrives.

The next morning, Wednesday, January 18, 1868, just after breakfast, as the ship gets underway, the crew is gathered about the gangway. During the night, the little whale was tried. Everything on deck is now clean, wet and glittering in the reflection of a bright, warm, morning sun.

On a quickly-rigged platform, beneath a slightly tattered American flag, lies the body of Paul Hicks.

After a few somber words about Ezekiel Jones and Paul Hicks, Capt. Lester clears his throat and begins to read from a shabby book that resembles a Bible:

We therefore commit his body to the deep, looking for the general Resurrection in the last day, and the life of the world to come, through our Lord Jesus Christ; at whose second coming in glorious majesty to judge the world, the sea shall give up her dead; and the corruptible bodies of those who sleep in him shall be changed, and made like unto his glorious body; according to the mighty working whereby he is able to subdue all things unto himself.

The sun has warmed the wet deck and now water evaporates as steam. It rises slowly about the flag-draped body as if Paul Hicks' soul is leaving, rising to heaven. When the captain is through, he nods to

Andrew and Jorge. They approached the platform, raise the planks upon which the body is resting, lifting the inside edge until the body, sewn in a piece of old canvas, slides freely under the open end of the flag. It gains momentum as it to races off the ship and plunges into a line of foam created alongside *Tranquility* as she and her crew move on.

"I was overcome by a strange feeling as the captain read from the book," Ben says to Andrew. "The steam rising from the deck was a sign of sorts. Was it Hicks?"

He later finds out that he wasn't alone in the experience.

CHAPTER 42

Once Again Seal Hunters

As they approach Juan de Fernandez Islands from the southeast, the crew on *Tranquility* sees two smaller islands on either side of a much larger island. They look more like the tops of the Himalayas rather than desert isles basking in a warm summer sun. Their profile is a continuous run of vertical cliffs and ravines, and where a level plain forms, it looks like the surface of the moon. Hospitable it isn't. On the north and west sides, it is almost a different island with verdant plains and jungle-like environments trapped in narrow valleys. All the rain that falls on the island, falls on this side, and accounts for the lush, tropical vegetation. But that is not what *Tranquility's* crew sees as they lower a boat in search of a rock-free channel that will lead them to a leeward anchorage hard against the island.

"What do you think?" Hiram asks his brother as they scan the island with their long glasses.

"I dare not take her in before finding a channel," answers Andrew. "From the exposed shore, it looks like the tide still has a way to fall. I would wait until the tide begins to rise before I take in the ship."

"Agreed," says Hiram.

"What of Abe Brown? Has there been any change?"

"None according to the watch, or his uncle. It is now five, maybe six days since he was brought out of the bilge. Ephraim says he's been able to get him to drink but not eat. He has yet to open his eyes."

"Something is likely to happen to him soon unless he comes out of the fog he is in." says Hiram.

Bringing the 300-ton bark into the lee of the island at dead-low tide is tricky for the crew. The half-moon bay created in its mid-section is studded with numerous small, rocky islets, exposed reefs and more in the water that cannot be seen. The passage is so narrow and difficult to maneuver that Andrew, after he has determined a course and returns to the ship, has all sails furled and lowers two boats to tow the ship shoreward. The anchor is lowered into 4 fathoms of water, just 500 feet off the beach.

At first, Capt. Lester is surprised by the great number of small boulders along the beach. As the ship gets closer, he sees the "boulders" moving. To better spy out the land, he puts the glass on them and discovers that they are fur seals.

"We may spend more than a day here," he says to his 2nd mate, who did not lower his boat. "We have come upon a virtual paradise of seals. I expect Mr. Brown will soon be upon us to insist that we turn our unexpected fortune into greenbacks."

"They do look a bit different from the last fur seals we hunted," says Andrew. "They are slimmer that the others. But I don't think Ephraim will mind."

"Who uses my name?" Brown asks as he approaches.

"Have you seen your nephew today?" asks Andrew.

"I did this morning."

"And how is he?"

"He fares no better. He looks terrible. He has lost weight. I do not think he will survive much longer. He will not, or cannot eat. Cook has been able to get some water into him, but not much. He is beginning to foul the mates' quarters. Hiram, I hate to say this but I must, you will soon have to make a decision."

"What decision?" Lester asks but he knows well what Ephraim means. "I think the decision is yours. After all you are his next of kin.

"Who had the Mid-Watch that day?" Hiram says as he turns to his brother and avoids commenting on the next move for Abe Brown. Andrew again senses his brother's inability to make quick decisions.

"Oh, yes, I recall now. It was Diogo. Is he handy?"

"I just passed him in the mess," says Brown.

"Andrew, will you fetch him?"

In a few minutes, 3rd Mate Diogo Pilla climbs onto the quarterdeck.

"You asked for me, Sir?"

"Yes, Diogo. I am still curious as to how Abe Brown got onboard without being noticed. Who was on watch with you?"

"Why the farmer….Jeremiah Kinder, Sir."

"Where is he now? Have him join us."

"Were you and Kinder always together on watch the last night in Concépcion?" Lester asks Diogo as Kinder stands off to the side.

"Why no, Sir. From time to time, when needed, we would relieve ourselves or go below for coffee. But, Sir, the gangway was always manned."

"Kinder, did you ever leave the gangway unmanned?" asks Lester.

"No, Sir. Never."

"Then how do you think Mr. Brown came onboard?"

"I have no idea, Sir."

"Kinder, I want the truth. Give it to me now and there will be no repercussions. If I later discover that you lied, I'll find a cat-o'-nine-tails for your back."

Unknown to the interrogators on the quarterdeck, a weak voice suddenly rises from below, from the hatch leading into the mate's quarters.

"There's no need for that."

"My God!" exclaims Ephraim who has turned toward the voice, "it's Abe!"

Suddenly all eyes are on a skeleton of a man. He clings to the sides of the hatch for support. Weakened after climbing the stairs, he gasps for air. His hands slip along side the hatchway, then he collapses onto the main deck.

Damn, says Hiram Lester to himself. Well, at least I won't have to heave his body over the side, he says with a sign of relief.

Abe is taken below and returned to his bunk. Cook brings him porridge to eat. He sits up as his uncle feeds him. Billy, the cook's helper appears with a bucket of water and some rags.

"What's that for?" Ephraim asks the boy.

"Mr. Andrew said you should help him wash. He is stinking the mates' mess. He said to tell you that he and the captain would be down here to talk to Abe. And, to remind you not to discuss the incident with him."

The boy leaves Brown and crosses over to Obie Jones who is still in the chair, on watch. He says a few words to him that no one else can hear, then returns to the galley.

A half-hour later, Capt. Lester comes down the ladder and turns aft and goes into the mates' quarters. Immediately behind him is his brother. Both Jorge and Diogo Pilla are sitting in the mess and rise to follow Andrew. Ephraim is sitting on his bunk, having finished with his nephew's cleansing.

"Jones," Capt. Lester addresses Obie Jones who has reclaimed his seat on the far side of the quarters from where he watched Abe and any visitors.

"I had to relieve myself, Sir," Jones said. "His uncle was with him and he told me he would watch Abe while I was gone. Because he still seemed in a coma I thought it was all right for me to leave them. When I got back, Mr. Brown was gone and so was Abe."

"No matter," says Lester.

"How do you feel, Abe?" asks Capt. Lester.

"Like shit," he answers. "How'd ya thinks I'd feel?"

"Have you your wits about you?"

"I never lost 'em."

"You must have, to get yourself into this state."

"Wad state's that?"

"It seems to be a state of pure stupidity," says Lester.

"If you cannot keep a civil tongue in your mouth I will send you below and lock you in irons!"

Abe Brown does not respond.

"What happened?" asks Lester.

"I'd's simple. I wuz rolled outside a tavern by a gang of Chilies. But dose bastards got more'n dey bargained fer."

"What happened to your companions, Jolly and Blackwell?"

"Dey wuz upstairs, 'bove the tavern. Dey found out dat dere were whores dere an' went to pay 'em a visit. I went outside wid 'em but waited on da street for dem ta git done. Dats when a bunch of Chilies came outside an' asked me fer money. I told 'em to go to hell an' reached fer my knife. Dey came at me wid knives an' I pulled mine. I tink I cut one bad. Duh udders jumped on me an' were poundin' me. I got free, an' smashed one in da face. De udder two went inside tuh git more men. I turned tail and ran down duh hill, ta da center o' town. I done quite 'member gettin' dere. I guess I was losing blood or sometin'.

"Somehow I made it ta duh dock an' sat down on a bench in duh park jus' afore duh wharf. I waited an' looked up duh hill fer Jolly and Blackwell. I guess dey didn't make it.

"Duh next ting I remember was you askin' me if I was alright."

"You're lying," says Lester. "Don't think you are going to lie your way out of this mess.

"Bo'sun," Lester says to Bellingham who has joined the interrogation, "Find Kinder and bring him here immediately."

In a few minutes Jeremiah Kinder enters the mate's quarters from steerage.

"You called for me, Sir?"

"Now tell me how Abe Brown came aboard this ship that last night in Concépcion. Before you answer, I want you to think about what you are going to say. If it is anything other than what I believe to be the truth, I will lock you in irons with Brown."

Kinder is slow to respond.

"Mr. Diogo and I was on watch. It was gettin' cold. He said he was goin' below to get a cup of coffee, to warm him up and asked me if I wanted one. I never say no to coffee. Besides, I, too, was gettin' cold.

"He no sooner went below than I saw someone staggering down the dock, headin' for the ship. The way he was walkin' I was sure he was drunk. As he got closer, I saw it was Mr. Abe. When he got on the bottom of the gangway I saw he was covered with blood.

"He said 'help,' not so loud that he would wake someone, but just loud enough for me to hear. Course, I went down to help him. I brought him up to the main deck and walked him aft to his companionway. He said no and pushed me to the forward companionway.

"'If ya tells anyone ya saw me, I'll kill ya,'" he said. "'You know I will,' he said again."

As Kinder reveals what happened that night he looks at Abe who is sitting up in bed. Brown stares at him, then in a swift movement he runs his fingers across his neck, under his chin, as if he had a knife in his hand.

"The last thing I saw was him going down the ladder. I got back real quick to the gangway. I saw in the lantern that I had blood on my shirt. Just then, Mr. Diogo came back with the coffee. I backed out of the light so he couldn't see it as he handed me the cup. For a moment, I didn't know what to do. Then I told him I had to relieve myself and went down the forward hatch. I found another shirt and returned. That's the God's honest truth, Captain. It all happened just like that."

"You're excused, Kinder. You may go," says Lester.

The quarters are silent for a few minutes. Then Capt. Lester continues.

"You may not know it, but Jolly and Blackwell are dead. They had their throats slit and all their clothes, shoes, and any money they might have had was taken. The police found them the next day.

"The police also found the young whore who you punched in the face. When she fell backwards, she broke her back. The police said she died instantly, if that is any consolation to you. The Chinese madam who accused you of punching the girl, then punching her told this to the police.

"Do you deny these accounts?"

Abe does not answer.

"To add to this, we know that you had organized a scheme to jump ship, which included Jolly and Blackwell. We have a signed note from Jolly to Roger Whetstone assigning his lay and ditty bag to him because he lent Jolly some money.

"It also indicates that you are supposed to have gotten more money from your uncle. Your uncle checked his chest and said there was $500 missing.

"Das a lie," Abe suddenly responds. "I tooks only $300. If he says I took $500, he's lyin'."

Lester looks over at Ephraim. "Your time will come, too, cousin," he says.

"Well," says Abe to Hiram, "wad does yuh plan tuh do 'bout it?"

"Too bad the cat-o-nine tails has been abolished, or I would use them. But, this is a homicide and more of a criminal than a disciplinary matter. This matter is done as far as you are concerned.

"In the meantime," Lester says as he turns to Bellingham, "Get some help and take him and his donkey breakfast back to the bilge. Find an appropriate post and shackle his legs and hands to it.

"Maybe he will have a change of attitude after a few days.

"Gentlemen," Lester says to his officers, "follow me into my quarters. Mr. Brown," he says to Ephraim, "you are excluded from this until I find time to consider your $500 claim. In the meantime, turn over the keys to your chest to the 1st mate. You will not have need of money for a while."

Now in the bilge again, within Abe's reach is a bucket for his sanitary needs. His only companions, excepting when food is brought down, is a candle and a bevy of rats.

Dat fuckin' uncle. Abe says to himself. He's as bad a robber as me.

The idea of money quickly mobilizes Abe into sitting up. His hands quickly go into both right and left pockets of his pants. Damn, he continues, I almost fergot da money. Duh dumbbells never searched me. A grin spreads over is face. Dis may be my ways out.

"Gentlemen," Lester again says to his mates as they assemble in the sanctity of his quarters, "I had not planned on this but have decided to modify the ship's itinerary. We will continue whaling and Abe Brown will be kept in irons. I had planned on taking *Tranquility* north to the Nazca Ridge then turn westerly in our hunt for whales. In light of what has happened, I must alter this plan. Instead, I will bypass Nazca and continue north to Lima. There's an American embassy where they can better handle the matter of what Abe Brown has done. He has three counts against him-- manslaughter, thievery and desertion--and I might even add attempted mutiny.

"In view of this, I am considering making Harvey Bennett the temporary 4th mate. Have any of you objections to this?"

"I don't think he has the respect of any of the men in the fo'c's'le," says Jorge. "Many think of him as being too close to Abe."

"I agree with Jorge," says Diogo, "but I know that he and Abe had a falling out after Abe accused him of screwing up that first whale. This is not his first trip on a whaler though at times I don't think he's learned much."

"What do you say, Andrew?" asks Hiram.

"At first thought, I would agree with you. But thinking more about it I believe there is a better choice."

"Who?"

"Ben!"

"Are you serious?" asks Hiram.

"I am," says his brother.

"The Indian has gained a lot of respect among the fo'c's'le," says

Andrew. "He has shown the ability to learn quickly. I have watched him rise in my boat from being a puller, to steerer to harponer. His strength and accuracy with the harpon are as good as any other harponer we have on board. He gets along well with the Negroes in our crew, something he learned as he grew up on his reservation. We do have an inordinate number of Negroes onboard. And, he is educated."

"He does get along well with the Portagee," interrupts Diogo. "I agree with Andrew, I think he will do."

"Naming either him or Bennett is a temporary position," said Hiram. "If he cannot handle it I can quickly replace him with Bennett. Who does not agree?"

No hands rise nor does anyone utter a nay.

"Andrew, will you tell Ben what I've decided? You know him better than anyone else."

"Good. Let's secure the ship. I think foul weather is again afoot."

Andrew climbs onto deck and scans the bow of *Tranquility*. He spots Ben there with two Greenies and approaches him. Ben sees him and leaves the two men and moves toward Andrew.

"Get your mattress and any gear you have stowed in the fo'c's'le," Andrew orders Ben.

A puzzled Ben does as he is told and is topside after a few minutes.

"Now, follow me!"

They enter the starboard hatch just ahead of the quarterdeck and drop below to the officer's mess. Andrew leads him forward to the mate's quarters.

"That one there is your bunk. That is your seat," Andrew says and points to the large table in the officer's mess where the mates eat.

"What is this all about?" Ben asks.

"The captain, with all the mates' approval, has just moved you up to acting 4th mate."

"What?"

"Is this a joke?"

"It's no joke," Andrew says. "You've earned it. But, be aware that this is a temporary position. If you screw up you'll be back in my boat as a haponeer. If you don't, you're likely to return to the reservation as a real 4th mate. Has anyone there achieved this rank?"

"I don't think so. Thank you, Mr. Lester."

"You may now address me as Andrew."

"Oh, by the way, Bennett will be your harponeer and Rusnak and one of the Chileans will be added to your boat. Any problem with either person?"

"No, Sir, none at all. Thank you."

The next day, the crew of *Tranquility* begins the business of harvesting fur seals. But before they do, several go up to Ben who is standing at the gangway opening and congratulate him. During this sealing operation, Abe, while confined to the bilge, is gradually nursed back to health, mainly by his uncle.

While the crew is cooking seal fat, a party of men comes down the mountain pass from the island's north side. The day before, one of the villagers had been in the mountains when he heard gunshots. He and others came to investigate. They had seen *Tranquility* at anchor and the smoke rising from the beach. They are part of a small community of Chilean fishermen who, for the past 40 years, have been living on the edge of Cumberland Bay. They tell the whalers that there are about 150 people in their village of San Juan Bautista. Several of the visitors are allowed on the ship, curious about how whales are rendered onboard.

The day after the fishermen return to their village Andrew finds his brother is extremely agitated. At first, Andrew thinks it is the problem with Abe Brown. Later, he discovers it isn't. Hiram confesses to him that he feels a change in the weather is about to take place and seeks out the barometer. It has fallen below 30 inches.

"I have had the same dream for the last three nights, a premonition that I am going to die in a storm. That is why the falling barometer has me so worried. Will it be this storm?"

"Hiram, everyone at sea fears hurricanes. But you seem especially affected of late by them. True, cyclones can mean disaster, but in the past they have never seemed to bother you as greatly as now."

"Andrew, I never told you about a dream that started this. It happened a few days before we sailed, the night I spent at the Mousetrap Tavern because the windows in my cabin were out for repair. That night I saw four whaling captains from Sag Harbor's past. They were all playing cards in the room next to mine. They made so much noise in arguing that it woke me and I went to their room to ask them to be quiet.

"All I had was candlelight and I'm not sure of what I saw. One told me to beware of cyclones because one would cause my death. That was ludicrous. In the morning, after I awoke I returned to their room. It was empty. This has plagued me ever since."

"Weather is always changing in these latitudes," says Andrew. "Cyclones at this time of year are common. Don't fret about it. It will change back before you know it."

Hiram is not eased by his brother's answer.

That night the winds rise, blowing hard from the southwest. By daylight they veer to the north, then back northwest. Capt. Lester fears that change is a foreboding signal of things to come. He knows what such low barometric pressure and the direction of the wind at this latitude means. It is the direction from which cyclones blow south of the equator. He hopes aloud that there is enough island between the ship and the wind to create a lee.

Immediately upon awaking the next day, Lester again checks the barometer. It has fallen below 29 inches. It is their only sure warning that a late summer cyclone is approaching. The winds are already rising. In order to secure his ship in its current position, Lester lowers two boats, each hauling one of the ship's two spare anchors. The heavy bitter ends of their lines are attached to large cleats on *Tranquility's* larboard and starboard stern quarters. The anchors are carried 200 feet from each corner of the ship and securely planted, wedged in the reef's rocky bottom. The slack is taken up on the shipboard cleats. The ship is now anchored at three points and will swing very little from her current position regardless of wind direction.

After the men in the boats secure the anchors, they go ashore to pick up the sealers on the beach. They gather all the pelts and any gear that can be blown away. They knock down their tents and add them to their cargo. Only the try works remain, a single, large cauldron overturned.

The next day, Saturday, February 1, 1868, just before dawn, with all its fury, the cyclone strikes. Throughout the morning, winds steadily rise and buffet the larboard side of the ship, throwing heavy sheets of spray across the deck. By noon, they reach, then surpass 76 knots. Unabated, they continue to rise and reach 100 knots by darkness.

The barometer in Lester's cabin continues to plummet and reads 28.25 inches of mercury. By the next morning, it is impossible to go on deck. Winds scream through the rigging like the proverbial horde of banshees as tension on the bow and stern anchors stretches their hemp lines into long, thin, rigid, unyielding arcs. Anything that hadn't been firmly tied down has blown into the bay.

"Good God," says Andrew as he and the other officers hang about their evening mess. "Can you imagine what it would be like if we were at sea?"

"I doubt we would be afloat," adds Diogo. "I have been in hurricanes in the Atlantic but I have never seen one blow as hard as this one. Maybe it's because the winds in the Pacific have a greater fetch."

"After a dozen miles of open water, I doubt the length of fetch is a factor affecting the wind's speed," says Andrew Lester.

"I agree with you," says Jorge. "I've been in two typhoons in the Indian Ocean and they were worse than any I experienced in the Atlantic."

"I don't think you can compare one typhoon, hurricane or cyclone, whichever you choose to call it, to another one," injects Capt. Lester, who has joined the mates in their mess. "All have their own characteristics. What these are depends upon the time of year, the temperature of the water in the latitude it is in, even the weather outside the storm, often a thousand miles away. These can all affect the winds that may be upon you."

"It is like women, comparing women," says Diogo in an attempt to change the conversation.

"How say you?" asks the captain.

"Not only it it foolish, but dangerous to compare one woman to another, especially when one is within hearing. You must enjoy each woman for herself, what she possesses, and not what you wish she possessed. We should thank God that they are all different. If they were not, it would be a boring world."

"Hear! Hear! Hear!" the officers respond.

"Diogo, do you speak from experience?" asks Andrew Lester.

"Only Portygee women," he answers. "I know nothing of American women. I have yet to explore that field. But I don't think they are different."

"Amen," says Lester. "But let's get out of here. The harponeers and steerers are outside the door, stomping their feet and coughing, wanting to get in here to eat."

Andrew is not quite asleep that night when he hears screams coming from the captain's quarters. He rushes and throws open the door. Hiram is sitting up in bed with a blanket pulled to his mouth. He looks at his brother and Andrew sees the terror in his eyes and sweat covering his face.

Hiram calms down as he recognizes his brother.

"It's that dream again. I fear this storm is building to drown me. There is nothing I can do. Help me, Andrew."

His brother hugs him for a few moments then Hiram breaks away.

"There is nothing I can do," says Andrew. He hugs him again for a few minutes then breaks away and rises off the bed. He looks at his brother and he sees a man he does not know. Never before has he seen him so lacking in control.

Hiram sees him staring and yells: "Leave me alone!"

Tranquility rides surprisingly well at anchor during the height of the blow. On the second day, while the shiphandlers and harpooners are in the galley eating supper, someone notices that the sound of the wind has disappeared.

"It's the eye, the eye. We are in the middle of this damned blow," says Joshua Edwards who is on his third whale hunt. "We are in the center of the storm," he repeats himself. He gets up, climbs the ladder to the main deck and for a moment holds open the door. "There's hardly a ripple on the water," he says as he returns. "It's deadly silent out there."

"What does that mean? Does it mean the cyclone is over?" asks the cook's boy who is serving salt horse.

"No, son," Edwards answers. "We are just half-way through this damned beast. It will come again. It won't let up until we are crashed on the beach or driven to sea dragging all three anchors."

"Stop it!" yells Jeb Blackman, the Barbados Negro, "you're scaring the boy."

"Scared! Scared! Damned well he should be scared of this wind. We all should be scared. Damn it. If I survive, this is the last time I'll go awhaling. I'm getting too old for this shit."

"I have weathered hurricanes at home, on land," Blackman addressed the boy and the rest of the crew. "We have a saying in Barbados, 'Two by one.' That means two days of wind before the eye and one day after. It is rare for a hurricane to stay in one spot more than three days."

Blackman is right. The winds return by midnight and now batter the starboard side of the ship. They blow throughout the next day but about sunset the winds begin to back. This is the first sign that the cyclone is moving on. During the night the winds continue backing from northwest to west, and by daybreak they are again out of the southwest.

"How did you sleep?" Andrew asks Hiram who is pouring a cup of coffee.

"With my eyes closed!"

Later that day, the sealers go ashore, re-establish their camp and continue the harvest. During that time, another party of fishermen comes over the mountain. They are looking for work. The men ashore tell them that they are almost done sealing, that there is only a week, two at most of work. The fishermen tell them that they want to work on the ship, not on the beach.

The crew ashore raises a flag, the signal that they want a boat from the ship. A half-hour later, Jorge beaches his craft, asks what is the problem, then takes three men back to the ship.

Captain Lester looks them over. He speaks to them but they tell him they know no English. Jorge is still on deck and awkwardly uses his native language to translate their Spanish.

"They want to work on the whaleship," Jorge says. "Fishing has been poor, they say, and that they all are without wives."

"What's the biggest one's name?" Capt. Lester asks.

"Juan," Jorge discovers.

None of the three Chileans is really "big." At most, the tallest is 5 feet. Instead of height, he is muscular but that is what Lester wants, another man in Andrew's crew.

"Do you think he can pull an oar?" Lester asks Andrew.

"He sure looks like he can."

"Tell them one, only one, the big one, Juan," Lester tells Number 2.

"What's his last name?"

"Colon," he answers.

"Does he need to return to the village? We are leaving in a few days."

After a string of mixed Spanish/Portuguese conversation, Jorge says that it isn't necessary, that there is no one there he needs to talk with.

"Good. Mr. Pilla, take these men ashore. Put the big one to work with the men on the beach and return with all the pelts and barrels that are filled. Tomorrow, we will begin breaking the try works."

Chapter 43

Abe's Plan to Escape

Saturday, March 21, 1868
Day 841

"This morning, I had the trypot knocked down and gathered all else ashore," Lester enters in his log. "From the crew's comments I see that the men are happy to leave the seals behind. Their stink is worse than whales. They worked hard as sealers, but everyone prefers to chase whales. I agree with them."

In 16 days of standing due north, at a cruising speed (3 knots), *Tranquility* has covered nearly 500 miles. To the captain's chagrin, her lookouts have not spotted a single whale.

"I would have thought this to be impossible in the Pacific," he writes in his log.

On April 6th, at 26° 21' S by 79° 53' W, they pass close to the east of Isla San Ambrosio, one of two uninhabited islands. It is a day or two sooner than Lester had expected to see them.

Lester had planned to use the islands only as a turning point in his route north, because just beyond them, two days sailing night and day to the northwest would bring *Tranquility* over the Tropic of Capricorn and the southern edge of the Nazca Ridge. They are a bit more than a hundred miles south of Lima, their immediate destination. After two days *Tranquility* is running north, paralleling the coast of Peru, so close that at times the high peaks of the Andes are seen poking above the eastern horizon.

"I fear we will not head home this year," Ephraim says during supper in the officer's mess. "There have not been as many whales as you hoped for," he says as he directs his comments to the head of the table. He has played a more subdued role since the incident with his nephew and the charge that he misrepresented the amount of money he lost. He has stopped criticizing Hiram Lester.

"Has anyone else something to say?" the captain asks.

"Ben?"

"No, Sir."

"The sooner we get out of here the better," adds Brown.

"Who has tomorrow's morning watch?" asks Lester.

"I do," pipes up Diogo Pilla.

"I would love to take the ship due west," says Hiram, "but cannot, at this time. We are a hundred miles southwest of Lima and for the moment, I plan to put whaling aside and deliver Abe Brown to the Marines at the American embassy in Lima. It will take us about two days, if the south-westerlies hold. Then we can head west along the ridge.

"After you finish here, Andrew, have the helm set the course at 90 degrees."

The mates break up after the meeting. As Hiram turns to head into his cabin he catches his brother's attention and waves to him to follow.

"Close the door behind you," he tells Andrew as he enters his quarters.

"How fares Abe?" he asks.

"I was down there yesterday," says Andrew. "He seems no better nor worse. He will make it. He refused to answer me when I spoke to him. Just as well."

"Andrew, I had that dream again."

"What dream?"

"You know, the one I had just before the cyclone struck us. I saw myself sinking in the water. I saw myself dead. What is the meaning of this?"

"I doubt there is a meaning. You are just under stress. It is Brown's fate that hangs heavily on you. Do not wear his mantle. In two days, you, and all of us, will be rid of him. Thanks be to God!"

Instead of returning to the mates' quarters, as did the others, Ephraim descends into the bilge, carrying several short candles.

"How are you?" he perfunctorily asks his nephew.

Brown doesn't answer.

"Here are a few more candles," he says and places them on the bilge deck where Brown can reach them.

"What do you want?" Brown finally asks.

"I want nothing of you. There have been some changes made in the ship's course. Lester plans to head directly from here to Lima. He says it is about two days away. As you know, he plans to turn you over to officials at the American embassy."

"What do you think they will do?"

"They certainly won't set you free. You're a wanted man. Most likely they will contact Chilean officials in Lima who will probably want to send you back to Concépcion, either by ship or maybe by the new train system they are building. You will probably wind up in a prison somewhere in Chile."

"Dat wone happen," says Abe.

"What do you mean, that won't happen?"

"Trust me, it wone happen."

"Do you have a plan?

"I gots somethin' in mind."

"What is it?"

"Ya don't needs tuh know. You ain't part of dis."

"Don't you trust me Abe?"

"I trusts no one. Trust's dat's whad gots me here!"

"I think this isolation has reached your brain." Ephraim says as he turns and climbs the ladder. He says, "Good Night." Abe doesn't answer.

"Two days ain't much time," Abe says to himself in a low voice. "Der's gotta be a way."

As he reaches for the candles Ephraim brought him the clamps on his legs, connected by a 3-foot chain, make a noise as they are dragged across the edges of a vertical post supporting the deck above the bilge.

"My god!" he exclaims in an epiphany, "da fuckin' answer's at my feet."

Abraham Brown has never been a person to be underestimated. He may not be especially intelligent but he is crafty and that has aided him in his life. Now he faces death, knowing that he will eventually be taken to Lima. He moves the lighted candle closer to his feet and notices the gradual wear that had taken place on the 4 by 4 post's square corners. He suddenly realizes that, if he constantly pulls the chain back-and-forth over the edges, he can wear a cut through the entire post.

"It's like a saw," he says as he lifts the chain slightly with one foot.

Abe begins a regular routine in doing so, but only when he hears no activity on the deck above him because the chain, wearing away the wood, doesn't do it silently. The action sends slight vibrations upwards. Immediately above him are the steerage quarters. Anyone sleeping there would surely feel the vibrations or hear the sound while in their bunks.

Abe figures that once he cuts through with the foot chain all he has to do is drop the hand chains down and pull it through. So no one can see what he is doing, whenever he has a visitor, he will wrap his legs around the enlarging groove to hide his work.

I gots two days ta finish, he says to himself. Dere's one problem. Whad if da weight of duh upper deck pushes down the post. I'd be screwed. I gots tuh try it now tuh see if'n it works. He works furiously, almost with disregard to the noise he is making. He is through and the post does not collapse on the chain. He pushes on the post and feels it move slightly. He pulls the donkey's breakfast under his body, leans next to the candle, and blows it out.

Chapter 44

The Final Assault

"We have a steady wind on our transom," Andrew says to his brother as the captain climbs the starboard ladder to the quarterdeck.

"We should easily make Callao, Lima's port, by late tomorrow or early the next day."

"Has anyone checked the log?"

"Bo'sun was at the transom a few minutes ago. He said we were making 5-and-a-half knots."

"That's good," says Lester. "We must be in the Humboldt to make such speed with these winds. I think you are right. We will be there late tomorrow…God willing."

"Did you sleep well?"

"No!"

As Lester steps down the ladder from the quarterdeck, he glances up and sees a lookout on the main and another on the fore. That should be enough, he says to himself. We are not in a whaling mode. We cannot get this business over fast enough.

In the bilge, Abe pulls the chain on his feet through the slice and stretches his legs as far as the chain allows. Next, he checks the chain on his wrists. It easily slides through the cut. He listens for any sounds on the deck above him. Then he stands up and stretches on his feet. He squats and rises in quick succession to exercise them.

Damned, he says to himself, I can't believe dey work so good after all dis time. He takes several quick steps to the casks and stops. He has heard something.

It's dat damn boy, he says to himself. He's bringing my morning shit ta eat.

Abe rushes back to the post, sits on the deck, and then runs the chain on his feet, then those on his wrists, through the cut and back up against the post, hiding the cut.

"Your breakfast, Sir," says Billy.

The youngster lays it on the deck then turns and scurries back to the ladder. He is fearful of Brown and is gone before Brown can reach the bowl.

"Ephraim said it'd take two days tuh reach Lima," he says softly, "and maybe duh morning o' the second. I am ready, more dan ready. I'll have my due afore dey can have der way wid me. They tinks me beaten. Dey be wrong."

The day ends without anything noteworthy for Lester to add to the ship's log. Maybe more tomorrow, he thinks as he takes his place at the head of the table for supper. The mates seem especially chatty this evening. Maybe it is in anticipation of docking in Callao, a port few have ever visited. Ephraim again eats with them as his reticence continues.

The next day dawns a duplicate of the previous days. Skies are clear and winds hold from the same direction, at the same speed. Again the Lesters are in the wheelhouse just as the sun clears the horizon.

"This has been one long tack," says Hiram.

"Were things always this way," answers Andrew, "it would make life at sea considerably easier.

"We should be approaching the coast of Peru sometime late in the day. I have never put into Callao, but I hear it is a rather large harbor."

"I was here on my second voyage," says Hiram. "It is large, but I don't think we should try to find an anchorage in the dark. Maybe we should slow our approach, wear ship at night, and go in with the sunrise."

"I agree," says Andrew. "I will see to it now."

He sees Bellingham with several crewmen next to the foremast and drops down to the main deck to approach him.

"Bo'sun," he says, "we're making too much speed."

"How can that be?" questions Bellingham.

"The captain plans on entering Callao Harbor in the morning and not this evening. And, at this speed, we will get there too soon. Instead, haul down the course and topsails on both fore and main. The ship should still hold this tack without undue effort for the quartermaster."

"Aye, Sir," says Bellingham. Out of habit, he touches the brim of his hat, as if to salute. The habits learned from four years in the Navy are difficult to overcome. He sends men into the yards and the prescribed sails are furled.

Before the sun sets, the watch in the main sees land. The highest tops of the Andes are snow-covered in summer, even this close to the equator. The ship is 50 miles south of Callao.

Deep in the bowels of the ship, in the bilge, Abe senses that the ship is slowing. The sound of water rushing against the hull has lessened and so has the forward-aft rocking as *Tranquility* no longer plunges into the backside of waves.

Two hours later, lantern light floods the ladder leading into the bilge. Brown sees it is not the cook's helper but his uncle. He is carrying a wooden bowl that contains supper. Abe sits up and with his legs covers the cut in the post.

"We'll be in Callao tomorrow," Ephraim says, as he places the bowl on the deck. "They'll probably take you to Lima as soon as we anchor or find a berth."

Abe says nothing.

His uncle rises, turns and silently climbs the ladder, taking with him all the light that floods the bilge, except that from the lone candle near Abe. He leaves the hatch door open, as it has been ever since Abe was chained in the bilge. Occasionally, when the wind is right, Abe gets puffs of fresh air that come down through the blubber hatch, if it, too, is left open.

Abe eats the oatmeal-water gruel. He finishes it then tosses the wooden bowl across the barrels. The bowl clatters as it falls to the deck. All is silent except for the creaking, moaning sounds of the ship as she slowly makes her way to Callao.

Abe does not sleep but lies on his mattress, with his hands behind the back of his head, watching the shadows made by the candle dance across the ceiling. He has no idea how long he has been there but is sure that everyone, except those on watch, is now asleep.

Cautiously, he slips the chain on his wrists through the cut in the post, then the chain on his ankles. He makes a contribution near the water bucket, missing it intentionally to maintain silence in the bilge. He is stiff and stretches for a while, then slowly makes his way to the foot of the ladder. The noise of the ankle chain startles him. Dis wone do, he says to himself. He thinks for a while then walks back to his mattress. In the candlelight he rips the mattress cover into strips then winds them around the chain.

He stands up and walks back to the ladder. The cloth strips now muffle the sounds the chain makes as it moves over the deck. Satisfied, he slowly, cautiously takes one step after another, almost soundlessly, on the ladder and reaches the top. He sticks his head just above the blubber room deck and looks around.

Steerage is just aft of the ladder. The hatch (door) into it is always open. He hears the many, varied sounds as more than a dozen men--harpooners, boat steerers and shiphandlers--snore, gasp for air and breathe loudly. He listens for a while and is about to step onto the deck when he hears someone cough, then get out of a bunk. Moments later he hears him urinate into a bucket that is not empty. A minute later he listens as the man returns to his bunk. All is again quiet.

He climbs onto the blubber deck and moves silently to the doorway leading into steerage. All inside are still asleep. A lone lantern, in the center of the quarters, swings gently from the ceiling as the ship slowly rolls from one side to another. Double bunks, filled with men, are along both sides of the bulkhead, just inside the door that separates steerage from the blubber room. Their trousers and oil slicks hang on pegs from posts on the outside edges of their bunks.

For the longest time, Abe stands there, studying the scene. Suddenly he catches a flash of light, then it is immediately gone. The light is the reflection of candlelight from inside the lantern.

Dats one, Abe says to himself and slowly, quietly, moves several feet to it. Abe sees a man's belt, taken off his pants, that hangs freely on a post. On it is exposed the handle of a knife. The blade sticks an inch above its sheath and is the source of the reflection. Silently, Abe pushes the knife deeper into its sheath then lifts the belt off the peg. He steps backward, without turning, to see if he has disturbed anyone. Back to the door, he is satisfied that he hasn't and turns, now making his way across the blubber room deck to the hatch leading into the forecastle. As he does, he buckles the man's belt around his waist.

A single lantern hangs there from the ceiling, much like the one in steerage. He stands in the hatchway, watching and listening to the noises created by nearly 15 men crammed into a space half the size of steerage. A man in the bottom bunk just inside the doorway, with his back toward Abe decides turns to sleep on his other side.

As the lantern light sweeps back and forth across the man's face, Brown sees that it is Kinder, Jeremiah Kinder. Dat son of a bitch, Abe says to himself. As he thinks, his mind is flooded with rage. I tol' dat bastard I'd kill him if he squealed on me.

Without thinking, Brown drops to his knees in front of Kinder as his right hand pulls the knife from its sheath. He places his left hand across Kinder's mouth. For a fleeting moment he sees Kinder's eyes pop open. In one smooth movement, as if it had been practiced, he runs the blade from right to left across Kinder's throat. For a few moments, there is a gurgling sound. Then he feels Kinder's body stiffen under him, then relax.

"I told ya I'd kill yah, yuh son-of-a-bitch," he quietly says.

"Mister Abe, is that you?"

Startled, Brown rises to his feet as he turns toward the voice.

It's Billy, the cook's helper, he thinks.

"Boy, wad yuh doin' here?" Brown asks him.

"I bin sleepin' here for the past few days 'cause it's been too hot at night in the galley," he says. "Besides, Cook snores so loud I can never sleep."

Just then, another man is awakened by the talk and throws his feet off the top bunk and jumps to the deck.

"What you doin' here?" asks Obie Jones, the Negro who watched Brown while he was recovering.

"You ain't supposed ta be here!" he says and moves to Brown.

The talking awakens others in the forecastle.

Brown, seeing that he is about to be trapped, lunges toward the boy and grabs him around the neck with his left hand. He pulls him between Jones and himself and yells, "Stop or I'll kill him," as he brings the knife to Billy's throat.

Jones cannot stop his forward motion and comes precariously close to Abe. Brown lashes out with his knife and cuts a slanting gash in Obie's right arm, between the elbow and shoulder. Jones quickly clasps the cut with his left hand and stops the bleeding. As he backs off he sees Brown's bloody shirt. Then he sees Kinder's bloodied body and blood on the deck next to his bunk.

"What's happening?" asks a sleepy Egas Sanchez as he, too, jumps down from his bunk.

"Come any closer," Abe says, "an' I'll kill 'im."

The noises have awakened several men in steerage. Kurt Müller, the shipsmith rushes to the hatch leading into the forecastle and sees what is happening. He turns and immediately runs to the mate's quarters. He stops at Andrew Lester's bunk and vigorously shakes his shoulder.

"Mr. Lester. Mr. Lester," he says loudly. "Abe Brown has escaped. He's causing trouble in the fo'c's'le.'"

As he passes Bellingham's bunk Andrew wakes him. "Come forward."

"What's going on here?" Lester yells at Abe from the entrance to the forecastle.

"What are you doing? Release the boy. Have you lost your senses?"

"Done come near me," Abe yells back. "Come closer an' dah boy's life will be on yur head."

"Bo'sun," Andrew turns to Bellingham who is immediately behind him. "Get his uncle. Maybe he can talk sense into him."

Bellingham turns and is about to head back to the mate's quarters when he sees Ephraim Brown rushing toward him.

"It's Abe," says Bellingham as he steps aside to let Brown pass.

"Get the Captain," Andrew says to Bellingham.

"Abe! Abe! What have you done?"

Ephraim looks down and sees all the blood. "Abe, have you gone mad?"

"Talk to him. Get him to release the boy," Andrew says to Brown.

Brown stares at the scene before him. Dumbfounded for a while, he finally speaks. "It's no use. There's no redemption for him. He is lost. There is nothing I can do here." Brown drops his head in shame, turns back, and walks past Andrew.

A crowd has gathered at the hatchway and opens it as if to let Ephraim pass. Instead, they have opened to let their captain come forward. He almost collides with Brown and asks,

"What is it?" Brown doesn't answer and disappears aft.

"My God," Hiram Lester says. He quickly surveys the scene with his eyes, moving from Abe and the boy, then to Jones whose arm is still bleeding and then to the mess on the deck and Kinder's body.

"What's your next move?" he coolly asks Abe.

Abe pauses for a moment.

I done tink it would be dis easy, he says to himself.

"First, I wants ya all to clear duh companionway ladder," he blurts out loudly.

"Do it now!"

Hiram turns to the bo'sun and says, "Make way. Let him pass. Do not attempt to jump him."

Bellingham moves the crowd away from the ladder. Hesitantly at first, Abe, trying to watch his back as well as move forward with the boy still in his grasp holds the knife precariously close to Billy's throat. He negotiates the ladder with difficulty because of the chains and moves on deck just forward of the foremast.

Daylight is just beginning to break in the sky over the Andes. Brown can clearly see everything around him. The seas have a slight chop and the ship bucks a bit more than it had throughout the night.

Brown takes the boy forward and stops at the anchor windlass. Secure in knowing that no one can now get behind him, he looks aft and faces Lester, who is now slightly ahead of the crowd.

"What now? Lester says.

"I wants yuh tu provision yur brudder's whaleboat an' lower it."

"As you wish," Lester says, "but that will take some time. We must heave-to, to stop the ship."

"Take as much time as yous needs but done plan ta trick me. I wone hesitate ta slit duh boy's throat."

"Jorge," says Hiram Lester, "stay here and keep the men in order. Do not let anyone approach Brown. Andrew, make ready to lower your boat, but first come with me."

Hiram drops down the forward hatch to the blubber room with Andrew behind him and stops. "First, I want you to find Whetstone and have him immediately come to my cabin. You come too and get a pistol. Then I want you to heave-to while you let your crew begin readying your boat. Now, get Whetstone. Hurry."

Once in his cabin, Lester unlocks the ordnance cabinet and pulls out one, then decides on two of the muskets used to shoot the elephant seals, and two pistols. In seconds, both his brother and Whetstone enter his cabin.

"Andrew, tuck this under your belt and work the ship," he says as he hands him a loaded pistol.

"Do you think you can fire this piece?" Lester lifts one of the muskets and hands it to Whetstone.

"Sure can," he answers as he takes it. "I used one in the war."

"What did you do in the war?"

"I was an infantryman, a sharpshooter. Just like Blackwell was."

"Did you kill anyone?"

"Yes."

"Many?"

"Enough!"

"How many is that?"

"I really don't want to talk about it. That's in the past."

"Do you think you can still kill a man?"

"Captain, I know what you are leading up to."

"Well? Can you? Can you to save a boy's life?"

"I took no pleasure in killing those Rebs. I had to. It was my duty. It was either thems or me."

"How about Abe Brown? Can you kill him?"

"I think so."

"Without hesitation?"

"Without hesitation!"

"Good. Load both muskets and follow me."

In a few minutes Whetstone is following Lester up the aft companionway.

"Keep the musket in front of you. I will do the same with this one," he says and takes it from Whetstone. "Don't let Abe see it."

Quickly they cross to the larboard ladder to the quarterdeck, slip behind the wheelhouse and come around the back to the door.

"Do you think he saw us?" Whetstone asks.

"I don't think so," says Lester.

"Moore, slowly open the forward window."

The quartermaster snaps the line on the wheel immobilizing it. He leans forward and pushes open the window. Whetstone crouches below the window and works his way to it. He leans the front of the gun on the window ledge, lifts its butt to his shoulder and immediately finds Brown just above the front sight.

"What now, Captain?" he asks.

"He holds Billy too close for a clean shot. I must figure a way to get him to free him, even temporarily. I know," he suddenly says. "Stay here, I think I have a scheme that might work. When you see him move far enough away from the boy, take the shot. We may not have much of an opportunity, but I would rather let him go free than kill the boy."

Lester brazenly walks out of the wheelhouse and sees Brown look his way as Lester descends the starboard ladder. He sees his brother Andrew at the gunwale with his boat still in the davit but ready to lower.

"Are you ready to lower away?" he says loud enough for Brown to hear.

"Aye, Sir," says Andrew, "we are ready."

Hiram then walks forward and the men open a path for him. He approaches to within a dozen feet of Brown, who is now sitting on the windlass, with Billy on his left knee and an arm wrapped around his waist.

"The boat is nearly ready," Hiram says to Brown.

"Do yah tink me dat stupid? Do yah tink I can row away?" says Brown. "Lower a second boat, bring it about, an' tether it to yur brudder's boat wid a short line. Den step duh mast on his boat. When I am far enough from duh ship, I'll put Billy in duh secon' boat, cut it free an' yous can come an' git him."

"Diogo," he says and turns to the crowd.

"Aye, Sir," Diogo says as the men around him move away.

"Gather your men and lower your boat," says Lester. Turning back to Brown, he continues, "Now, is there anything else?"

"Oh yeh, da mos' important ting. Duh key. Duh fuckin' key ta dese chains."

Andrew's boat is immediately lowered. Ten minutes later, Diogo's boat has been lowered and is being secured.

"Now, where's duh key?" Abe asks.

While the crew opens a pathway on the main deck, Lester walks through it and stops short of the foremast, a dozen feet away from Abe. He pulls the key from his pocket, holds it up, and momentarily dangles it for Abe to see.

"Dat better be da right one," challenges Abe.

Lester then purposely throws it at Abe's feet rather than toward his free hand where he might catch it.

"Lester," Abe says to Andrew who is in the front of the crowd, "get yur crew back. Back them up a fathom. Ya, too, skipper."

Andrew motions the crewmen to fall back six feet.

"How's that?"

"It'll do. If anyone rushes me, I'll git back ta duh kid afore dey can reach me."

"No one will rush you," says Hiram.

"Have I gots yur word on dat?"

"You do."

"Dat's shit," says Abe. He waits a moment, eyeing everyone in the front line.

"Billy, reach out an' git dah key. I'll be right behind yah an' I'll git ya afore dey gits me. Understan'?"

"Yes, Sir, Mr. Abe," the 12-year-old says.

He slips off Brown's knee and drops down to pick up the key while Abe leans forward but still holding his left arm around the boy's waist. Billy's arm is inches short of reaching the key. As he tries, Abe moves off the windlass so he can reach it then stands erect as Billy is about to rise.

The unexpected sound of the musket shot sounds like a cannon, momentarily stunning everyone.

Abe grabs for his chest. He holds his hand against his heart as blood gushes forth between his fingers. He stands there for a moment, not believing what has just happened. His knees buckle and he slumps to the deck.

The crewmen yell with joy.

A Hasty Burial At Sea

"I see no need to continue on to Callao," Hiram says to his brother and Jorge who still stand next to him. "Delivering the bodies to the Peruvian authorities would only complicate matters and delay us."

"Have the men retrieve the boats. Get the sailmaker here and have two men help him bring up Kinder's body. Sew him and Brown in canvas. Also, get some men to wash down the deck where Brown was shot. The sooner everyone can forget about this the better it will be. We have a whaleship to fill before we can turn homeward."

After the two boats are hauled back into their davits, the 1st mate sends men into the rigging to add more sail. The ship's course is changed and *Tranquility* heads west.

Capt. Lester is in the wheelhouse with Andrew and the quartermaster.

Lester is surprised to see John Daily emerge from the aft companionway and climb the ladder to the quarterdeck. He is not prohibited from being there but it is unusual for him to be there. Lester steps outside and addresses Daily.

"John, is there a problem?" he asks as Daily stops at the top of the ladder.

"I have a surprise for you, an' maybe Mr. Brown" Daily says.

"I was fitting Abe's body in his canvas suit when I spotted a bulge in one of his pockets. Lo an' behold, it was a roll of money, mostly 5 dollar bills. It would have been shameful of me to let it be. He'd have no use for the money unless Davy Jones was awaitin' there for him," Daily said as he chuckled.

"You're quite the comic," Lester says as he takes the bills.

By mid-day, everything appears to have returned to normal except for disposal of the bodies. The crew is called on deck while the bodies are hoisted onto the burial stage. Andrew tacks an American flag over Kinder's body but not on Brown's. The move is a message for everyone to see, even Ephraim Brown. Captain Lester reads a short prayer as the bodies are slid into the sea. Finally, he says, "It is over. It is done."

"I am amazed how quickly everyone turned to their tasks," says Ben to the other mates at dinner. "It was as if we all wanted to get over what had just happened, to set it behind us. I helped Dibble build the burial stage this afternoon. He chatted about everything except what happened this morning. It seems as though the captain went out of his way to have everybody doing something."

"Work did take our minds off the murder and the shooting," says Jorge.

"I did see you," he addresses Andrew, "take Billy aside and talk to him for a while."

Chapter 45

Running West Just Below The Line

Sunday, July 19, 1868, Day 945
05° 13' S by 095° 2' W

"31 days since we turned to the west," Lester writes in the logbook. "42 days since we saw the last spout. Temperatures are intolerable at this latitude. This is said to be the coolest month of the year. God help us if we don't pass some distance farther south by September to find relief. No one sleeps below. There is just enough wind to move the ship at 2 knots. I thought the Southeast Trade Winds would push harder than they do. They did the last time I was here. It is as if we are in the doldrums. Thanks be to God we are not.

"Three days prior we weathered a gale. Its relief was appreciated. We gathered 12 casks of drinking water. The fo'c's'le seems especially quiet. I worry when they do not complain. Maybe they are still feeling the affects of Abe Brown's action. I hope not. Tomorrow I will change tactics. These seas are barren of whales. We will cruise until we reach 130 degrees longitude, then alter course southwest for the Marquesas Islands. Maybe hunting there will be better, God willing. It cannot be worse than here."

Friday, August 7, 1868, Day 962
04° 08' S by 130° 03" W

"We would have been at this longitude three days sooner that I expected, even though en route we lowered for two sperms," Lester logs the day's events. "One was huge. A schoolmaster. An unusually large bull that tried-out 75 barrels and the other 45. Today, I reset the course for the Marquesas, at 250°. Mr. Brown again counted the casks. He told me he was surprised by the count. I, too, was surprised that he did not count every barrel as it went into the hold. I told him again to do so. He doesn't take correction kindly. We have 1,800 in the hold and are at three-quarters of the ship's capacity. We may well be home by Christmas. I, too, am surprised that we have accumulated so much oil. Thank God we didn't depend on the Atlantic."

Capt. Lester's immediate objective now is the village of Taiohae on Nuku Hiva, the largest of 12 islands in the Marquesas, 800 miles away. En route, the Southeast Trade Winds rise to light-gale winds and moderate rains. Rain falls intermittently for the next seven days. Because of the weather, Lester does not unbox the sextant but instead depends solely upon his chronometer to tell him where he is.

"Mr. Brown," says Capt. Lester as his mates gather around him on the gangway. *Tranquility* has just dropped anchor about 2,000 feet off a sandy beach and is still weathercocking. "Cook is again in need of fresh food. I know these islanders raise pigs and chickens. Also, they grow breadfruit. Get some. The crew might enjoy it. Please go ashore with the second boat and see if you can procure them."

"Andrew, please return the key to Mr. Brown's treasury. He will need hard coin to negotiate with these islanders.

"By the way Ephraim, how is your French?"

Before Ephraim Brown can answer, Diogo Pilla volunteers, "I am not fluent but I can get along some in French."

"Good," says Lester, "you then will take the second boat with Mr. Brown. Cook will join you. The cook is from New Orleans and he must speak some French. I know his younger brother does. Maybe you can also ask which port the ship anchored to our east is from. She flies no ensign and has no name on her transom.

"Number 1, you make the necessary protocol moves with the authorities. Also, ask about that ship at anchor. And, ask if any whalers have been in here of late and if they were successful.

"Lower away! Lower away the whaleboats."

"What is the name of your ship?" a uniformed man asks Brown as he steps onto the dock. Andrew Lester recognizes it as a tropical customs uniform.

"*Tranquility!*"

"*Tranquillité?* That is a strange name for an American vessel."

"Why so?" asks Brown.

"Because," the Frenchman answers, "the Americans I have seen are not such *tranquillé* people."

"Maybe you have been looking in the wrong places."

"Maybe so. Maybe so."

Late that afternoon, Diogo's boat with Brown is the first to return. When it is hauled on the davits, Hiram Lester sees that Cook has acquired several pigs, with their feet tied together so they can not run, and three crates of chickens.

"Did you have any difficulty with the natives understanding you?" Lester asks Brown as he and Cook step onboard.

"The French would not let us barter directly with the natives," Brown says, "We had to work through them."

"The French here are not nice people. At first, they refused to take American dollars. They said our greenbacks were no good. They insisted that we pay in French francs. They acted as if our money was shinplaster.

"One of the islanders, who knew what a whaleship would be after, and who had pigs with him, saw that we were getting nowhere with the French. He started to complain to them. We were walking away when the native yelled for us to come back. He must have said something powerful to them. The French hastily decided that they would take our greenbacks.

"I picked up some coconuts and yams with the breadfruit. The cook spotted them and insisted that our potatoes were running low, that we needed the yams," concluded Brown.

"Mr. Pilla, did you discover the home port of the vessel?" Lester asks next.

"Not really," Diogo replies. "I asked several in the market places but did not get a straight answer. The best I could determine was that it is an island ship, a trader that goes from island to island. She's too big for such a task."

"I don't like the looks of her," says Lester.

"Nor I," says Diogo. "She'll bear watching. I think she is a *pirata*."

"What is that?"

"A pirate," answers Jorge Pilla.

A half-hour later, Andrew Lester's boat is alongside. The tackle is lowered and the whaleboat is raised by its davit.

"Well, what did you discover?" Lester asks.

"The customs man answered me in French when I asked about the ship. I thought that was odd because until then, most of our conversation was in English. I failed to get him to tell me in English. He acted as if he didn't know the correct words in English to describe the ship. That, too, piqued my curiosity."

"That **is** strange," says Hiram Lester, "because Diogo was able to obtain no more information than you. And what of any whaleships?"

"None. He said the last whaleship was here more than six months ago."

"What was her name? From where did she hail?"

"He didn't know either. He said he had been reassigned here and had arrived from Papeete just six months ago."

"There are still pirates operating in these waters," says Capt. Lester. "For all I know they are natives in cahoots with the French, or vice versa. I wouldn't put it past either of them. I have had the glass on her from time-to-time this afternoon and I have seen almost no activity onboard. One boat came alongside, hoisted a few bags of something, then departed.

"After sunset, I want you to put watches on both bow and stern. Also, send a man aloft on the main. Make sure he ties himself into the hoops. I don't want anyone falling asleep and landing on deck. Replace all the watches every two hours. Also, I want all three men armed with loaded muskets. Whetstone can see to that. We should be on extra alert this night."

Chapter 46

Into the Den of Pirates

Friday, August 14, 1868, Day 969
9° 00' S by 139° 30' W

"At midday today, we entered the bay leading to Taihoe, on the south side of Nuku Hiva, one of the uninhabited Marquesas Islands," Capt. Lester writes that evening in the logbook. "I was here, about 20 years ago, as a young man. The French had just declared sovereignty over these islands. That did not please the *Kanakas* (Polynesian: the men). It wasn't too long before that, that they ate visitors. I remember how feared our crew was when we went ashore. No one was eaten."

"Do you see what I see?" asks Andre LeBlanc of a half-dozen men, some sitting and others lying on an overturned boat about 50 feet from the water's edge. A collection of palm trees towers over them, providing ample cover from the day's stifling heat.

"I see *beacoup d'argent*," one man answers. "Not in francs but in Yankee dollars."

"What kind of ship is it," another asks.

"A *baleiniere*," answers LeBlanc.

"A what?" asks a man with a decided Cockney accent?"

"A whaleship," says LeBlanc.

"Too bad," says the Brit. "Those guys probably don't have a coin to rub among them."

"Why's that?" asks another lying on the boat.

"Because they don't get paid until the oil is sold back in port."

"Shit," he responds.

"That ship is worth much more than what they may have locked in their chest," says LeBlanc. "The winds blow in our faces. It is a fortuitous sign. Tonight we will see."

Two hours have passed since 8 bells, midnight, was rung on *Tranquility*. In the damp, hot, night air, the sound quickly spreads across the bay and reaches the beach where the men are gathering. Silently two boats are turned upright and carried to the water.

LeBlanc picks three men to go with him and assigns the others to the smaller boat. After the smaller boat is in the water, LeBlanc's boat is pushed off. They are some 50 feet off the beach when someone in the smaller boat yells, "*Merde!*"

"What is wrong?" asks LeBlanc.

"The damned boat she is leaking. We are sinking."

"Go back," he says to the men paddling the boat.

Silently, LeBlanc's boat approaches *Tranquilty's* bow.

LeBlanc wraps his arm around her heavy anchor line as a second man pulls on it and brings the boat closer. As the two hold on, a third man goes forward as he pulls out a large kitchen knife.

"Slowly, quietly," LeBlanc tutors the man.

Just before six bells is rung, at 3 a.m., a shot rings out on *Tranquility*. Almost immediately, it is followed by a second shot. The winds are light and the night is especially silent. The sound of the muskets shatters the silence. A moon without horns is nearing the horizon and floods the bay and ship with its reflected light revealing a boat at the ship's anchor line.

Capt. Lester springs out of his bunk as the sound of the first shot fades. He runs up the ladder, two steps at a time. Except for his shoes, he is fully dressed, having pulled a blanket over himself as he went to sleep that night. Immediately behind him are his mates and Brown.

"Who goes there? Who goes there?" the watch in the bow continues yelling.

"What did you see?" Lester yells aloft.

"A boat was holding to our anchor line," the bow watch responds.

"I saw the flash of metal," the mainmast watch yells. "Someone was cutting the anchor line so I fired."

"I saw it, too," says the bow watch as Lester runs forward. "I know I hit one man. There were four in the boat. There they go, toward the beach," he says and points.

"Shall I put a shot in them?" he asks.

"No, I don't think that will be necessary," answers Lester.

"Jorge, lower your boat and check the state of the anchor line. Yell back as soon as you discover what occurred. Lower away when your men are ready.

"Number 1," he says as he turns to his other mates. "I think an early departure is called for. I don't want the Frenchees coming aboard and asking questions or quarantining our ship for an investigation, or even a trial. I suspect they would like that. Daybreak is less than three hours away. I want us underway before that time."

"What was their intent?" Ephraim asks Lester as they draw cups of coffee in the galley.

"That's easy to determine," Lester says. "The winds are light but from the southeast and a loose ship would have quietly drifted ashore. I'm sure there were others, many others, on the beach who were ready to lay claim to *Tranquility* as salvage."

"But under the law of the sea, we're still in possession of the ship," says Brown.

"Not if we were foundering. Besides, the laws of the sea are what you make them. Here, they make the laws as they see fit. The laws of the sea are in your arms, in your strength and what you can get away with. The problem is not with the laws of salvage, the law those on shore had hoped to employ, but with those scoundrels who would endanger our vessel."

Andrew discovers that the anchor line, just above the water, had been partially cut. Knowing that a strain might cause it to break and the anchor lost, he orders two more boats to be lowered. They tow the ship forward until there is slack in the anchor's cable.

Stars in the east are fast receding, quickly yielding to the light of the rising sun as the bo'sun, commanding four men on the windlass, begins the task of loading line on the warping drum. At first, it is hauled onto the drum by hand as the three whaleboats continue to tow the ship toward the anchor, creating still more slack in the line. When the cut section is onboard the ship and buried under several layers of line, the bo'sun signals the boats. They return to their davits and are hauled out.

Ten minutes later, the bo'sun yells astern that the anchor is weighed and firmly secured with extra lines. He then turns to the men in his crew and says, "Remain here unless you are ordered aloft. We must unravel the warp on the drum to the cut. We will either make the cut complete and re-splice the ends, or bend the line directly to the anchor. I must get the captain's choice on that matter."

Crewmen are already on the yards, waiting to loosen the gaskets (light ropes used to tie furled sails to the yards) and set the sails. As during most times when getting underway, Number 1 is in charge and quietly gives the signals. The sails immediately unravel and catch the wind. The wind, as if in anticipation of the rising sun, has picked up a few knots and quickly fills all canvas. They snap and billow forward in response.

The quartermaster feels the telltale force on the rudder as *Tranquility* begins to move and spins the wheel clockwise to turn the transom more fully to windward.

Ashore, all is quiet. Lester glasses the dock and beach to see if anyone has been alerted by his ship's movement. He knows that the ship surely is under the eyes of the would-be salvagers. Maybe they are tending to the one who was shot. Only a few lanterns flicker here and there along the distal ends of two small wharves that end at the village's main street. Lester hears a dog bark. He tucks the glass under his arm and smiles to himself as he turns. Taihoe is now to his back.

Chapter 47

A Whale's Revenge

Saturday, September 18, 1868, Day 1,003
20° S by 168° 13' 109" W

"We have cruised nearly 2,000 miles in the 32 days since we left Taiho," Lester enters in the ship's logbook. "Never once in all that time have we heard those magic words: There she blows. It is as if all the whales in the world's oceans have been stuck and tryed. This is the longest we have been in the Pacific without seeing a spout."

On Sunday, just after sunrise, they spot an oncoming whaleship. The seas are tumultuous and neither ship makes an attempt to come about. The crews have great difficulty even understanding what is said because of the weather. Frustrated, they pass in opposite directions.

"She is out of New Bedford," says Andrew. "A whaler. I guess she's in a hurry to home."

Tranquility has been under near-gale winds almost since she departed the Marquesas and is soddened to the core by the constant rain. Sunday is the first day in several weeks that the sun shines. At midday Hiram is at the gunwale and takes a reading.

"That island is the island of Niue," Hiram says to the mates who surround him.

Niue is like many of these volcanic islands in the Pacific with steep cliffs surrounding its perimeter and a plateau on top. The crew does see some islanders fishing.

"There is nothing about the island that would encourage me to stop here," says Hiram. "We are about 135 miles east of the Dateline. We should cross it by noon tomorrow, Sunday. "

For the next week, Lester drives *Tranquility* eastward, not cruising but under full sail, though he does hove-to each day after sunset. The weather is mixed, alternating between hot, sunny, stuffy days and hot, overcast, drizzly, stuffy days. The dearth of whales now makes him believe that he should see as much water as possible during the day so he spreads as much canvas as prudent under the conditions. On the last day of the month (Sat. Oct. 31st, 1868) he turns the ship northeast, rounding the north side of Mangaia Island, on the western end of the Austral Seamount Chain, an 1,800-mile long string of widely-separated islands. Then he turns *Tranquility* and runs her southeasterly, through a 400-mile corridor, with the Tuamotu Archipelago on the port and Australs on the starboard side.

The crew has not seen a whale in two months and is becoming increasingly bad tempered. One day, there is a fight in the fo'c's'le between the Negroes and the Portygees. Knives are flashed and some are cut.

"I don't know why they dislike each other," Ben says to Jorge as they sit on the bunks. "The Portygee in our crew, the men from Brazil, are as black as the Negroes. They are mixed blood and don't look at all like you or your uncle, or even Egas Sanchez.

"I think it is more their personality rather than color that sets them off," says Jorge. "If we had whales to try this wouldn't have happened."

"Actually, I'm surprised that we all got along as well as we did when I bunked there," said Ben. "The tight space in the fo'c's'le has been their home for nearly three years. Even the best families fight among themselves when they live in a small house."

The fo'c's'le is a miserable place and everyone in the whaleboat crews prefers to be topside or even in their boats. It is a cramped, filthy place that is always hot when the ship is in the tropics. One either sits on his bunk or on a sea chest. The air is foul with smoke and the smell of men who don't wash. The only bathing takes place when they are sent into the rigging while it is raining. Few seek water on their own.

The place is alive with bedbugs and roaches, and rats are the crew's constant companions. What makes it grubby is that they eat where they sleep. The galley is without tables so the cook's boy brings them their food in tubs and ladles it out into each man's greasy, wooden or tin bowl. Half the time it winds up on the deck. And there are always some Greenies who still get seasick when the weather is rough and frequently they don't make it on deck in time. As little time as possible is spent in the fo'c's'le."

October 17, 1868, Day 1,036
22° 26' S by 151°20' W

"It is a grand day," says Pierre Batiste as he firmly grips the gunwale railing just outside the larboard hatchway. He inhales deeply, savoring the morning air before the day turns hot. He is about to repeat the breathing when he hears Captain Lester call him from below. He hastily disappears down the hatch.

"Have you seen your bother?"

"No, Sir."

"When you do, tell him there is no coffee ."

"I will, Sir."

Tranquility is running down the north side of the Austral Islands. About midday she is off Rurutu Island, south of Tahiti, when a lookout spots activity to her starboard. The wind still has a morning freshness as it blows lightly out of the north.

"To starboard! To starboard!" yells the lookout, who sees a pod of whales spouting.

Everyone on deck rushes to the starboard side of the ship.

What a glorious sight they are, Andrew says to himself as other join him at the gunwale. The bright sun glistens off their wet backs each time they rise out of the water. It is like watching a troop of dancers moving together, in unison, all in syncopation.

"They are humpbacks," Hiram Lester yells from the quarterdeck as the ship nears them. "Come about," he says to the quartermaster. Then he turns to the men on the gunwale. "Prepare to launch your boats."

Fourth-Mate Ben, on the tiller of what had been Abe Brown's whaleboat, makes for the closest whale. Bennett, his harpooner, exchanges his bow oar for the harpoon as they draw near to the whale. Ben waits a few moments then sharply turns the tiller, bringing the boat quickly alongside the whale. He watches as Bennett rises, pulls the harpoon back, then sinks the iron. Unexpectedly, the whale bolts and the iron is torn free. The whale doesn't sound but lies motionless on top of the water.

Off to the starboard of Ben's boat, no more than 7 or 8 fathoms away, is Diogo Pilla's boat. "We were about to stroke when we saw Diogo guide his boat onto the whale and Nuno Dias lay on the iron," Ben later tells Captain Lester when he queries him and his crew. "The whale immediately sounded. A second later, Diogo, rose to go forward as Nuno ran astern.

"The warp was pouring through the bow chock, when I saw it suddenly dance off the loggerhead. It looked as though the peg (a wooden or whalebone pin that would keep the line confined in the chock) was missing or broken. The towline was bouncing as it came out of the tub and over the oars. It must have had a twist, a kink in it to cause it to do that. It had not been coiled correctly.

"We watched in horror, in the blink of an eye, as the line wrapped itself around Nuno's leg and hauled him over the bow and into the water. It was still fouled and somehow wrapped itself around the hands and neck of Paul Norman, the tub oarsman. He had been trying to remove the kinks in the tub when the line again popped off the post. The strength of the gallied whale was so great that it yanked him out of the boat and into the water as if he were a feather. As he was pulled forward, he knocked Diogo overboard.

"There was no one in the bow to cut the warp. The boat shot into the air when the warp jammed onto something else and it took off with three men in it. Whetstone told us he was wearing his knife. That saved his life and the lives of the two Negroes in his boat.

"We rushed to Diogo and fished him out of the water. The whale had towed his boat about two miles from where it was struck, and we rowed to it with all haste. The men in the boat were alive but had been battered around badly. One of the Negroes had a broken leg.

"We never found Dias or Norman, nor the whale. After that, you signaled for us to come back the ship."

In vain, Andrew tacked the ship back and forth looking for the men. They did so for the entire next day and saw nothing.

Chapter 48

Amorality Among the Bajans

Friday, December 4th, 1868, Day 1,093
27° 35'30"S by 144°17'45"W
Off Rapa Island

"Today we marked the end of our third year at sea," Capt. Lester enters in the logbook. "I have *Tranquility* underway just north of Rapa Island, the most south-easterly island of the Australs. During the preceding month-and-a-half, I had the boats lowered three times and tried-out but two humpbacks in all that cruising and searching."

Lester stops writing, drops his pen alongside the worn ledger and leans back in his chair. He folds his hands across the back of his head and peers through the portals on the stern bulkhead of his cabin. These windows are a godsend, he thinks to himself. I've never seen windows across the transom of a whaleship. Thanks, Nehemiah Hand. Feeling a bit awkward, he lifts his legs to the edge of the desk, a more comfortable supine position. For a moment, thoughts race through his mind. Thank God, I have been too tired of late to dream.

The Pacific now is better for hunting whales than the Atlantic, he says to himself. But there still is no comparison to the past. I cannot believe the changes that have taken place in the 35 years since I first went to sea. Can we have slaughtered so many whales that there is only this pittance remaining? The oceans then seemed so filled with them, so full of life when I first cruised the coast of South America. I was 15. Whales were always in large schools, sometimes 40 and 50 in a herd. Can they all have been turned into oil and corsets?

He stops, uncouples his hands, drops his feet to the deck and leans forward to retrieve his cup of coffee. It has turned cold, he thinks, but it still tastes good. How sad life would be without coffee. He returns to leaning backward and his eyes peer aimlessly though the window. He continues gathering wool.

It has been 48 days since the loss of the two men in the fouled-line incident but it still lies heavily on Hiram's mind and disturbs his conscience. He thinks to himself, two more men are gone since we left five in Chile, two off Peru. This has been an expensive voyage in men's lives. Nor has the crew come completely to grips with what happened last. It was stupidity. The last event was a rare occurrence. Such a thing never happened on my previous voyages. Jorge, however, in an effort to soften the affect, recounted a similar occurrence on one ship he had sailed. Lester's thoughts are suddenly shattered by a loud bang on the deck above his deck.

"My God!" he exclaims and rushes topside to seek the cause. He sees several of the crew on the quarterdeck. This area is prohibited to them; only mates and shiphandlers are allowed there. As he climbs the larboard ladder he sees two men fighting and a third lying on the deck. Several Greenies surround them as the quartermaster jumps out of the wheelhouse to break up the fight.

"Stop this," yells Hiram. "Stop immediately!" he yells again as he reaches the quarterdeck.

He looks behind and sees Bo'sun Bellingham is on the ladder.

"Get some help," he orders bo'sun.

"I don't need help for this," he says as he is atop the deck rushing toward the two fighters. He pounces on John Coachman just as Coachman lands a blow on Jeb Blackman with a belaying pin. Immediately behind bo'sun is Ben, who seems to have appeared out of nowhere. He lands on Blackman and holds him down on the deck. Jorge Pilla has joined the fracas and lends Ben a hand.

"There's no need," the Shinnecock says. "I think he is out cold. See to Blackman. He may need help."

"You men," Lester addresses those watching, "get off the quarterdeck. I'll deal with you later."

Lester dashes to Jeb Blackman who is lying prostrate on the deck. He turns him over and reveals a pool of blood surrounding his head. Lester sees his eyes open and calls for someone to get Cook. Cook arrives with his bag of medicines, and Ben and Jorge begin to lift the injured man to a sitting position.

"No," yells Cook. "Let him be or he'll drain what blood he has left."

"Take the other two below and lock them up," Lester says to Bellingham, who now has several men to aid him.

Late that afternoon, Lester with his three mates and Bellingham is in the bilge just outside a makeshift cell, a large cage. Coachman and Blackman stand up in the limited space as Lester approaches. Towering over Blackman, Coachman is a formidable man in a fight.

"What caused this?" Lester asks. "I thought you Bajan's were all friends. At least, that is what I thought when I brought you onboard in Barbados."

"We were," says Coachman, "until he started talking stupid."

"What do you mean…stupid?"

"I done know," Coachman says in a clipped voice. "I think he was drunk."

"How could he be drunk?"

"He got some rum stashed an been sippin' it from time to time. We was outside, sittin' on the anchor windless when he started at me. I didn't mind him doin' dat. Drinkin' dee rum. Den he begin talking about all the women he had on the island. I told him he was crazy. He was braggin'. Dat dee rum was talking. He say he wasn't just talkin' an' could prove it. I ask him how he gunna prove it out here in dis ocean.

"He say, 'I had your wife, two or three times. She say she love me.'

"I say, 'You lying. Done talk 'bout my wife.'

"Den he say, 'Think about Reggie, your tird son. Done you ever tink he looks different? He done look like you. Think about it, man. He be MY son.'

"Den Blackman say he was right. He say she a whore. Dey started laughin' and run down the main deck. I chased dem and got a pin on the way. Dey ran up the quarterdeck and Mr. Moore yell for us to get off. I caught Blackman and lay it on him. I couldn't help it, captain. I exploded inside. Dey done me wrong. I hadda hit him."

After a few minutes of silence Lester turns to Jorge.

"What do think?"

"I'd do the same thing."

"Diogo?"

"Me, too."

"Ben?

"I have no children. I don't know what I would do."

"Andrew?"

"I would never have to face what Jeb had to. My wife would never have done that to me. Never."

Lesters thinks deeply for the next few minutes.

"Bo'sun, release Coachman. Release Blackman as well. Blackman, I want you to show Bellingham where all your rum is. Rejoin your watch for now but be prepared. You are on borrowed time. I plan to put you and Blackman ashore, if he lives. Whether it is a port or island, you will be off my ship. And, if I hear you and Coachman at it again, I will throw you off the ship, even while underway. Do you understand that?"

Blackman doesn't answer but nods his head.

Lester returns to the wheelhouse to read the compass. He has the ship turned southwest.

A week later, on December 10th, *Tranquility* is at 30° S and 140° W. Late that morning, they encounter a pod of pilot whales, called blackfish or pothead whales by American whalers. The oil of bowheads is inferior to sperm or right whales. Normally, whalers would scorn them for more productive species but given the straits in which the crew of *Tranquility* now finds itself, they are a blessing.

The whales show little fear of boats and are easily approached. In four days, they boat six. The "fish" are all about 20 feet long, except for two females that reach 16 feet, and range from 2-1/2 to 3 tons. In the aggregate, they yielded but 190 barrels of oil, a quantity as well as quality less than that of the coveted sperm whales.

"How goes the cask count?" Hiram asks Ephraim as they meet on deck.

"I have not been below since I last took food to Abe," answers Ephraim. "I have no stomach for that place.

"By the way," says Lester. Daily prepared Abe's body for the trip into the deep. He noticed his pocket bulged and retrieved close to $100 of the Company's money. Do you wish to count it?"

"I don't think that will be necessary," answers Brown.

"But do count the casks," says Lester. "I need the figure for the log. Wouldn't it be good to know how much more oil we must gather before turning homeward? Get me a count. Take Chips to help you and look for any leaking barrels. Go!"

An hour later Ephraim is back on deck and sees Lester on the quarterdeck leaning on the taffrail.

As he approaches the captain, he begins speaking. "Hiram, I could never have imagined what we have accumulated. We have defied all those dire predictions that everyone espoused before we left Sag Harbor. *Tranquility* now holds 2,090 barrels of oil stored in her."

"What? 2,090 barrels? Did you also find some rum down there?"

"You know I don't drink rum. But, I think I might. This surely is a moment, an accomplishment to celebrate. Might it not be appropriate, as you say, time to splice the main brace?"

"I don't know how much rum may be left in the flagons, but for once I agree with you. Let the men before the mast know. They, too, will be delighted."

Capt. Nicholas Stevensson Karas

Monday, December 14th, 1868, Day 1,103
30° S by 140° W

"We are again at a crossroads," Lester writes in the log. "This afternoon, we crossed 30 degrees South by 140 degrees West. If we go much farther south we will encounter the winds of the Roaring 40s. And, temperatures will fall. It is mid-summer here. Even so, this is still a hellish part of the world.

"Our holds are almost full. Though we have had long, fruitless periods, the oceans have been better to us than we expected. We should thank God for this bounty. Maybe it is time to strike the furnace and deep-six the greasy bricks. I must address my mates."

"I was below yesterday with Chips," Brown says to Capt. Lester as they eat supper. "I hear there is some talk of heading home. But, there is still plenty of space that could be filled. I think we can easily store 300, maybe even 400 barrels more. And, still more in places that are too narrow for the full-sized barrels. Chips said he could make smaller casks to fit these spaces. If we did that, we might even add a hundred or so of these to properly fill out the holds."

The mess was silent for a few minutes.

"I don't know where you heard it. Maybe you are clairvoyant. But, I do plan to head homeward," Captain Lester says without addressing Brown's comments.

The words startle the mates and catch Brown off guard.

"But...but," Brown unsuccessfully tries to interrupt.

"This is an opportune time to safely pass Cape Horn Island. I know you mates will agree with me," Lester continues. "Winds at this time there should be less though they seldom drop below 25 or 30 knots. But they do not rise to the tempest we experienced getting into the Pacific. Best of all, they will favor us by blowing on our backside.

"I have calculated that we are approximately 5,600 miles away from the Cape. If the winds do not range above 30 knots most of the time, *Tranquility* will be able to carry a full, or nearly full, complement of sail.

I estimate that we should reach Cape Horn in 39 to 40 days from now, or about January 22nd."

"But we are still 310 barrels short," Brown again interrupts.

"I'm sure," responds Capt. Lester, "that we can find enough whales in the south Atlantic, on our way home, to fill the voids if you think that is so necessary. What is more important is that we cross as soon as possible to take advantage of the fair winds that now blow across Cape Horn. I intend to bring *Tranquility* and her crew safely back to Sag Harbor."

"I agree with you, captain," adds Jorge. "I have been twice in the Pacific and going back now is the right thing to do."

The other mates mumble an audible agreement.

"But remember, cousin," Brown says, "our time in the Atlantic was not at all worth the period nor the effort. What makes you think we will do better on a return trip? And, too," Brown adds without waiting for an answer, "that may be our profit with which you are willing to gamble."

Outwardly, Lester is infuriated that Brown should address him as cousin and not captain in front of his officers. He is formulating an answer when Brown repeats himself.

"That may be our profit," Brown adds to his argument. "You are aware that the price of whale oil has steadily declined since kerosene was introduced."

"We can and will fill the hold in the Atlantic," answers Lester. "I will not strike the pots." His voice is showing signs of irritation. "It is but five or six whales of which you speak. If, en route to The Horn we are successful, I will then strike them."

The mates again speak an agreement.

"But the Atlantic was not that favorable to us when we were there," Brown again repeats himself. "I vote we continue here until the barrels are full."

"Mr. Brown," Lester says in a raised voice, "you forget where and who you are. You are on my ship and it is not run as a democracy. I am the ship's master and my word here is not only as good as the law, it is the law."

"This is not your ship!" Brown yells back and jumps to his feet. As he does, his chair falls backwards. "The ship belongs to the Company. The Company owns it."

"Damn you, Brown. There is no Company here. There is only me. And, you will do as I command, as I desire, as I damned well please. The Company, as you call it, gave me this authority and only I can and will exercise it! This IS my ship and I am its captain. AND, my word is law. I do not need your permission as to where she can and cannot be sailed."

The mess is quiet. No one speaks. Only the sound of the wind blowing across the open door of the companionway on deck comments on what has just taken place.

"But....," Brown was about to continue.

"Shut up and either sit down or leave these quarters. If you don't do it immediately, I will chain you below, among the barrels.

"Besides," says Capt. Lester as he rises from his seat, and the mates all rise in respect, "I don't like the weather we are currently about to face."

Brown, seemingly in defiance, again takes his seat. His elbows are on the table and his hands are clenched with each other.

"It has been squally of late," says a now cooler Lester as he addresses his officers, "and the barometer has been low for more than a week. I sense the weather is about to change. Remember, it is still the hurricane season on this side of the line. We should have been out of these latitudes weeks ago. The farther south we can get, into colder water, the better are our chances of avoiding them.

"On the morn," Lester says as if to break the pall of silence that now looms in the mess, "we will change the heading. Number 1, see that the quartermaster is told of this as soon as he takes the wheel from the Morning Watch. Sail 90 degrees, due east, along the 30th latitude. We will change course only when we reach 100 degrees west, where we should encounter southwest winds and should be close to Chile and eventually The Horn.

"Do you all understand my orders?" Lester asks of his officers.

Each in turn answers with an aye.

In reality, they all agreed with his decision the minute he announced it. Ephraim Brown, disappointed in that he could not sway the captain's mind, remains seated at the table, staring into the mug of coffee still tightly clasped in both hands, as the others make for their quarters.

Chapter 49

A Dream Come True

December 15th, 1868, Day 1,104

Weather on the first day homeward bound continues to be on the squally side. Rains seem unusually heavy and the changeable winds blow from almost every direction. On the next day they finally settle down from the southwest.

"It doesn't look good," Jorge tells Diogo, who is on deck with him.

"I know," he says. "The captain is concerned."

Believing that the weather ahead will be trouble, Lester resets the barometer dial. The mercury is at 29.9 inches. By evening, it drops to 29.3 inches but for the moment is steady. Winds have increased to gale speed and now are building past 35 knots. Lester sends his steward forward to call all the officers. They, too, know that there is something in the offing.

"Gentlemen, I fear we are in for really bad weather. We are near the end of the cyclone season but I don't think it is over. I believe a cyclone is building. This area of the Pacific has generated many hurricanes in the past. The barometer has been falling all day. There's no need to tell you that the winds are on the increase.

"I know it is dark on deck but before the winds rise even more, I want you all to go topside and have your men secure anything that can be moved by wind or water. Andrew, reduce our sails to the three jibs and the foremast royal. That should be enough to give us some control in this blast!

"Those who go aloft to shorten sail should go in pairs. Have one man mind the other who is doing the work. Also take the spare boat off the platform and anchor it to rings in the deck. Bend added lines to the boats on the davits and run lines across the tops of all gunwales.

"Also, run safety lines down the center of the ship, from mizzen to foremast. And, double the watch on the helm. It will take more than one man to manage the wheel. If you've a mind, also say a prayer or two."

By morning, winds are reaching 50 knots. They show no sign of lessening. To the contrary, they continue to rise and are at whole-gale force, above 60 knots, at noon. By evening, they reach 70 knots, and there isn't a man on board who doesn't realize that he and the ship are in the clutches of a cyclone.

The next day is horrendous. Rains are heavy. Most of the time the bow is awash under huge waves. Tremendous claps of thunder add to the confusion making everything on *Tranquility* that is sympathetic to its sound vibrate. She quivers as if she is shuddering in fear, and she may well be. Certainly, the foremast crew is. From time to time, those in the wheelhouse are entertained by flashes of lightning that just barely miss the bow.

The sails had been lightened earlier but, the main's royal, as an afterthought by Andrew Lester, had been left alone. Without it, there isn't enough sail aloft to maneuver the ship. Now it is in shreds and its remains flap violently, constantly, in the wind. Two of the jibs were torn free after the first day, swamped by waves that ripped them off with ease. Somehow, the new bowsprit added in Concépcion, is still attached.

Early in the afternoon, the rain squalls ease. Dark clouds hang so low and heavy that it looks like the period between daybreak and sunrise or after sunset. Diogo is in the wheelhouse with Capt. Lester. Miguel dos Santos is at the wheel helping Quartermaster Moore steady the rudder.

They have no course to follow. Their immediate and only goal is to keep the ship from broaching; they point her directly downwind, in winds that now have blown continuously out of the southwest for three days. At times, the ship skitters ahead, surfing into the back of the next wave, like a child skipping flat stones on a millpond.

Ben volunteers to spell off Miguel as a second on the wheel. The wheelhouse on *Tranquility* isn't especially high, and he must keep his head down to avoid hitting the ceiling. Everyone inside declares that this is the worst storm they have ever weathered.

"This morning," said Ben, "the captain stated that the barometer was at 28.5, and again falling. He said he thought it might even fall off the scale."

The winds are now above 125 knots, and from time to time Ben catches sight of the lone jib sail. The two others are torn and their remnants flap aimlessly in the wind. The intact jib is so strained that it is likely to go at any time.

"What happens if we lose the last jib?" Ben asks Miguel.

"Then we have only the rudder to steer by. It is not much."

In the morning, the winds finally begin to fall off and by noon they are completely gone. *Tranquility* glides on a quiet ocean, one that honors her name. It is as calm as a millpond.

At daybreak, Lester confirms that there is no canvas left aloft. The sticks are bare. He orders new sails raised on the bow and replaces the royals on the main and fore. Sails on the mizzen have little control on the ship's direction and omitting them reduces the windage. Two sheets (lines) to the main were torn loose and lie scattered on yards and on the deck. He says to Andrew that it was not worth the effort to raise new lines. When Ephraim asks why, Lester says: "The worst is yet to come. We are becalmed in the middle of the hurricane, in the center of its eye. This calm will last two, maybe three hours."

Even the sun comes out and the captain takes a reading. Lester is amazed, almost speechless by what he reads on the sextant. "In five days," he says, "we have not progressed an inch to the east. In fact, the hurricane has blown us nearly 500 miles to the northwest. We are off Oeno Island. God only knows why we were not smashed upon one of several islands that lie near here."

All too soon Captain Lester's prediction comes true. By midmorning, the winds are back. The clouds are so heavy that it again looks like daybreak. Then the rains begin. The clouds are emptying themselves. At first, the winds are heavy but not so fierce as they had been the night before. But once night falls they gather renewed power. There is no building-up time. They start at 125 knots and rise. Their strength is unimaginable. Then lightening returns seemingly with even greater intensity.

Lightning strikes everywhere around *Tranquility*. Most fear that this time it will hit the ship. *Tranquility* suddenly shudders as a massive bolt strikes the water just ahead of the ship. Simultaneously the masts and yards glow in a weird, eerie light that travels down the masts, lighting their entire lengths.

In the wheelhouse, Diogo and Miguel fervently bless themselves.

"We've been hit," yells Ben, who has never seen this before.

"No, we haven't," says Capt. Lester who is in the back of the wheelhouse.

"What you see is St. Elmo's Fire. I expected to see it sooner. This always happens when the lightning is most severe. It lasts but a minute or two and then fades."

"This is a bad sign," says Miguel. "God has marked us for death." He intensifies his blessing.

"Just the opposite," the captain says. "When this happens it usually signals the end of a storm or hurricane."

"I didn't know who to believe," says Ben who is again helping Miguel. "My people never saw anything like this. It is unnatural. I am awestruck."

The cyclone rages throughout the night and the next morning. As daylight is still but a glow in the east, the watch on the wheel sees the larboard stern boat banging wildly against its davit. He sends his helper below to tell the mate in charge of the watch.

Andrew comes topside, with his brother directly behind him.

"Send men out to secure it," says Hiram. "Make sure they all go with safety lines tied about them."

"Immediately," answers Andrew.

Andrew goes forward below the main deck, through the mess, through the galley and to the fo'c's'le. Getting there is a chore because the ship bucks and heaves so violently that he must brace himself continually to avoid being thrown against a bulkhead. Ben and his crew are about to climb topside on the companionway ladder when Bellingham stops them. "Return to the fo'c's'le," he says. "It is too late; the boat is gone!"

Ben alone goes topside and is once again stunned by the size of the waves. They easily reach 30 to 40 feet. Every time they hit, the ship's bow is pushed into the back of a wave, and a wall of water sweeps aft over her decks. They break only when they reach the wheelhouse. Ben quickly closes the larboard hatch to keep the ocean from entering. He is soaked but amazed by the scope of the violence the waves impose upon the water. He makes it to the wheelhouse and for a moment leans against it to catch his breath before entering. As he enters, yet another wave engulfs him and he feels the wheelhouse shudder as the waves slam into it. Its connection to the deck is tenuous.

"I don't know how we'll mange if the wheelhouse is swept away," Moore says to Ben as he secures the hatch behind him.

"We'll tie you to the wheel," answers Capt. Lester who is behind Moore. "When I started whaling, there were no wheelhouses. The wheels were always exposed. You could always see better."

"In this kind of weather?" Moore asks.

"Yes, in this kind and any kind of weather," answers Lester.

Throughout the day, the seas unmercifully batter *Tranquility* and her crew. There is no relief in the darkness that overcomes them.

Near midnight Ben and two other mates are violently thrown from their bunks. Ben picks himself off the deck and steadies himself against the bunk. Now wide-awake, he hears and feels the grinding, the wrenching, splintering of wood somewhere beneath his feet. The ship is being driven over a shoal, a reef. All the men are up, yelling, cursing, hollering, trying to get to their foul weather gear. The scene is bedlam.

For a moment, Ben feels the ship level herself.

"She is afloat," he yells immediately feeling some relief. He had feared the worst. "I think we have just passed over a sandbar," he says to Diogo, "only a sandbar."

As words escape his lips the stern strikes bottom. For a short time Ben and the others feel the wind slowly turning the bow of the ship. Then she stops dead. It is such a jolt, so strong, that it knocks everyone to the deck. The lone lantern in mates' quarters swings madly back and forth as they scramble to put on boots. There was no need to dress because most slept in their clothing. Then the ship begins to list to starboard and stops.

Ben grabs whatever weather gear is on the pegs and scrambles up the ladder. He is in the lead. As he gets on deck he cannot see anything because it is still dark. Only a weak light in the wheelhouse breaks the stygian darkness…and the flash of lightning. He feels the force of a wave break over the larboard side, abaft of the mizzen side of the ship. The ship shudders and moves a foot or two. The wind pushes a wall of water across the deck that quickly drains off the starboard side.

Ben hesitates to get out of the forward companionway because he cannot see what might be on deck. He is being pushed from behind by others trying to get out. Only when a bolt of lightning lights the ship can he see what misfortune lies ahead. The fo'c's'le, with the wind from the transom, is filling with water that races across the deck and down the ladder, into the companionway. Two men climb against the inrushing water but only one, John Rusnak, makes it outside.

There is a safety line from the companionway aft to the main and then another to the mizzen and a third to the wheelhouse. Ben sees a faint light in the wheelhouse as wave after wave crashes on the ship's larboard side. With each wave, the ship leans more and more to starboard, unable to right herself.

Ben makes it to the wheelhouse and then hears someone on the main deck scream above the roar of the wind. He turns, only to see a wave that washes him to the safety ropes. He is about to head back down the ladder to help the man. He can faintly see a Negro holding onto the line as yet another wave strikes. It is Coachman, he thinks. When the wave clears, the lifeline is empty. The ship now leans 30 degrees to starboard, making it difficult, if not impossible, to go safely to the foremast.

Ben climbs the ladder and enters the wheelhouse. Andrew is there with the quartermaster. Moore is hanging onto the wheel. He feels the ship's life depends upon him. Mr. Lester yells for him to let go.

"There is no need to control the rudder," he says. "There is no rudder. The ship isn't going anywhere."

Egas Sanchez comes into the wheelhouse behind Ben just as another large wave strikes the ship. The water pours, unstopped, across the main deck and up to the quarterdeck to the wheelhouse. The house shudders and then moves a foot across the quarterdeck. The next wave picks it up, flips it over and smashes it against the stern whaleboat that is still in its davit. Moore is still tied to the wheel; its support saves him from being crushed when the wheelhouse flips. Lester and Ben are swept against the toppled wheelhouse and struggle to get to their feet. Ben suddenly realizes that the forward boat is missing. As lightning flashes, he sees the davit collapse on the waist boat.

Moments later, another wave sweeps over the quarterdeck and washes Andrew and Ben against the lifelines. Lester and Ben pull hand over hand on the starboard safety line toward the only boat left. Ben sees Moore at the wheel and yells for him to work his way to the boat.

Andrew's is the only whaleboat afloat. It hangs precariously by its forward tackle still attached to the davit. A wave momentarily pushes the boat's stern away from the ship. In the wind, its empty aft tackle bangs aimlessly against the ship. Its stern hook had been torn from its ring on the cuddy board and the boat now clings to the ship by its bow tackle. The starboard bulkhead of the ship is now partially submerged.

A safety line from the mizzenmast ends at the larboard safety line and crosses in front of the companionway ladder that leads below. Andrew grabs it and pulls himself to the now hatchless opening. He looks down and sees two or more feet of water on the lower deck. He is about to drop down the ladder when another wave sweeps over the opening and a flood of water carries him below. There is no light except the occasional flashes of lightning. He hears someone cursing in the direction of the mate's quarters as water and debris rush forward between his legs.

His first concern, however, is his brother, whom he has not seen or heard since he left him in the mess and told him he was going to try to get some sleep.

"I would try to sleep," Hiram had said, "but I fear to close my eyes. I am afraid of what I might see if I dream. I fear this moment. It is my dream coming true."

Andrew had watched his brother enter his cabin and close the door.

Now Andrew turns aft, opens the door to Hiram's cabin. He cannot see in the darkness until a flash of lightning floods Hiram's quarters. He is shocked to see that all the stern windows have been blown out. At will, water rushes in and out of the gaping hole. He yells but there is no answer. The cabin is empty. He knows not what has happened to his brother.

Maybe he got out, Andrew hopes to himself.

Again, above the roar of the wind, he hears the almost inaudible sounds of someone talking, coming from behind, from the mates' quarters. Maybe it is Hiram, he thinks. Andrew turns to seek the sound's source when something bangs against his leg. Floating on top of the water is a packet tightly wrapped in yellow oilskins. Immediately, he knows what it is. It is the ship's logbook. He picks it up. Knowing the ship might be in danger of sinking during the cyclone, Hiram must have stored the logbook in this packet, Andrew thinks. Was this his last act?

For a moment, Andrew thinks about discarding it. It's of no use now, he says to himself. He is about to cast it back into the cabin when he changes his mind. Maybe I should keep it. Maybe there is something in the book that should be kept, if any of us gets out of here alive. It records the events of almost 4 years in the lives 44 men. Maybe someone will want to know what we did.

He tucks it into the back of his trousers, wedging it between his wide belt and his back. Then he turns toward the mates' area. A lone, lighted lantern, driven by the wind, swings madly from a hook on the quarter's ceiling. In the dim candlelight he is able to see Ephraim Brown, on his knees, trying to unlock his flooded footlocker. Water sweeping over it makes it impossible for him to insert the key.

"Damn your locker! Save yourself," Lester yells to him.

Brown pays no heed to Lester as another surge of water pours down the ladder. Brown turns and heads forward in the mates' quarters, pulling the heavy chest to a corner of the deck that is almost free of water. But the wave now floods that corner, too.

"Not there," yells Lester. "Come this way. Come this way!"

Brown pays no attention to Andrew. He seems driven by the need to save what money remains in the locker. Instead, he drags the footlocker toward the door that leads to steerage. A wall of water greets him, washing him back as it floods the mates' quarters even more deeply. Jarred from its hook, the lantern falls into the water. Blackness engulfs the quarters.

Lester makes it to the top of the aft ladder as water quickly rises about him. The blubber hatch must have collapsed, Lester fleetingly thinks, and water is now coming in from the bow. It races him to the top step. The mess is now totally filled. Somewhere in it is Ephraim Brown. Lester waits for a few moments but sees no one come afloat. The returning surge must have pulled him back into steerage, Lester thinks. Damned idiot. His own greed has caused him to die.

Lester makes it back to the starboard gunwale and sees that the whaleboat is still afloat and tethered by its davit haul. He grabs the tackle and pulls the whaleboat to him. It won't be much longer, he thinks. Every wave that sweeps over the deck tries to tear the boat away from the ship. It is only a matter of time until that happens. *Tranquility* is now hard on her larboard side; the gunwale and part of the main deck are awash.

"Get in the boat and find something to hold on to," Andrew yells to Ben who has been waiting for him to return. He isn't far from Andrew but can barely hear the words above the roar of the wind.

Ben jumps into the boat, grabs a thwart seat, and wraps his arms around it. Close behind, Lester begins a leap for the boat. At the same moment, the wind catches the boat and pulls it away from him. He lands in the water but his hands have caught the boat's gunwale. He holds there for a moment then feels Ben grab his arm. He assists with the other and falls into the boat.

They see Sanchez still on the ship just before he makes the leap into the water and grabs the gunwale of the whaleboat. He expertly pulls himself in. The trio watch as Adrian Moore hesitates, waiting for the boat to swing back toward the ship. He never learned to swim. From the starboard side, a wave sweeps over the deck and washes Moore into the water. When it clears, he is gone.

Quickly Ben leaps into the water and dives. In seconds he is up and lifts Moore's waterlogged head above the water. Sanchez does not hesitate; he jumps in and both bring Moore to the boat where Andrew grabs his shirt and lifts him over the gunwale. In seconds, both Ben and Sanchez are back in the boat and help to pull Moore inside.

"One more," Andrew yells as they see Rusnak pulling himself forward though the water by the safety line attached between the main and the quarterdeck. As he approaches the whaleboat, Ben grabs an oar and extends it to him. Rusnak grabs it and is pulled to the boat where Sanchez grabs him under the arm and pulls him into the boat.

"Any more?" ask Ben.

The boat still clings to the davit by its bow tackle but is in danger of capsizing with every wave.

"We dare not wait any longer," says Andrew. He works his way to the bow, finds the ax, and is about to chop the line when another wave sweeps over the ship and into the whaleboat that had moved alongside *Tranquility*.

Tranquility is constantly being pounded by large, wind-driven waves. For a moment she acts as if she might even right herself. In doing so, the pull on the bow davit's lines is extreme. The ring to which the tackle is attached tears loose from the water-filled boat and five men are carried away.

Waves on the larboard side of the ship, the leeward side, are smaller. But, they still have the power to carry the whaleboat downwind for 300 or 400 yards from the ship and the reef. The boat is half full of water and the four men inside cling on to anything they can. Unexpectedly, they find themselves entering the surf as it pounds and crashes upon a sandy beach. In seconds the boat is aground as it moves short distances up and down the beach. A larger wave lifts the boat and carries it a bit farther up the beach. All the men except Moore slip over the side, and feel soft sand under their feet instead of sharp coral. They are in only three feet of water.

"We better save what we can of the boat," Lester says. "We may need it later. Let's pull it as far out of the surf as we can."

Standing against the boat, ready to begin pulling it, Andrew realizes that the packet he had stuffed into the back of his belt is gone. He momentarily loosens his grip on the boat and quickly feels his back with his hand to confirms its loss.

Ben doesn't know where they got their strength but he and the others pull the boat until it is on dry sand.

"I hope it isn't low tide," he says to Andrew.

Rain pours down like a waterfall as Ben collapses from exhaustion. The last thing he remembers is sand in his face and mouth and rain pelting on his back.

Chapter 50

The Wreck of the Whaleship *Tranquility*

December 19, 1868, Day 1,1490

Rain is still falling the following morning when Ben feels someone shaking him. He looks up and sees Andrew. Standing behind him is Sanchez.

"Ben," Lester says as he shakes him. "Are you alive? Ben! Ben! Oh no, not you too."

"I'm not sure," Ben answers as he begins to stir.

"He's alive," says Sanchez. They help him sit up.

"The hurricane has passed," Lester says. "Even the rain is letting up. The beach is littered with debris and drowned men. We found Michael Astor (the cooper) and Whetstone (bum/oarsman), barely alive, lying farther up the beach. Henry Dibble was just a few feet past Whetstone. A bunch of canvas wrapped around a yard was washed up high on the beach. When Sanchez passed it he saw something underneath it move. He peeled back the canvas and found John Daily, waterlogged and just barely alive. He was still spitting up water when Sanchez turned him over."

"It seems right that a sailmaker should turn to his sails to survive," says Sanchez. "Luckily the sailcloth was still attached to a yard and floated him ashore.

"Mr. Lester, have you found your brother?" asks Ben.

Startled by the question, Andrew quickly rises from his knees and looks out over the water. He stares at the ship, not responding to Ben.

"We have all been scouring the beach," interrupts Sanchez. "We found no sign of the captain.

"Last night, Mr. Lester and I lifted Moore out of the boat after we dragged it up the beach. I guess he swallowed too much water when he went under near the ship. He didn't make it. He may have crawled a bit after we put him down because his body was just a few yards down the beach from our boat.

"We didn't find any from the foremast crew. I wonder why?"

"When I first came topside," says Ben as he sits up and brushes sand from his face, "I was looking forward to see if the men were escaping. A bolt of lightning cracked just off the bow and lighted the ship. I saw a large wave sweeping over the deck and running forward. The hatch cover was missing and before the light was gone I saw the wave pouring into the fo'c's'le. I don't think the Greenies had much of a chance. I know only one made it."

"I owe you a real big thanks," John Rusnak said to Ben. "When I got on deck I didn't know where to go until you called. Thanks. *Djakuvu duzi.*"

"What about the captain, or Mr. Brown?" Ben asks again.

"We never found him or Ephraim."

"I had to stop running down the beach, looking for survivors," says Sanchez. I was out of breath, but not Mr. Lester. He ran far down the beach, looking for his brother or his body. When he came from covering the beach on the other side he acted crazy because he couldn't find him. He ran the other way still acting like a madman, overturning anything on the beach that might be big enough to hide someone. A lot of the crew is still missing."

"Maybe they're still alive and on the ship," says Ben.

"I doubt it," says Sanchez.

During the morning, a dozen natives come out of the woods to pick over the debris. At first, Ben thinks he might be their dinner, but they turn out to be friendly. Later he learns that French Jesuits had Christianized them. When they see Ben and Sanchez hauling the bodies back from the beach to bury them, they help. Both Astor and Whetstone remain in bad shape. They had swallowed so much water, and had been battered about the coral reef that surrounded this island, that later that day they died. Daily seems to be recovering.

"The beach is still a mess," Ben tells Sanchez late that afternoon. "I saw my boat, Abe Brown's old boat. It was filled with water and being pushed and pulled back and forth by waves hitting the beach."

Ben leaves Sanchez and walks to a large stand of palm trees. From there he spots the ship, or what is left of it. She is about a quarter-mile away, on the outer reef that surrounds this island. She lies on her port side, as if careened and waiting to be caulked.

Only half, maybe less, of the main deck is out of the water. The mainmast is broken and its lines, still attached on one end, are scrambled on the water. The fore- and mizzenmasts, however, are unbroken. Their yards and lines foul the water and trap some of the decking that had been torn from its beams. In places where the main decking is missing the second deck is exposed. Where the second deck is open, tied-down barrels of whale oil are exposed, trapped in the bilge. She moves slightly a little, lifting a bit each time a wave off the open water hits her.

Tears flood Ben's eyes. She was so beautiful, he says to himself. There is nothing more beautiful that a full-rigged whaler. She was my home for a long time. Now she is gone. He feels his throat choke up and clears it, then wipes his eyes. He sits on the sand and wonders to himself what has happened to Jorge and Diogo. They were nice. They made becoming a real mate a lot easier. And what happened to Joshua Edwards? He was my real teacher in the whaleboat.

Quietly, Andrew comes through the trees and stands for the longest time next to Ben without speaking as they look at the wreck of their whaleship.

"I guess there is nothing we can do," Ben says to Lester.

"Maybe we should try to go out to her. Maybe there are still men alive," says Andrew.

"I watched her while you were still asleep," Andrew continues. "I saw no signs of life. Besides, the whaleboat did not escape damage. The garboard plank, on the larboard side, opened."

"We didn't see you for a time," says Ben. "Were you searching the beach?"

"Yes," answers Andrew. "I was hoping to find the captain or anyone else."

"What else?" asks John Rusnak.

"While I was on the ship looking for survivors, I found a yellow packet wrapped in oil skins. It was the ship's log. The captain must have wrapped it in hopes it would survive the sinking. I guess it, too, didn't."

Just before the sun sets, a band of natives comes out of the woods and gestures for the survivors to follow. They speak Tahitian and a little French but are able to communicate what they want the survivors to do. Their village is on the far side of the island. They arrive just as the evening winds begin to blow. The seamen are shown to a large hut with a fire pit in the center. Minutes later three women arrive carrying palm baskets with food---fish, bread and strange fruits. One lights the fire and goes to a corner where several sleeping mats had been rolled and stored. As the men eat, she spreads out the mats against one of the hut's walls.

Outside, the winds howl as they pass through openings in the hut. "Sounds almost like a hurricane is upon us," says Sanchez who is lying next to Ben.

"I don't ever want to go through one again," says Rusnak.

The winds, now laden with rain, blow north across the island. The storm continues throughout the night and into the next day. The men stay in the hut as natives come in and out during most of the day just to see the survivors. Ben, because of his slightly darker complexion, gets most of the attention. Some of the men even rub and pinch his skin. Two women seem enthralled with his straight black hair and he watches with a grin as one tries to pull hers straight.

Ben notices that Andrew has spoken but little during the time they are in the hut and seems to prefer to be off to one corner by himself. That night they find it difficult to fall asleep. Just after midnight Andrew's screams wakening the others. He rambles incoherently, occasionally calling out Hiram's name, then Rebecca's and Noah's names. Sanchez and Ben quiet him down as they realize he is not awake.

"He is still living in the past," says Sanchez.

"This is strange," Ben says. "You are right."

"No," says Sanchez, "It is not really strange. I have seen this happen before to men who have lost someone. Just think, not only has he lost his brother, but his wife died while he was with us and he has blamed himself for not being there for her"

"How do you know this? Asks Ben.

"From idle talk when on watch together at night," says Sanchez. "And he does not know where are his sons and daughter. His problem is that he is a too-caring man. This makes the hurt worse."

By the third day Lester is extremely anxious, agitated. He tells the other he is going back to see the ship, to see if anyone else has been washed ashore.

"We will go with you," says Sanchez. Ben and Rusnak join them.

The rain is reduced to a drizzle and snippets of blue sky begin to appear in the south. "I guess the storm has blown itself out," Ben says as they march through the trees.

"*Meu Deus!*" exclaims Egas who is in the lead and first onto the beach. "The ship is gone."

"How can that be?" asks Ben. "That's not possible. Are we in the right place?"

"Anything is possible in these storms," says Andrew.

They turn to Lester whose eyes are fixed on the waves that break on the reef where *Tranquility* met her end. He does not speak again.

There is no sign of anything on the reef.

"The rising tide must have lifted her just enough off the reef to let the storm's winds push her into deeper water," says Egas. "The ocean has claimed its booty."

They spend the next several hours going first up then down the beach and find no one or anything worth bending over to retrieve.

Rusnak does find a sea chest. Ephraim's name is carved into the wood. There's no lock on it and the lid is partially open. All it contains is water.

Lester's personality has drastically changed. The men are keenly aware of it. He is never again quite the same. He becomes even more remorse, withdrawn after he sees the ship is gone. He must have finally accepted that his brother, too, is gone.

Back in the village, confused, he says to Ben that they must fix the whaleboat boat and go out to the reef to see if anyone is still onboard. That statement startles the men. He keeps repeating it to himself. Most of the time no one can understand what he is saying. Ben does not try to correct him.

Occasionally, Andrew talks about Rebecca.

Six months pass and the survivors still don't see any of the French nuns whom the natives said visit the island from time to time. The men are slowly becoming acclimated to life on a small, isolated island in French Polynesia.

Unknown to anyone, two large, ocean-going canoes land on the far side of the island where *Tranquility* went aground. Gaudily-painted armed men quickly disembark and hurry up the beach to the trees. Just before they reach the trees one man sees sunlight reflecting from something at the base of a stand of sea grass. He stops, picks it up, then unwraps a cord made of sailcloth. Others eagerly crowd next to him to see what he has found. It is a book. The man opens it and leafs through its pages. Seeing nothing, he grabs the book by its spine, shakes it a few times, hoping something valuable is between the pages.

Nothing falls out.

Disappointed, he rips a fistful of pages from it then throws them into the wind and drops the book. The wind scatters the pages on the beach sands. Another man grabs the book and does the same. It has no value to him so he, too, throws the book toward the water. The logbook falls just short and the men continue their trek toward the village. They catch a few natives on the village beach by surprise and enter the village killing all the men that they see. The raiding party is after women and boys because they had lost many of their own in other wars with other islanders.

Someone in the village reaches a gong and forcefully, repeatedly strikes it. People run out of their huts. Men grab their shields and war clubs. Women gather the children that had been playing and rush them inside.

Ben and Egas had been splitting coconut shells and are armed with machetes. They run with the village men toward the raiders.

"Where's Lester?" Ben yells to Egas who is running alongside.

"I don't know. I haven't seen him today."

"There he is," yells Ben, "sitting on the beach."

"Why doesn't he move?" Egas says as they rush toward him.

The approaching horde of raiders reach Andrew first.

Lester is frozen in thought, in another world, oblivious to what is happening around him. He doesn't heed the wave of screaming men coming upon him. The lead man runs to Lester and for a moment stops and quizzically looks at him. He lifts his cumbersome war club and smashes Lester's head. John Daily and John Rusnak are fleeing together and are about to fade into the woods when another band of raiders emerges from it and strikes them down.

In the melee the raiders subdue the islanders.

Still wearing worn, tattered shirts and trousers, Egas and Ben look different, more like the natives. They are taken captive along with a dozen native men. Ben and Egas see the raiders take one man at a time into the middle of a circle they've formed. They kill one after the other with their fancy, carved, wooden clubs.

Somehow Ben and Egas break free. Ben knocks down one of the raiders, takes his killing club and crushes his head. Another raider comes at him with raised club. Ben swings his club and a sharp hook on the end cuts the man across his chest. He collapses almost on Ben. Still another is behind him and Ben turns as the club misses his head but his club catches the man across the jaw.

A bunch of raiders have Egas surrounded, and that is the last Ben sees of him. Ben starts running and two islanders who had been in the circle break out and follow him into a dense stand of palm trees. Huddled together, they hide there for a moment. As as they hear the raiders coming closer, they break their cover and run deeper into the trees before they are seen. The two natives take the lead and Ben follows them into the hills in the center of the island.

After several days Ben, from his mountain location, sees four big canoes break through the surf and cross over the reef. The raiders are leaving. Two more canoes have bolstered their number, and all carry off women, young girls and boys.

The islanders who had escaped with Ben noted how well he fought against the invaders. They tell the others upon their return to the village. Ben is now accepted as an equal among them. The task is made easy because his skin has turned as brown as theirs after a summer in the sun.

Eventually the nuns come. There are seven and they stay three months, teaching the children how to speak French and how to become Christians. During that period the surviving islanders are asked to construct a chapel. The chief at the time isn't too impressed by what they are doing to his people, or to his authority, but the nuns have brought medicines. He isn't sure if he should oppose them, or if what they are telling his people about someone named Christ is true or not. But he is smart. He knows they will eventually leave. After the nuns depart, the natives return to their old ways. The chapel sits empty until a few years later when a cyclone, one as big and as bad as the one that drove *Tranquility* onto the reef, blows it down.

Chapter 51

Another Beginning On a Tahitian Island

February, 1942
Paui Akua Island in the South Pacific

"Father! Father!" a young boy yells in Tahitian as he runs from the water up the beach toward a group of men untangling fishing nets in a boat pulled out of the water.

One man stands upright as he recognizes his son's voice.

"What is it?" he asks as the boy stops at the boat.

"There is a strange boat outside. Like one I have never seen. It is about to come into the lagoon."

The man and the others look toward the cut in the coral reef that surrounds Paui Akua. They see the boat.

"It is a lifeboat," one of the men says as they all drop the net and head to the water's edge.

"Go tell the Old One," the man says to his son.

The lifeboat slides between the breaking combers, riding on top of the temporary rush of water in the stream. In moments, it is inside the lagoon. Men in the lifeboat hear cheering and see waving from the growing crowd on the beach. Several small, outrigger canoes are push off the beach and men being paddling toward the lifeboat. As the lifeboat nears the white, sand beach, several natives run into the water, grab the lifeboat's gunwales, and pull it onto the beach.

Children clamber into the lifeboat and over the crewmen, curious as to who they are and from where they have come. They, as well as the adults, try to communicate with the survivors but it is useless. None of the natives speaks English. They do know some French because of infrequent visits by Catholic missionaries.

"For Christ's sake," Fred Leach yells in frustration, "doesn't anyone here know a word of French?" Toni Gucci tries his second-generation Brooklyn-Italian, but to no avail. There is real confusion as to what is about to take place. The Americans, aware of tales of cannibalism among some of these islanders in the past, are fearful of what the natives might do. At first, the crew bands together in a tight group as they climb out of the boat. The natives, through hand gestures, guide the survivors a few hundred yards inland, to a collection of palm-thatched houses.

"What have we gotten ourselves into?" Leach wonders aloud as he begins to move up the beach. The other men follow. Suddenly, the natives form a barrier in front of him. The leader of the band holds out his hand signaling Leach to stop. He then turns to one of a dozen youngsters at his feet and gives him an order. The boy dashes through the sand and climbs the stairs to one of several high-gabled, palm-thatched huts in a grove of palm trees.

The men wait impatiently.

Gucci wonders aloud if anyone has taken the Very pistol from the lifeboat.

"It might be of some help," he says.

But before they can decide where it is, a commotion at the top of the beach, near the houses, commands their attention. Several natives pour out of the hut and form a path between them. Slowly, an old man, a very, very old man, appears in the doorway. He glances down at the beach and then, with carefully measured steps, and with the aid of two men, he slowly walks down the steps of his hut and onto the path. The others follow at his side and behind. Two children run up to him and cling to his hands.

John Albright immediately knows there is something different about this man. Even though he is ancient he stands a head taller than the others. His hair is not the black, curly mass the others wear. Instead, it is straight, long and pure white. His face is thin, his cheekbones high and exaggerate a prominent, finely-shaped aquiline nose. His brown eyes are dark, piercing. And though his skin is the same bronze color as the islanders, as he gets closer to the men, Albright sees that it has a bluish tint to it. He is covered with tattoos. The other natives have tattoos, but this man's entire body is adorned with them.

In French, he welcomes the survivors to his island.

He must be the elder, Albright says to himself as the old man slowly approaches the seamen. He looks them over, one by one, and for a while listens to them asking questions about him. He finally lifts his right arm. The natives around him, as well as the crew of the *Atlantic Star*, become silent. In faltering, little-used English, he finally speaks.

"I not of these islands," he address the seamen. "I am 4th Mate Benquam of whaleship *Tranquility* out of Sag Harbor."

"Is this guy nuts?" says Gucci. "There ain't no whaleboats anymore."

"Shut up," Albright says to him in a hushed voice.

"I was called Ben by my people. I am from Paumanok. I am a Shinnecock Indian!"

"Where the hell's Paumanok?" Leach asks as he turns to his companions.

It isn't so much where he is from that astonishes Albright, but who he said he is. Finally, Albright speaks: "It's the Indian name for Long Island."

To most of the other seamen, his speaking in English is startling enough. A few think aloud that it is unique that he is an Indian and not a south seas-islander. They wonder among themselves how he has gotten to this out-of-the-way-island. To John Albright, the message is unbelievable.

"How did you get here?" asked Albright. "Are there others? What happened to them?"

"My ship was wrecked on this island. It was big cyclone that pushed it on the reef. But is a long, sad story," Benquam answers as his mind tries to locate English words he knew in the past. "You tired, hungry. First you eat, then rest and sleep. Tonight, I tell what you want to hear."

Paui Akua is a small island in a widely-spread, 2,500-mile long chain of islands, the Tuamotu Archipelago, located about 200 miles north of Tahiti. Hundreds of small islands make up the chain. Most are extinguished volcanic peaks that range in size from bare atolls, only acres in scope, to several that are 40 and 50 miles long. Included is Pitcairn Island on the archipelago's southeast extremity. There is little or no traffic to Paui Akua because of its distance from Tahiti. Because of its diminutive size, it produces only small amounts of salable crops. The 200 or so natives who live on it are dependent primarily upon the sea to sustain them.

Early in the evening, eight enthralled men are gathered near and around the tall Indian. Most are seated on the steps that lead to his elevated hut. A large fire, a dozen feet away, casts its shadows on the hut's grass sides and palm-thatched roof. Benquam is seated in a chair provided for him on the sand near the base of the stairs but not far from the fire. Slowly at first, words from his past begin to enter his mind, clouding his thoughts, then race back-and-forth inside his brain. He clears his voice, pauses, then begins speaking.

"First," he says as he points to Albright. "How you know Paumanok?"

"I was born in Greenport. In school I learned that Paumanok is the Indian word for Long Island."

"Which Indians you know?"

"I know Shinnecocks. When in high school I made extra money as a caddy on the golf course in Southampton. The reservation is there. I met some Shinnecocks who also work on the course, but not as caddies."

"How you and boat get here?"

"My ship was sunk by Japanese torpedoes. We are at war with Japan after they bombed our naval base at Pearl Harbor last December."

"Who win war?"

"I don't know. We are just seamen taking farm machinery to Australia. But, you said you would tell us your story."

"You smart kid."

"This my story. Is December in year war among Americans end that whaleship *Tranquility* goes out from Sag Harbor."

"My God," blurts Jerry Mullholland, "he's talking about the Civil War!"

"There 36 others on ship. I be kidnapped by super.., supersti...," Benquam labors with the word and finally blurts out in perfect English, "superstitious men. They believe they must have Indian in crew to have good hunt for whale."

Benquam pauses for a moment to recollect his thoughts. At the onset, he finds it difficult to speak in English. From time to time during his life on this island, he has spoken to the occasional Englander or Australian who found their way here, but only during brief encounters. As he addresses the seamen, he experiences a lessening difficulty in finding the right word to express what he wants to say. This improves gradually as he unfolds the story of his life as a whaler.

Still, he wonders to himself before he speaks again, if he can talk to them. He senses that their language has changed since he left Long Island. I hear them say words, he says to himself, words I never heard before or know what mean. I must try!

"Mine is story of brave men and cowards," says Benquam. "And, there was one among us who was evil. It is story of some who believe in God and others whose god is money. And, is the story of a few who believed in nothing at all.

"It not best times in the country or on reservation. Most people, Whites and Indians alike, still feel loss war gave them. Wounds were many and deep. It was still time to mourn. But there was no time to mourn."

"How old are you?" Albright interrupts.

"I not sure," Benquam answers. "I told I was born during the great fires in San Francisco. And same year was a great show in London."

"I think that was about 1851," said John Duran, the *Star's* chief engineer and one of eight survivors in Albright's lifeboat. "How old were you when you put to sea?"

"I was 14…no 15. I not quite sure."

"Good God," says Duran after mentally calculating the dates, "that makes you 90, aaah 91 years old."

"Is too late now. I old. You sleep. Tomorrow we talk more."

CHAPTER 52

Where My People Now?

Near noon the crew of the *Atlantic Star* sees Benquam finally emerge in the doorway of his house. They've been milling about during most of the morning waiting to see him and to see if there is still more to his adventure. When he appears, they quickly reassemble on the stairs that lead to his elevated hut. By late afternoon his story is told.

Albright is in the forefront and is about to ask a question when Benquam takes command of the interview.

"What happened to my people? Are there still Shinnecocks who go to sea? Are there are more whalers who put out from Sag Harbor?"

"There are no more Shinnecock Indians," Albright says with authority, "at least, not as you knew them."

Benquam is astonished by what Albright has just said. He has difficulty absorbing what the young sailor has just told him. Before he can speak, Albright continues.

"The Civil War changed the lives of many people on Long Island, White, Black and Indian. Those bad years and their affects were felt by everyone and lasted a long time. Your reservation, and that of the Montauks, but mostly yours, was overrun by Negroes who escaped from the South, looking for work in the North. You knew that, didn't you?"

"Yes," Benquam answers. "I saw this happening when I was boy. Anything is possible."

In the comparatively few short years spent on Long Island, Benquam had seen his life and the ways of his people rapidly changing. All of Long Island and the nation had been undergoing change. His kidnapping was proof of the way White Long Islanders, whose ancestors Ben's ancestors had befriended and taught how to eke a living from the gravid sea, had also changed.

"When Negroes couldn't find work," Albright continues, "they settled on reservations on Long Island or those in Upstate New York. They quickly outnumbered Indians. After a few generations, mixed-breeds dominated and controlled the reservations."

"How you know all this?" Benquam asks Albright.

"My knowledge of the Shinnecocks is sparse, but I do know of such things. I grew up in Greenport. If you can remember, it is no more than 20 miles from the reservation. Most of what I do know comes from newspapers that I read or what others who visited the reservation told me. While in high school, I worked one summer as a caddy on a golf course in Southampton, near the reservation."

"What is golf course?"

Albright gives him a quick explanation.

"That seems silly thing for grown men to do!"

"While in school," Albright continues without further commenting on golf, "I read about Long Island's 13 Indian tribes in a New York State history book. It told of the deaths of the last remaining Shinnecocks."

"When was that?"

"About 20 or so years ago. I'm not certain of the date."

"Are Shinnecocks no more? Maybe they move away. You be wrong?"

"I don't think so," answers Albright. "There are pure-bred Indians on the reservation today but they are from other tribes in the United States. Many Indian men came to Manhattan because there was work there for them. They were fearless, especially while building skyscrapers. Some did not return home after their jobs ended and moved onto reservations.

"There are no pure-bred Shinnecocks because they intermarried with the Negroes long before the western Indians came to New York. And, while the reservation still exists, it no longer has the status it had when you lived there. The courts decided sometime in the late 1800s that there was not enough Shinnecock blood in the people who then lived there, so it lost its federal reservation status.

"And no, there no longer are whalers in Sag Harbor, nor in America, nor for the most part in the world. There is no need for whale oil and there are no square-rigged ships to seek them out. Diesel fuel drives the engines of all the ships today.

"But why didn't you return to the United States?" Albright asks Benquam. "Surely this island is not so isolated that there never was the chance for you to return."

"I told you about raiding party that take our women soon after I come here? We need women or people here will disappear. Many times that happens among people here. We make raid on small islands and brought back women.

I took one and had son. She was good squaw. Soon villagers treat me with respect. Respect is new feeling for me. I never know it living among Whites on Long Island. Maybe it is because people here don't know who or what I was. They know I had a connection to them from somewhere far in past. I did stand taller than any man and maybe that alone was why.

"I could go Papeete with nuns and find way back to Sag Harbor, but I saw no reason. I was happy here.

"I had more sons, many sons and many daughters. And they have sons and daughters. My family grow bigger and bigger. Look about you; almost everyone now carries some Indian blood in them. I don't think it is that different, do you?"

"Where are your sons? Your wife?" asks Albright.

"They all gone. I outlive them. I outlive three chiefs. When there is no one else they choose me as leader. In way, is family election. Some here still look at me with awe and ask who I am. At times, I, too, wonder who I am."

"Chief Benquam, I know who you are," said Albright. "You are the last pure-bred Shinnecock alive. And, you come from a family of whalers. Benquam, you are **the last whaler!**"

EPILOG

Three weeks after John Albright and his shipmates landed on Paui Akua, French nuns arrive burdened with medicines and Bibles. The nuns are surprised when they see the Americans but not for long, because they are familiar with the new and strange events occurring in their part of the world ever since the Japanese bombed Pearl Harbor. They take the survivors back to Papeete where a French destroyer is stationed. The destroyer captain has just received orders to move to Sydney to join several other Allied vessels in a defense of Australia.

Before departing Albright seeks out Benquam.

"You have no desire to return with us…do you?" Albright asks.

"Why would I?" asks Benquam. "This is my world now. It has been for nearly 75 years. There is no one back there who would know me. Should I start life all over again? No, there is no life there for me. Even if I could, I am too old to change, or make the journey back.

"No, Albright, I will stay here. I will die here."

"Goodbye," says Albright.

"Goodbye, Albright."

"I swear I saw a tear in his eye," Albright says to Toni Gucci, as they climb into the boat with the departing nuns.

THE END